D0205029

From Provinces into Nations

From Provinces into Nations

DEMOGRAPHIC INTEGRATION IN
WESTERN EUROPE, 1870–1960

Susan Cotts Watkins

PRINCETON UNIVERSITY PRESS

PRINCETON, NEW JERSEY

Copyright © 1991 by Princeton University Press
Published by Princeton University Press, 41 William Street,
Princeton, New Jersey 08540
In the United Kingdom: Princeton University Press, Oxford

All Rights Reserved

Library of Congress Cataloging-in-Publication Data

Watkins, Susan Cotts, 1938–
From provinces into nations : demographic integration in Western
Europe, 1870–1960 / Susan Cotts Watkins.
Includes bibliographical references.
Includes index.
1. Fertility, Human—Europe—History. 2. Europe—Population—
History. 3. Nationalism—Europe—History. 4. Regionalism—Europe—
History. I. Title.
HB991.W38   1991   304.6′32′094—dc20   90-36900

ISBN 0-691-09451-9 (alk. paper)

This book has been composed in Linotron Times Roman

Princeton University Press books are printed
on acid-free paper and meet the guidelines for
permanence and durability of the Committee on
Production Guidelines for Book Longevity of
the Council on Library Resources

Printed in the United States of America by Princeton University Press,
Princeton, New Jersey

10 9 8 7 6 5 4 3 2 1

Contents

Figures

Tables

Preface

THIS BOOK describes and attempts to explain a single finding. In 1870 national boundaries were faint on the demographic map of western Europe; by 1960, they were deeply etched. In the late nineteenth century, and presumably earlier, levels of marital fertility, illegitimacy, and marriage differed greatly from one part of a country to another; by 1960, these demographic differences had diminished. I call this hardening of national demographic boundaries "demographic nationalism"—not organized social movements or deliberate state-led attempts to influence births or marriages, but evidence, I think, of the creation of a national community that paralleled the integration of national markets, state expansion, and nation building.

Most work on demographic changes in western Europe over the last century has concentrated on the massive declines in mortality and fertility that are termed the demographic transition, and, to a lesser extent, on changes in the age at marriage. In the past two or three decades, specifying the determinants of fertility decline has seemed particularly important, largely because of a concern with the consequences of rapid rates of population growth in developing countries. My own interest in the field was stimulated by just this set of questions as they were set out by Ansley Coale when I was his student. Subsequently, I became involved in the Princeton European Fertility Project, an attempt to describe the fertility decline in western Europe and to specify the circumstances under which it occurred (Coale and Watkins 1986).

While trying to understand the fertility decline, I became dissatisfied with the framework in which most of us worked. At the core of the dominant models of demographic behavior were individuals calculating the costs and benefits of another child, or the costs and benefits of marrying earlier, later, or not at all. Primacy was given to individuals (or couples) and to economic circumstances. Both academic demographers and ordinary people, I think, consider birth rates and marriage rates the outcomes of many individual, or couple, decisions. Moreover, we usually give economic calculations a major role when we try to explain why people have the number of children that they do, or why they marry at the age that they do, or remain single. When we speak informally, we might say that it is difficult to pay the high college tuition these days for more than one or two children, or that it is not a good idea for a couple to marry until they can support themselves without help from their parents. Academics are likely to explain these decisions more formally, by including measures of income as explanatory variables, for example. But the point is that most people think demographic decisions are private choices by individuals who are influenced mainly by their pocketbooks.

This view seemed increasingly inconsistent with what I had experienced in my own life, talked about with others, and learned more formally. Thinking back over my own childbearing, it seemed to me that the number of children was not really much of an issue—we knew we wanted some children, we felt it was not a good idea to have an only child, and we never even discussed having a third. Two was the right number to have. When I gossiped with friends, we wondered when a mutual acquaintance was going to have her second child, not if she would, or why one friend was having a third child, not why another was stopping at two. Norman Ryder, in lectures that I attended and in writings that I read with pleasure and intellectual profit, formulated a challenge to the conventional wisdom that resonated with my own experience: "My premise is that the ultimate level of explanation of fertility is macroanalytic, that fertility is an aggregate property, a characteristic of the groups to which the couple belong and not directly of the couple themselves" (Ryder 1974).

If the focus is turned to groups, then the question is what groups. I chose to look at relatively small, spatially defined groups, such as counties in England, departments in France, cantons in Switzerland; these are generically called provinces. To a much lesser extent, I also consider groups defined in other ways, such as occupation and religion. My central concerns have to do not with changes in level—why was fertility high in the past and low in the present—but with changes in demographic diversity. I examined both diversity *among* countries (how different were the countries from each other between 1870 and 1960) and diversity *within* countries (how different were the provinces within each country).

I found that fertility varied less across provinces within a country in 1960 than it had in 1870. The same was true of marriage and of illegitimacy. It is easier to think of reasons why marital fertility would be uniformly low; we can immediately point to the efficiency of modern contraception and to the high cost of children in the modern world. Why marriage also became more national seems less obvious; it is harder to think of reasons why marriage ages should be similar in Essex and in Cornwall, or in Morbihan and Allier.

In seeking explanations, I examined markets, states, and nation building. I did not ask the more usual questions—how economic development affected the costs and benefits of children, or what was the effect of governmental pronatalist policies. Rather, I found myself asking how the integration of national markets and the expansion and elaboration of state functions might have drawn provincial populations into networks that increasingly encompassed the entire nation. Charles Tilly greatly aided in crystallizing these themes; the citations to him are only a weak measure of his influence on this work.

Finally I realized that it might be possible to use demographic differences among provinces within the same country as a measure of social integration. If two groups are demographically quite different from each other, I think one can assume that they are different in other ways. If they change from demographically distinct to demographically similar, one can usually assume that other differences have diminished as well. Demographic homogeneity might be accidental—variation in the level of marital fertility, for example, is limited by biological constraints. But it increasingly seemed likely that often—although not always—demographic similarity was a sign of social integration.

Since my first days in graduate school, Marion J. Levy, Jr., has told me that demography is wasted on demographers. I would not fully agree with him, of course, but I do think that examining demographic diversity can speak to some of the questions that sociologists, historians, anthropologists, and political scientists traditionally have asked. Demographic data can be used to talk about the shift from the little traditions to the great tradition, from Gemeinschaft to Gesellschaft, from peasants into Frenchmen, and it can also be used to talk about convergence and about social mobilization. I cannot answer Durkheim's questions: "Why does the individual, while becoming more autonomous, depend more upon society? How can he be at once more individual and more solidary?" If, however, one is willing to take rather crude demographic measures for territorially defined aggregates as relevant evidence about social solidarity, it is possible to show that in 1870 such solidarity was largely local, whereas in 1960 it was largely national.

The demographic nationalism that I am writing about would not have been evident had this study not used demographic data and had it not covered many countries and a long time period. The problems are obvious.

First is the problem of telling a story in numbers. Some of those who are interested in the themes of this work will be unused to this language. I have assumed that most readers have no knowledge of either demography or statistics, and I have thus kept tables to a minimum and have tried to translate the tables into language more familiar to nondemographers. The measures and the few statistical techniques I use have been deliberately kept simple and, I trust, fully explained. Issues of more interest to experts in these fields have been relegated to footnotes, appendixes, to one section of chapter 2 (where I evaluate the quality of the data), to one section of chapter 3 (where I try to make sure that differences in demographic diversity across countries are not illusory), and to chapter 7 (where I test some of my explanations more formally).

My friend and colleague Jane Menken gave me a great deal of moral and technical support, reading chapters carefully, checking calculations, redrafting tables, and insisting on greater clarity. I consulted frequently with friends who are also experts on historical demography; particularly helpful were George Alter, Jack Caldwell, Myron Gutmann, Roger Schofield, Daniel Scott Smith, Etienne van de Walle, David Weir, and Tony Wrigley. Ewa Morawska, also both colleague and friend, helped translate from the numbers that are the language of demographers to English; when she wrote "statistical jargon'' or ''I don't understand'' in the margin, I figured no one else would understand either, and clarified.

A second problem is that the numbers are bloodless, a skeleton that one intuitively wants to flesh out. Indeed, I think it is precisely because demographic data are considered the precipitates of the intimate lives of people of the past that the story of demographic nationalism is so compelling. But no amount of translation or clarification will make the numbers that describe provincial aggregates speak precisely about individuals, couples, or families, much less about passion or its lack, or about the routes that led from markets, states, and nations to the bedroom (and back again). The shapes of the connections—how they actually worked out on the ground—are necessarily speculative; they require knowing about the networks that linked individuals to one another. In this work, which covers fifteen countries over a century, the study of such networks is ruled out by the lack of data, and even were data available it would be a formidable task, precluding the sort of comparison that was necessary to illuminate the outlines of this story. Thus, the networks have to remain largely invisible and imagined.

Pushed to imagine—particularly by David Levine and John Gillis, who have been consistent readers of various versions—I have usually imagined women. This is appropriate because the numbers I use describe the births, both legitimate and illegitimate, of women and the marriages of women. But it was also easier for me to imagine women gossiping about the intimate details of reproductive life. Men surely gossiped too, but I imagine that they were less likely to gossip about these topics. Leslie Moch helped me to visualize these women in motion, as migrants who knit villages, provinces, and nations together.

Lastly, comparison is of the essence here. I had to try to account both for similarities and for differences in the historical experiences of each of the fifteen countries examined. Some countries are given less attention because I cannot read the language in which the most important works are written; other countries, such as England and France, are given more weight not only because I can read the literature but because I was expertly guided through it by Lawrence and Jeanne Stone. The attempts at explanation required delving into the secondary literature in a variety of disciplines. I received important assistance from friends and colleagues in other disciplines—Stanley Engerman, Stefano Fenoaltea, Eric Jones, Kenneth McRae, Jane Schneider, Wally Seccombe, and Julian Simon, among others—but I am still not sure that I have gotten right the parts of this story that fall in relatively unfamiliar disciplines, and thus my explanations are tentative.

Many readers made valuable comments on parts or versions of the manuscript: James C. Davis, Douglas Ewbank, Jack Goldstone, Tim Guinnane, Michael Hanagan, Sam Klausner, Miriam King, Barbara Laslett, Jim Lehning, and Jay Winter. Conversations with Marvin Bressler sharpened my sense of the theoretical implications of my findings, and conversations with James Beniger, Peter Brown, and Geoff McNicoll stimulated me to think about things differently.

I received much assistance with computing from Mark Keintz and Barbara Vaughan; with statistical issues from Paul Allison, Michael Bracher, Charles Denk, Mariah Evans, Alan Gray, Hallie Kintner, Phil Morgan, Noreen Goldman, Sam Preston, German Rodriguez, Herb Smith, and Zenas Sykes; and from several generations of work-study students, particularly Kerry Ogata and Jennifer Mall. A year at the Institute for Advanced Study in Princeton, funded by the National Endowment for the Humanities, provided the opportunity to work in peace, as did two summers as a fellow in the Research Schools of Social Science at the Australian National University.

I also am grateful to my New Haven women's group—Jan Marmor, Sylvia Tesh, and Marcie Schuck—and to my Philadelphia women's group—Marion Howell, Jane Menken, Nina Segre, Anita Winston, and Tobia Worth—for opportunities to gossip. And, finally, to my children, Katherine and Timothy, who supported me indirectly by managing their own lives very well indeed, and directly by their encouragement.

From Provinces into Nations

CHAPTER 1

Introduction

THE TERM "the demographic transition" refers to the major declines in fertility and mortality that occurred in western Europe between 1870 and 1960 and subsequently in many countries of the developing world. Social scientists have given much attention to describing these changes and to understanding why they occurred. In this book, I ask another question: What happened to demographic diversity in western Europe during this century?

The answer, as it turns out, is rather simple. In 1870 there was a great deal of diversity in childbearing and in marriage within each of the countries of western Europe. In Switzerland, for example, in the canton of Lucerne about half the women of childbearing age were married, whereas in Glarus only one-third of such women were married. By 1960 differences in marriage patterns had diminished, so that one canton of Switzerland was more like another. In 1870 a demographic map of western Europe would have shown that national boundaries were faint, provincial boundaries vivid; by 1960 this situation had reversed—provincial boundaries were faint, but national boundaries quite visible.

Insight into the sources of these changes comes from a comparison of the move made by a French peasant in the sixteenth century with a trip made by a villager from Chanzeaux to Paris in the middle of the twentieth century. In 1527, Natalie Davis tells us, Martin Guerre's father, Sanxi Guerre, moved from the French Basque country near the Spanish border, to a village in the county of Foix, also in southern France (Davis 1983). The move took three weeks, on foot. For Sanxi, the Foix was a new world: he found changes in language, names, and dress; different household arrangements; a more active market in land and less identification between a family and its land; more use of the written word; and distinctive courtship customs (Davis 1983, 6–18). In the Foix, there was greater freedom to engage in sexual activity before marriage. Although we do not have records of illegitimate births for the Foix or the Basque country in this period, we would expect more illegitimacy in the Foix. The difference in language was probably the more meaningful difference between the two areas, however, for language often marks the boundary between communities.

In the early 1960s, more than four centuries later, Laurence Wylie accompanied a friend from Chanzeaux, a village in one of the most traditional parts of France, to visit his city cousins in Paris. Initially the country cousin seemed subdued, the city cousins condescending. As the conversation between the cousins developed, however, it gradually became obvious that the country cousin was as well informed as the city cousins on politics, on farm policy, on social security, on the Common Market. Wylie concludes the story by saying that "As all this became clear, the country-mouse, city-mouse situation faded. These three men were much more on a level than they had thought" (Wylie 1966, 342). Had they discussed when they intended to marry and how many children they wanted, the conversation would probably have reinforced the view that the cousins belonged to the same national community. Their ability to converse as equals was predicated on speaking the same language. It was also due in part to citizenship in the same state, which provided them with a common education; to participation in a national economic market and national welfare systems; and to a press that kept them informed about national issues.

Asking about demographic variation leads to consideration of a set of demographic behavior determinants rather different than the usual. It is customary to analyze modern fertility or marriage as if the number of children a woman bears and the age at which she marries were the outcome of decisions made by individuals (or couples). Such an interpretation is enhanced by a tradition that interprets progress as the increase in the control exercised by individuals over their fates. There has certainly been a relentless increase in the *rhetoric* of individualism, a rhetoric that has legitimized personal choice over an expanding range of activities. Lawrence Stone has documented the early stages of the effect of individualism on the family in England, and its logic is played out in today's tolerance of a wide range of sexual practices between consenting adults and the use of highly personal therapeutic language to describe family obligations (Stone 1977; Bellah 1985). Thus, more couples in 1960 than in 1870 would feel that the use of contraception to limit the size of their families was a private decision, one rightfully made by themselves alone.

Specifying a target family size was more reasonable in the 1960s than a century earlier, because such goals were more easily achieved. By the 1960s contraceptive information was available through national public health ministries in Northwestern Europe and Scandinavia. Even though the pill was not yet in widespread use, the techniques of fertility control were less demanding in personal terms and more effective in 1960 than in 1870. In addition, declines in infant and child mortality made it far more likely that parents would see all their children survive.

It is reasonable to believe that individuals would vary considerably in their intentions with respect to family size as well as marriage. In an exuberant passage written after the introduction of oral contraceptives, Ruth Dixon expresses the potential for diversity that this technology promised:

Instead of living in a society where three out of four women get married between the ages of 18 and 23 and in which 19 in 20 have married by the time they reach 40, we could look forward to a society in which some marry young, others marry in their thirties or forties or choose not to marry at all. Instead of concentrating our child-bearing in the mid-twenties and producing the socially appropriate three or four children, more women could remain childless, more could have just one, and the rest could spread out according to individual temperament. We could even begin to share each other's children. Instead of having to search out our own small burrows each with its mother and father and babies, some could choose such a private world freely and others choose larger and more fluid "families" of men and women and children, or of single friends or whatever. (Dixon 1970, 92)

Individuals are not evident in the demographic measures used in this book. An increase in diversity among individuals is compatible with a reduction in diversity among provinces. But finding that diversity in marriage as well as in fertility diminished calls into question the role of changes in contraceptive technology and infant mortality for changes in diversity in fertility and marriage. More importantly, it also makes it unlikely that membership in local and national communities did not matter for demographic behavior. By communities I mean networks of individuals who talk to each other, such as the nineteenth-century Frenchwomen who gossiped about neighbors as they washed their clothes, as well as the "imagined communities" of Benedict Anderson's newspaper readers, who keep in touch with each other by reading the same news on the same day (Anderson 1983). These communities appear to have been predominantly, although not exclusively, local in the nineteenth century, but predominantly, although not exclusively, national in the twentieth century.

When we look for the sources of the creation of national demographic communities, we are led to consider what Charles Tilly has called the two master processes of the modern era, the formation of states and the expansion of capitalism (Tilly 1981), as well as to nation building. It might seem that these processes would have little to do with such private behavior as marriage and childbearing. But state formation, market integration, and nation building increasingly drew local communities into national networks. Where these processes were derailed—for example, in Belgium and in Ireland—it is notable that demographic diversity increased rather than decreased between 1870 and 1960.

This book has two aims. The first, and the one to which most attention is given, is to describe as precisely as possible the changes in demographic variation in western Europe between 1870 and 1960. The second aim is to try to account for the change from demographic diversity to greater demographic uniformity.

In chapter 2, I introduce the measures of marital fertility, illegitimate fertility, and marriage that will be used. These describe the demographic behavior of spatially defined aggregates, called provinces: the populations of departments in France, counties in England, and *lan* in Sweden, for example. The demographic measures were calculated by the participants in a large project to analyze the demographic transition in western Europe (the project is described in Coale and Watkins [1986]). For most of the fifteen countries and approximately five hundred provinces of western Europe, the measures are usually available at ten-year intervals from the first date that censuses and vital registration systems permit their calculation (usually about 1870) to 1960. Although these boundary dates are dictated by the availability of data, in fact they encompass the fertility transition; at the earlier date the fertility transition had hardly begun, whereas by 1960 fertility was low everywhere. Subsequently, changes in family patterns, especially the increase in cohabitation, are sufficiently great that it is reasonable to treat the post–1960 period as distinctive.

It would be desirable to include eastern Europe, but changes in the borders of the provinces as well as the borders of the countries make accurate comparison over time impossible. It would also be desirable to give equally close consideration to demographic variation by class or occupational group and by religion, because these are often considered to be important influences on demographic behavior. The lack of comparable data for these groups within each of the countries of western Europe for the century makes a systematic and comprehensive analysis impossible. Where evidence about social group differentials is available, however, it suggests that the story of reduced demographic diversity would probably be much the same for groups that are socially defined as it is for groups that are spatially defined.

In chapter 2, I also evaluate the accuracy of the demographic data and consider whether poor measurement might bias the examination of demographic diversity. Readers who find discussions of data and measures tedious might wish to skip these sections. I then flesh out the numbers. I consider the main determinants of marital fertility, illegitimacy, and marriage before the onset of widespread fertility control and ask how the local setting—particularly the daily interactions with others in the community—might have influenced them.

When the focus is on all the five hundred–odd provinces of western Europe around 1870, as it is in chapter 2, the degree of demographic diversity appears striking. But were there limits to demographic diversity? Were there some things that western Europeans did not do, or some things that Norwegians did but Italians did not (or vice versa)? To national historians, and perhaps particularly to local historians, differences between one community and another often seem so enormous that similarities in demographic behavior across an entire country (and much less across all of western Europe) would seem unlikely. For those who think of reproduction as a function that has to be successfully accomplished by any society, it is clear that in principle a variety of ways must exist to ensure this; those who think of fertility as closely linked to material structures would also expect the diversity in fertility to be as great as the diversity in these material structures. In either case, variety would seem probable. But it is a strictly limited variety. In chapter 3, I show that the location of local communities in western Europe, as well as in a particular country, appears to have limited the range of demographic options. Examining the limits to local diversity, therefore, pointed to national and international communities.

When we ask which countries were relatively diverse, which relatively homogeneous, we find that the more diverse countries were usually Belgium, France, Germany, and Switzerland, all multilingual countries. Those people who spoke a common language appeared to behave in similar ways with respect to reproduction, but they behaved quite differently from those with whom they could not communicate. Linguistic boundaries, it seems, were also community boundaries. In chapter 3, then, I examine two countries—France, which was relatively heterogeneous demographically, and England, which was relatively homogeneous demographically—to explore further the limits to demographic diversity.

In chapter 4, I examine the long-term decline in marital fertility. I use the fertility transition to examine the integration of western European societies, much as the injection of a dye into the body permits tracing the circulation of blood. I argue that the deliberate control of fertility within marriage was a time-specific innovation and that the process of fertility decline has much the same characteristics as the diffusion of an innovation. Although we can rarely glimpse this diffusion—we cannot see individuals spreading the word over the back fence, or at cafés—we can observe rapid changes in fertility and, thus, roughly track change in behavior. This points again to networks that stretched across provinces and helps us visualize the boundaries of social systems.

In chapter 5, I compare demographic diversity in 1960 with diversity in 1870. Convergence theorists, who emphasize the functional interdependence of modern social systems consequent on industrial modes of production, would predict that countries would become demographically more like each other, and this turns out to be the case. More striking, however, is the reduction in within-country demographic diversity; the differences among the provinces within most countries in 1960 were smaller than those in 1870. This was so for marital fertility, for illegitimacy, and for marriage. The countries of the Mediterranean (Italy, Portugal, and Spain), where the fertility transition had begun later than elsewhere, were exceptions to the general pattern; on at least one measure of demographic behavior, they were more heterogeneous in 1960 than they had been earlier. Other exceptions were Belgium, Ireland, and Norway, where political and cultural conflicts seem to be evident in demographic differences.

In chapter 6, I show that roughly paralleling the decline in demographic diversity was a decline in linguistic diversity. In most countries, a national standard language either replaced local languages or dialects, or became a lingua franca—inhabitants of any province could talk to inhabitants of any other province. The change is striking in France, where Eugen Weber and others have estimated that before the last part of the nineteenth century many spoke local languages rather than French (Weber 1976). By 1960 few, if any, did not speak French, if only as a second language. Roads and schools had turned peasants into Frenchmen, explained Weber; they also, it appears, created Frenchwomen, whose fertility and marriage differed little from one part of the country to the other. In Belgium and Switzerland, however, significant proportions of the population did not share a common language, either in 1870 or in 1960. In Switzerland, linguistic differences seem to have been subsumed in a widespread commitment to a common political culture; in Belgium, this had not happened by 1960.

In chapter 7, I specify more precisely some of the links between state formation, economic integration, nation building, and demographic behavior by considering one country, France, in greater detail. I distinguish more sharply than in earlier chapters two alternative accounts for reduced demographic variation. The first would emphasize the creation of a national community, captured especially by increased ability to speak French, in addition to or instead of local languages and dialects. The second would postulate that demographic behavior became more uniform because the economic circumstances in which provincial populations lived became more homogeneous. Participation in national markets, for example, would reduce provincial disparities in wages and prices, and the expansion of state welfare policies would also diminish economic differentials among the different areas of France.

The results of the analyses in this chapter are quite consistent with a conclusion that it is the first of these stories rather than the second that accounted for the greater demographic homogeneity in 1960 than in 1870. Particularly persuasive is my finding that *past* language—that is, whether or not the provincial population was largely non-French speaking in the middle of the nineteenth century—is statistically more significant in accounting for variation in patterns of marital fertility and marriage in 1960 than are current levels of income. In other words, even though all the departments of France were more like each other in 1960 than they had been a century earlier, those departments that were linguistically the most distinctive in the past were demographically among the more distinctive in the present.

In chapter 8, the conclusions, I put all these pieces together. Both the general overall patterns that were described previously and the exceptions to these patterns suggest that our accounts of demographic behavior—and, by implication, other kinds of social behavior—would be enhanced if we made more effort to embed individuals in the context of their communities. That nineteenth-century western European countries were demographically diverse, whereas in the middle of the twentieth century they were more homogeneous, suggests that individuals are influenced by what others are doing. In 1870 the relevant others were those who lived nearby and who spoke the same language. By 1960 the relevant others were members of a national, rather than a local, community.

CHAPTER 2

Western Europe around 1870

THE PRIMARY aim of this chapter and chapter 3 is to set the stage by describing demographic variation in western Europe before the demographic transition. Establishing these parameters is important, because the characteristics of western European populations before the transition influence their subsequent trajectories. I begin by introducing the data and measures used in this and subsequent chapters. Attention will be paid to ways in which either the data or the measures of variation might exaggerate the demographic diversity of pretransition Europe and so bias the comparison with later dates. I then examine the ways in which local communities might have influenced demographic behavior.

DATA AND MEASURES

The countries examined in the analysis that follows are introduced in table 2.1. I distinguished between Northwestern European countries and the Mediterranean countries because of historical differences in their marriage patterns (earlier and more pervasive female marriage in Italy, Portugal, and Spain), because of the later marital fertility decline in these countries, and because they have a degree of cultural unity (Tortella 1984). I grouped the Scandinavian countries because they have a long history of interconnection, most obvious in their similar languages and religion but also in political and economic ties. Danish, Norwegian, and Swedish are all varieties of Norse, and educated speakers of all three can communicate with each other; for various periods two or more were ruled by the same monarch; most of the population was Lutheran, with close connections between church and state; and trade among them has been extensive (Haugen 1976; Hoffman 1969; Mead 1981; Trudgill 1983).[1]

Levels of Aggregation

The social groups of interest here are defined spatially. There are two levels of aggregation, the country and the province. Provinces are units smaller than

---

[1] Strictly speaking, Finland is not usually considered part of Scandinavia, and Portugal is not usually considered a Mediterranean country.

TABLE 2.1
Country Characteristics

Country	First Date[a]	Number of Provinces[b]	Area[c] (Millions km²)	Population Size[d] (Thousands)
Northwestern Europe				
Belgium	1880	41	.03	5,520
England and Wales	1851	45	.15	17,928
France	1831	78	.55	35,569
Germany	1871	71	.36	40,997
Ireland	1871	31	.08	6,552
Netherlands	1859	11	.03	3,309
Scotland	1861	33	.08	3,062
Switzerland	1870	25	.04	2,507
Scandinavia				
Denmark	1852	19	.04	1,415
Finland	1880	8	.34	2,061
Norway	1875	20	.32	1,819
Sweden	1880	25	.45	4,556
Mediterranean				
Italy	1861	14	.30	25,017
Portugal	1890	21	.09	5,060
Spain	1887	48	.50	17,550

[a] The date is that at which all three demographic indexes are first available and is (or corresponds closely to) the date at which the population size was measured. Although Knodel calculated the indexes for Germany in 1867, those for 1871 will be the first ones used here, because there was likely to be more consistency across provinces in recording the data upon which the indexes are based after the unification of Germany. For Portugal, I_m is available for 1864, but the other indexes are not available until 1890, the date used here.

[b] There are 50 provinces in Spain, but it is possible to calculate the indexes for only 48 in 1887. For Switzerland, I_m is available for 25 cantons in 1860, but I_g and I_h are available for only 23 cantons at that date, so 1870 is used. The indexes were calculated by Livi-Bacci for 75 smaller units of Italy as well as for larger units. The latter are used here because they were corrected for the effects of heavy male outmigration on marital fertility in some provinces. Antrim-Belfast and Down were combined into one unit because of boundary changes.

[c] Data are taken from McEvedy and Jones (1978), who report area in millions of square kilometers measured around 1975. Few changes in national boundaries over the period significantly affected the size of the area; thus, the area around 1975 is used to represent the area at the first date. Germany includes both East and West Germany; France includes Alsace-Lorraine; Ireland includes what are now the Republic of Ireland and Northern Ireland.

[d] Population sizes at (or close to) the first date are taken from Lesthaeghe (1977), Mathiessen (1985), Teitelbaum, (1984), Knodel (1974), Livi-Bacci (1971; 1977), Mitchell (1976), and the United Nations Demographic Yearbook (1955).

countries but larger than villages (departments in France, counties in England, cantons in Switzerland, and so on).

The choice of provinces as units of analysis is not without problems. The crucial issue is whether the provincial boundaries do encompass distinct and coherent social entities. If they do not, then an analysis based on these units would not have much meaning. Ideally, one would begin with demographic measures about individuals or couples and determine inductively the effective boundaries of the demographic community—drawing a map, as it were, based on demographic similarities much as van Gennep did for folklore practices (Belmont 1979, 127). Because demographic data for individuals or even very small geographical groupings are not available for many areas or many dates, the advantage of a comparative perspective covering a century of major social change would be lost. In practice, the province is the smallest possible unit for a study of this sort.

But were the provinces so heterogeneous as to be meaningless units of analysis? Historical demographers have provided evidence for what Chaunu has called "micro-demographic regimes," demographic communities not much larger than a village or a city neighborhood (Chaunu 1973; Spagnoli 1977; Smith 1978). And as we shall see later, the face-to-face interactions among members of the same small community were probably important in shaping demographic behavior. Nonetheless, there is other evidence, both statistical and anecdotal, that provincial boundaries were often significant for demographic behavior. Although there could be substantial variation across smaller areas within a province, these small areas were more similar to each other if they were in the same province than if they were in different provinces. In England, Italy, and Germany, smaller administrative units within the same province were more similar to each other than they were to villages or parishes in another province (Livi-Bacci 1971, 113; Knodel 1974, 86).[2] The correspondence of demographic behavior within a province is also evident in the high correlations between the rural and urban portions of a province in the nineteenth century (Sharlin 1986).

In addition to statistical evidence, there are other reasons to believe that provincial boundaries mattered. The fact that statistics were tabulated and published for provinces with the same name and usually the same boundaries over a century is an indication that those who collected the information considered the province a relevant unit. In England, for example, the county was

---

[2] I am grateful to Robert Woods and Patti Watterson for estimating the importance of county boundaries in accounting for demographic variation among smaller units in England in 1861. There were approximately 600 registration districts and 45 counties. Their analysis showed that county location was highly statistically significant in accounting for variation across these registration districts. In 1861 county location accounted for 31 percent of the variation in marital fertility (I_g), 35 percent of the variation in illegitimacy (I_h), and 31 percent of the variation in marriage (I_m) (Watterson, pers. com., August 1986).

recognized as the appropriate administrative unit for the Marriage Act of 1653. In Spain, an area that had been first a fief, then an administrative district for centuries, developed as a result ways of sharing land and services that helped tie the area's villages together (Christian 1972, 16). And there is some evidence that the provinces were a meaningful unit to their inhabitants as well as to administrators. For example, in England between 1600 and 1800, short-distance migrants appeared to be reluctant to cross county boundaries (Phythian-Adams 1985). And outside observers attributed personality to provinces:

> Even an inhabitant of the neighbouring county of Lancaster is struck by the peculiar force of character which the Yorkshiremen display. . . . Conscious of the strong sagacity and the dogged power of will which seem almost the birthright of the natives of the West Riding, each man relies upon himself, and seeks no help at the hands of his neighbors. (Gaskell 1857, 9)

In summary, although provinces mask diversity, sometimes extreme diversity, among villages or parishes, they do appear to be meaningful social units. In the nineteenth century and earlier, the communities in which people married and gave birth were almost certainly smaller than the province. In many of them, much daily life went on within sound of the parish church bell. Nonetheless, there is statistical reason to believe that diversity among villages within a province was less than that between villages in different provinces. Furthermore, the stability of their boundaries over time as well as the evidence that they were sometimes meaningful units to individuals makes them an acceptable level of aggregation.

Demographic Indexes

Fertility and marriage can be measured in several ways that differ in the data they require and in their interpretation. Because the analysis that follows will be comparative, it is necessary to use the same measures for all the provinces at all the dates of interest. Some measures that could be calculated for some areas at some dates cannot be calculated for other places and other dates. The demographic measures that will be used here are the indexes developed by Ansley Coale for the Princeton European Fertility Project. They are based on the information most widely available: vital registration of live births by legitimacy status, and census distributions of women by marital status (single, married, widowed, and divorced).[3] Three indexes will be used: one to summarize the childbearing of married women, one to summarize the childbearing of unmarried women, and the third to represent the proportion of women of childbearing age who are currently married.

The index of marital fertility, I_g, compares the number of live births to married women with the highest well-recorded fertility schedules, those of Hut-

---

[3] The indexes are described more fully in Coale and Treadway (1986).

terite women.[4] Note that the measure is based on live births, not surviving children. An I_g of .75 means that the level of marital fertility in the population is three-quarters what it would have been if fertility in the province had been like that of married Hutterite women. An I_h of .10 means that there were only 10 percent as many illegitimate births as there would have been if unmarried women had the same fertility rates as married Hutterite women. The marriage index, I_m, is a measure of the proportion married. It is the ratio of legitimate live births to the number of legitimate live births the population would have if all women ages 15 to 49 were currently married and had the same fertility rates as married Hutterite women. An I_m of .33 means that one-third of the women of reproductive age in the province were married.[5, 6]

The indexes are all summary measures and thus hide interesting information. The same level of the marriage index (I_m) could be produced by different combinations of age at marriage, spinsterhood, and widowhood, though in fact I_m is usually influenced more by the proportion married among younger women than by the proportion remaining single at age fifty. Similarly, two provinces might have the same relatively low level of marital fertility for very different reasons. In one province, migration might separate spouses (as it did in southern Italy and northern Portugal in the late nineteenth century), whereas in the other, fertility might be low because women customarily nursed their children for long periods, thus making it less likely that they would become pregnant again.

Despite their disadvantages, the indexes have several advantages. First, they exist. They were calculated by collaborators on the Princeton European Fertility Project for all the provinces of fifteen countries over approximately a century.[7] Second, they are reasonably reliable. Much attention was paid to the

---

[4] The Hutterite fertility schedule thus serves as a standard. If another fertility schedule were used, the absolute levels of the index would differ, but it is likely that the relative levels would be preserved.

[5] Strictly speaking, an I_m of .33 means that one-third of the women of reproductive age is married only under the assumption that women of all ages are equally fertile. Since I_m is fertility weighted, it gives more weight in the calculation of the index to younger women whose fertility is higher.

[6] I_g is defined as

$B_L/\Sigma m(i)F(i)$, where B_L is the number of legitimate births, $m(i)$ the number of currently married women in the population at age i, and $F(i)$ the age-specific fertility rates of Hutterite women.

I_h, the index of nonmarital fertility, is defined as

$B_I/\Sigma u(i)F(i)$, where B_I is the number of illegitimate births, and $u(i)$ the number of unmarried (single, widowed, divorced) women in the population at age i.

I_m, the index of marriage, is defined as

$\Sigma m(i)F(i)/\Sigma w(i)F(i)$, where $w(i)$ is the total number of women in the population.

[7] These collaborators were: E. Harm (Finland); J. Knodel (Germany); R. Lesthaeghe (Belgium); M. Livi-Bacci (Italy, Portugal, Spain); P. Mathiessen (Denmark); C. Mosk (Sweden);

accuracy of the data, and census or vital registration data that appeared to be faulty were adjusted.[8] Third, they have intuitive meaning.

Let us take as typical of western Europe in 1870 a community with a level of marital fertility (I_g) of .700, where half the women of each childbearing age are married (an I_m of .500), where illegitimacy is negligible ($I_h = 0$), and where life-expectancy at birth is 40, and see what this would mean for couples. If all women between the ages fifteen and forty-nine were married and reproduced at Hutterite levels of age-specific marital fertility, women would reach age fifty with, on average, just over twelve children (the Total Fertility Rate would be 12.44). With a level of marital fertility (I_g) of .700, the Total Fertility Rate would be only 8.7 (.700 × 12.44). If the proportion married (I_m) is taken into account, the level of fertility would be halved; on average a woman would bear 4.35 children. If just under two-thirds of the children born survived to age twenty, only 2.82 children would live to the beginning of adulthood.[9]

Two issues need to be considered before we proceed. The first concerns the timing of the onset of the fertility decline. The second is whether the three demographic indexes do indeed capture three distinctive aspects of demographic behavior or whether they are so highly related to each other that they are in effect measuring a single demographic system.

In the analysis that follows, to minimize the effect of early fertility decline in some provinces on the measurement of diversity we will be measuring diversity at the first date for which data are available. As was evident in table 2.1, the dates range from 1831 (France) to 1890 (Portugal). Most are around 1870, so that the term "around 1870" will be used. There is some awkwardness in comparing countries at different dates. The advantage of doing so, however, is that we can be more confident that we are measuring demographic diversity before the transition in marital fertility began. In addition, in some countries the decline in marital fertility was accompanied by an increase in the proportion married, so that we would also like to measure marriage as early as possible in the period.

In all countries except France, at the first date for which we can calculate the indexes for provinces few or no provinces had begun the fertility transition (Coale and Treadway 1986). That few provinces outside of France began the fertility decline at the first date for which the indexes can be calculated means

---

M. Teitelbaum (England, Ireland, Scotland); E. van de Walle (France, Norway, the Netherlands); and F. van de Walle (Switzerland). Roy Treadway prepared a computer tape containing these indexes; it is available from the Office of Population Research, Princeton University. They have also been published in *The Decline of Fertility in Europe*, edited by Coale and Watkins (1986).

[8] Coale and Treadway (1986) gives a full discussion of the sources of the data and the corrections made to them.

[9] This calculation uses the West Model Life Tables for females (Coale, Demeny, and Vaughan [1983]).

that the term "pretransition" can be used to refer to western Europe around 1870. (This issue will be discussed in more detail in chapter 3.)

Second, it is possible that marital fertility, illegitimacy, and marriage are but different aspects of a single unified demographic regime. For example, when marriage was late illegitimacy might have been high, or delayed marriage and control of marital fertility might have been alternative ways of limiting reproduction, so that when marriage was early marital fertility was low, whereas when marriage was late marital fertility was high. Examination of the interrelations between the three indexes using correlation coefficients (not shown) shows that in general the indexes are not tightly linked with each other. In Belgium and in France all the correlations are statistically significant, but in the other countries most of the correlation coefficients are small in magnitude and not statistically significant. Thus, we can conclude that the indexes do indeed measure distinctive demographic behaviors.

Demographic Diversity in Western Europe around 1870

The extent of local diversity within western Europe can be shown by ordering the provincial values from highest to lowest. This distribution can be described with three simple measures. One is the median, which is in the middle of the distribution (half of the provincial values are higher, half are lower); it thus represents the average level of all the provinces. A second measure, the range, is the difference between the maximum and minimum provincial values. For some purposes this is a useful measure of diversity, but it has disadvantages; we might expect, for example, that something is odd about the extremes. A more robust measure of diversity is the midspread (sometimes called the interquartile range), which excludes the upper 25 percent and the lower 25 percent of the provincial values.[10] In general, the midspread will be much smaller than the range. Table 2.2 presents, for all of the western European provinces, the maximum and minimum provincial values, the median, and the range and the midspread.

Examination of the median level of marriage (I_m) in table 2.2 shows that in the median province, fewer than half the women of reproductive age were married. Marital fertility (I_g) was high compared to modern levels, but less than the highest reliably recorded fertility, and illegitimacy was quite low. Although subsequent comparisons with diversity in 1960 will provide a yard-

[10] The midspread is preferable to the standard deviation for this analysis. Although the distribution of provincial values on the three indexes is rather even in most countries, ordinarily one or two unusual provinces (usually the capital city or another large city) have disproportionate weight on the standard deviation. In addition, the midspread can be translated into intuitively meaningful differences in number of children or proportions married in a way that the standard deviation cannot. Because the analysis in this and subsequent chapters treats provinces as units, they are not weighted by population size.

TABLE 2.2
Descriptive Statistics for Indexes of Marital Fertility (I_g), Illegitimacy (I_h), and Marriage (I_m), All Provinces, First Date

	Median	Maximum	Minimum	Range	Midspread[a]
Marital fertility (I_g)	.698	1.052	.348	.704	.113
Illegitimacy (I_h)	.042	.140	.004	.136	.033
Marriage (I_m)	.462	.691	.290	.401	.105

Source: The demographic indexes used in this and subsequent tables are published as appendix A of Coale and Treadway, in Coale and Watkins (1986), and are available on tape from the Office of Population Research, Princeton, New Jersey. For some countries, more than one series of indexes were calculated. In this book series 0 was used except for Italy, where series 1 (corrected for male outmigration) was used and Spain, where series 1 (smaller provinces) was used.

Note: This analysis includes all the provinces of Western Europe at the first date for each country for which data are available to calculate the indexes (see table 2.1).

[a] The midspread is the difference between the upper quartile and the lower quartile.

stick against which diversity around 1870 can be compared, examination of table 2.2 shows considerable differences among the provinces of western Europe. The maximum marital fertility, in the Flemish arrondissement of Dendermonde in Belgium, is higher than the standard set by Hutterite fertility. The minimum I_g, (.348 in the French department of Eure where marital fertility had presumably been declining for decades) is close to the average level for all of western Europe in 1960. Because Hutterite women who married at twenty would have borne about ten children, Dendermonde and Eure differed in their levels of marital fertility by more than six births.

The range of marriage patterns is also evident. In the southern province of Cáceres in Spain, over two-thirds of the women of reproductive age were married, whereas in the Swedish lan of Stockholm and in Sutherland, in the Scottish Highlands, under one-third were married. Variation was, of course, much greater when measured by the range than by the midspread. The range, however, is anchored at the low end by a French province, which means that it does not adequately represent pretransition diversity. In contrast, because the midspread excludes the one-fourth of the provinces with the lowest fertility and because fewer than one-fourth of the provinces have begun their fertility decline at this date, the midspread is not affected by early fertility decline. Because the large differences in the median levels of marital fertility and marriage on the one hand and illegitimacy on the other compromise comparison of variation, these measures cannot be used to compare variation across the indexes.

It is obvious that these measures describe only what people did, not what they wanted. It may be that wishes were more similar than outcomes. In developing countries today, desired fertility is more similar across individuals than is their achieved fertility (Cleland 1985), and it may have been that wishes were more uniform than outcomes in the past as well—especially given the local variability in infant and child mortality. Even had that been the case, however, the difference in outcomes between the extremely different provinces affected other aspects of people's lives; a family with nine births over the couple's reproductive lifetime surely functioned at least somewhat differently than a family with three or four.

LOCAL COMMUNITIES AND DEMOGRAPHIC BEHAVIOR

What role might local communities have played in influencing demographic behavior? I will begin by discussing illegitimacy; because we usually do not think of an out-of-wedlock birth as an outcome desired by individuals or couples, it is rather easier to visualize the role of the local community.

An illegitimate birth is the outcome of a sequence of events—courtship (however abbreviated), sexual relations without effective contraception, pregnancy without abortion, and a failure to marry before the child was born (Shorter 1975, 93). In addition, the birth would have had to have been registered as illegitimate.

Most illegitimate births were probably conceived within an accepted courtship, especially in small rural communities (Levine 1977). Both partners were much like each other in social status, so that a marriage between them would have been appropriate (Laslett 1980). The age at which the courtship began was probably much the same whether its outcome was an illegitimate birth or marriage; the age of the mother at the birth of her first child was similar whether the child was born out of wedlock, conceived before marriage but born after marriage, or conceived and born after the marriage (Laslett 1980; Watkins and McCarthy 1980). What constituted an acceptable courtship, and whether or not it included sexual relations, was probably determined by the community rather than by the individuals involved. In some provinces illegitimacy rates were so low as to suggest that community controls were sufficiently strong to ensure that either most couples were chaste or that births out of wedlock were not registered. In other areas, such as Verviers in Belgium or northeast Portugal, illegitimacy was so high as to suggest that the stigma of illegitimacy was not great (Alter 1988, 114; O'Neill 1987).

Local economic circumstances probably also influenced illegitimacy. Because in most areas couples were expected to set up a new household upon marriage (Dupâquier 1972; Laslett 1972), unexpected reversals in economic fortunes might have dictated a delay (Levine 1977; Wrightson and Levine 1979). Where markets were poorly integrated, so that income and prices in one province bore little relation to income and prices in another, these reversals likely occurred at different times, thus accounting for some of the demographic diversity in a single year. More than income was involved, however.

When expectations that births would be legitimate conflicted with expectations that couples would set up a new household of an appropriate standard at marriage, the conflict could have been resolved in two ways. In some communities, the principle of legitimacy probably dominated—in others, the insistence that the new couple live on their own.

The local community also accounted for variations in the level of marital fertility. Before the last quarter of the nineteenth century, when the long-term decline in marital fertility began, these variations do not seem to be due to deliberate attempts to control births within marriage.[11] Nor are variations in marital fertility in the pretransition period well explained by differences in economic circumstances. Income and occupation were rarely associated with pretransition differences in marital fertility (see the monographs of the Princeton European Fertility Project cited earlier). In particular, the fluctuations in the real wage that have been shown to correspond roughly to fluctuations in marriage in England and France had little effect on marital fertility, which was much more stable over time than marriage (Wrigley and Schofield 1981, 1983; Weir 1984a).

It is likely that there was little deliberate regulation of marital fertility in most western European populations around 1870, although this will be discussed more extensively in chapter 4. In the absence of deliberate attempts either to space births or to stop childbearing once a desired number of children had been reached, differences among communities can probably be accounted for fairly well by differences in breastfeeding practices. Studies in developing countries based on surveys that record both contraceptive use (modern as well as traditional methods) and the duration of breastfeeding show that among women who do not use contraception much of the observed variation in marital fertility can be attributed to lactation (Casterline et al. 1984). Coital frequency, fetal mortality, and sterility play a much smaller role (Bongaarts and Menken 1983).[12] While direct evidence of these proximate determinants of marital fertility is not available for historical populations, the conclusion that breastfeeding accounts for much of the variation in marital fertility is compatible with evidence from English parish registers between 1600 and 1799 and from German village genealogies in the eighteenth and nineteenth centuries; in Germany, information on local practices of breastfeeding from surveys in

[11] The evidence that couples did not terminate childbearing before the physiological capacity to produce children was exhausted is persuasive. Couples might, however, have spaced births. This issue is discussed at length in chapter 4.

[12] Simulations show that the observed range of postpartum infecundability associated with breastfeeding (from three months to two years) can account for a difference in the total fertility rate of five children. In contrast, differences among groups in the waiting time to conception (primarily determined by coital frequency) only account for a difference of slightly less than one child and spontaneous intrauterine mortality accounts for about .25 of a child (Bongaarts and Menken 1983, 44–45).

the late nineteenth and early twentieth centuries substantiates these inferences (Wilson 1986; Knodel 1988).

Patterns of breastfeeding varied widely from one community to another. An examination of regional variations in breastfeeding in Germany shows that in some areas of southern Germany women did not breastfeed, giving their children pap instead; in other provinces, between 85 percent and 100 percent of the women nursed their children (Kintner 1985). (See also Knodel and van de Walle [1967] and Knodel [1988]). The areas of never-breastfeeding customs included southern Bavaria, the neighboring province of Donaukreis in Württemberg, and parts of the Kingdom of Saxony, as well as parts of Bohemia, the Austrian Tyrol, and Switzerland (Fildes 1986, 264; Kintner 1985).

Extended breastfeeding or never-breastfeeding customs seem to have been longstanding. In fourteen German villages studied by John Knodel, those villages where breastfeeding was most common among women who married at the end of the eighteenth century were also those where it was most common among women married at the end of the nineteenth century (Knodel 1988, 324). In southern Bavaria, the practice of never breastfeeding was evident by the fifteenth century; scripts of the Christmas plays of farmers in Oberbayern show Mary cooking the Christ Child a meal of pap rather than breastfeeding (Kintner 1985, 168).

What accounted for these variations is unclear, but whether or not women breastfeed seems to be associated more with women's work patterns and with community customs than with the individual characteristics of women. I have found only one study that connected breastfeeding with women's work in pre-transition western Europe. Ulla-Britt Lithell studied records for Petalax, a Swedish-speaking province in the western part of Finland and Umeå, a rural county in Sweden. Both parishes were known for not breastfeeding. In both, women worked hard in the fields during the summer, and a surge in infant mortality rates during the summer months suggests that they weaned their children then. In other areas, women who worked in the fields took their children with them (Lithell 1981). Thus, while women's work patterns probably were relevant for breastfeeding, apparently the manner by which women's work outside the home was integrated with childcare varied from community to community.

Religion might have influenced variation in breastfeeding practices. In England and Germany, women of the stricter Protestant sects were more likely to view breastfeeding their own children (rather than sending them to a wet nurse) as a religious duty (Fildes 1986, 99). In the provinces of Limburg and north Brabant in the southern part of the Netherlands, both of which were approximately 90 percent Catholic, children were breastfed for a shorter period than elsewhere in the Netherlands; a contemporary wrote that Catholics "omit breastfeeding out of a sense of shame or out of tradition. That is to say the bosoms of young girls were laced in such a way that their breasts could not develop fully'' (quoted by van Poppel 1983, 29).

Whatever the reasons for variation in breastfeeding customs across communities, and despite changes in these practices over time, the communities themselves seem relatively homogeneous in this respect. In southern Bavaria exceptions to the practice of never breastfeeding "were subject to severe social sanctions, including ridicule from neighbors and threats from husbands," which suggests the mobilization of village opinion (Kintner 1985, 168). Although there is little direct evidence about variations across social groups in breastfeeding customs, variations in infant mortality can serve as indirect evidence. Knodel's study of fourteen German villages in the eighteenth and nineteenth centuries found that village customs of breastfeeding account well for village differences in infant mortality. In these villages, infant mortality differed little among occupational groups within a village. Knodel concludes: "The fact that all social strata within a village appeared to have shared a more or less common risk of child loss emphasizes the probable role of local or regional infant-feeding customs, common to all classes, as a key determinant of infant mortality" and thus of marital fertility (Knodel 1988, 447). Even if the practices of elites were different, there were relatively few of them in these small communities, so their practices would not be evident in demographic measures based on total village populations.

What about marriage? The distinctive western European marriage pattern—relatively late age of female marriage and a relatively high proportion of spinsters—has been associated with nuclear family households, a tolerance for unmarried women (Watkins 1984) and a close correspondence of the spouses' ages (Laslett 1972; Gaskin 1978). These were found throughout western Europe and were apparently quite longstanding (Hajnal 1965; Hajnal 1982). Within this broad western European pattern, however, were regional patterns (the distinctive marriage in the Mediterranean countries [R. Smith 1981]) as well as sharp local differences.

What was local about marriage? Most young people married those they had met, which meant that the marriage market was circumscribed by their movements. For the upper classes, the relevant community extended beyond the village and the province; in England, the marriage market for the nobility was national (Stone and Stone 1984). For ordinary people, parish registers show that the marriage market was far more local. In France in 1865, 52 percent of couples marrying in rural communes in Ardèche were from the same commune; in the department of Loir-et-Cher, in only 13 percent of marriages between 1870 and 1877 did one of the spouses come from outside the department (Sutter 1958). And three-quarters of brides and grooms in the Bavarian village of Hetzenhausen in the first half of the nineteenth century came from settlements within a radius of one mile from the village (Lee 1981, 102).

Because the ability to set up a new household at marriage depended on economic resources, presumably economic circumstances were important in the timing of marriage everywhere; this would lead to considerable variation in the age of marriage. Additional variation probably came from substantial flexibility in the interpretation of the rule linking marriage to economic circumstances. But what satisfied the prerequisites for a new household seems more likely to have been defined by the community than by the individuals themselves. If it were simply resources that mattered, one would expect the women of the aristocracy to have married very early, perhaps just after menarche (as seems to have been the practice in other parts of the world). In nineteenth-century western Europe, however, the marriage age of aristocratic women was well within the range of the general population, which suggests a widespread consensus across social groups that marriage in the early teens was too young. Moreover, there is some evidence that occupational differences in the age of female marriage were surprisingly small (Knodel 1988; Kertzer and Hogan 1989).

This brief discussion of the determinants of demographic behavior in late nineteenth century western Europe points to the role of the community, and particularly the local community, in influencing demographic behavior.[13] This is not to say that individual decisions, based on individual circumstances, were not relevant. But it seems likely that relatives, friends, and neighbors had a say.

New mothers would have learned how to feed their children from their own mothers and from their neighbors, both through observation and from conversation. There are glimpses in the historical records of the circumstances of these conversations. On market day the women of the French village of Auffay walked together (without men) to the market seven miles away, where they sold their yarn and made purchases; we can imagine them chatting as they walked (Gullickson 1986, 84). Martine Segalen, in her account of peasant life in France in the nineteenth and twentieth centuries, cites a work on Brittany that says,

> The wash-house is one of the principal places of gossip in our region. Women of all ages meet there, and soaping and beating their linen often seems only a secondary activity, so enthusiastically do they exchange scandal, and tell each other of the loves, marriages, births and other major events of the district. (Segalen 1983, 138–139)

The picture of Breton women washing and gossiping together does not seem to me to be peculiar to Brittany or to France, and it is at least plausible that among the topics women discussed as they laundered was how to feed a new

---

[13] Only rarely is there evidence of community control at its most extreme form, as in some areas in nineteenth-century Germany, where marriage was forbidden if the couple was judged not to have sufficient resources to support the new household and thus would be a burden to the community (Knodel 1967).

infant and that the scandal they exchanged would have included stories of women who did not do it "right."

More direct evidence comes from the accounts of *Spinnstuben*, gatherings for work and sociability that were common across western Europe. Sometimes mixed-sex and sometimes single-sex, they were "one of the places around which the sexual culture of youth concentrated" (Medick 1984, 323). Here the women talked about everyday problems of the household economy, and "the censuring and settling of village conflicts were in the forefront" (Medick 1984, 334). A contemporary observer (from a publication of 1799) wrote that women "talked intimately of one's babies, of a cousin, of a neighbor, of flax, spinning; of geese, ducks, chickens, and eggs. . . ." (Medick 1984, 334). Men, in their own Spinnstuben, would also gossip, but apparently about somewhat different topics: agriculture and everyday life.

Evidence from trials of infanticide in rural Bavaria in the nineteenth century demonstrate the kind of detailed knowledge of each other's activities that members of small communities had (Schulte 1984). Women witnesses told what led them to be suspicious that an unmarried woman was pregnant; they recalled that she wore bulky clothes in the summer, that her diet changed, that she had not had a period for months. "From such talk it is clear that people in the village—and, in the case of Munich, particularly the milieu of tradesmen, shopkeepers, small dealers, and employees in the immediate neighborhood—knew everything that was happening" (Schulte 1984, 95).

Memoirs of rural Lancashire life around the end of the nineteenth century bring village tales even closer to the date of the analysis in this chapter. The author's Aunt Bridget was the first in a line of housemaids-cum-mistress to a certain rector. The sequence was one of seduction, enjoyment, pregnancy, dowry, and marriage (to someone else). The rector's immorality was talked of over port and coffee cups, but the "village made no trouble because the parson was charming and gentle," and if he left they might get someone worse (Robinson 1977, 28).

Gossip, as Patricia Meyer Spacks has written in her fine analysis of the parallels between gossip and the realistic English novel, has often been scorned as idle and malicious talk, particularly associated with women (Spacks 1986). Gossip is certainly a form of social control; some behaviors are condemned, others praised. But, Spacks argues, at its best gossip provides narrative, explanation, and judgment; in the stories of others, the talker narrates a sequence of events that imply an explanation, and talker and listeners alike speculate on the meaning of the events, reach a common point of view, and reassure themselves of what they share. Although the stories need not be local—one can gossip about anybody—it is likely that it is those who are "like us" who would be the most common topics of gossip, and that in the nineteenth century those who are "like us" would be members of the local community.

The village community was not undifferentiated socially or economically, nor was it the only community to which individuals belonged. Class or occupation channeled conversations; religious communities were not necessarily congruent with political communities (Macfarlane 1977). That differences in demographic behavior within villages were relatively small compared to the larger differences among villages suggests, however, a sort of village demographic culture. Why were the differences not larger? It is likely that individuals' choices of action were limited and defined by the context in which they thought and planned (Levine 1987, 8); important in that context, I think, were their conversations with other women.

It would be a mistake to picture western Europe in the decades around 1870, or even during the previous century, as isolated or locked into immobility (Tilly 1975). People came and went. The institution of service made young men and women quite mobile (Chatelain 1976; McBride 1976; Moch 1983; Mitterauer and Sieder 1982), and they could travel quite widely (Gillis 1974; Kussmaul 1981). Already by the seventeenth century, one-seventh of Englishmen had spent some time in London (Wrigley 1967). People went out to markets in nearby villages or towns; peddlers, tinkers, and vagrants came in; the state took some away to war; temporary migrants crossed provincial and regional boundaries.

A description of marriage patterns in Korle, in northern Hesse, meshes extra-village networks of trade and marriage (Wilke and Wagner 1981). In Korle marriage across the social boundary between goat and cow farmers was permitted, but not between these and horse farmers. Horse-farmer families used a go-between to arrange marriages. "The matchmaker was usually a cattle-dealer or a grain-dealer—someone who got around in the district and was familiar with the financial and social situation of the various farms with sons and daughters of marriageable age" (Wilke and Wagner 1981, 137). This suggests that marriage markets may have coincided with marketing regions, as William Skinner has argued for China (Skinner 1964, 1985); news of nubile young women could have been exchanged along with grain, introductions made, courtships developed.

Even those who traveled little would have heard what was going on outside the local area. News of political events was carried by newspapers and periodicals, as well as by peddlers and other visitors. One observer (from an account published in 1798) commented: "If a stranger comes travelling through, he will generally show up to the *Spinnstube* in order to share his store of novelties, and if a newspaper reader came from the village into the room, he was hardly allowed to catch his breath" (Medick 1984, 334). Politics came to ordinary life via newspapers in towns of eighteenth-century England; in Graz (Austria) in the late eighteenth century, peasants "heard about abolition of feudalism in France and demanded the abolition of their own feudal dues" (Burke 1978, 268).

It seems likely that in the past the local, face-to-face community had the most influence on demographic behavior. It was probably largely those who shared the same geographical space, who spoke the same dialect or language, whose interactions were frequent and regular because they were neighbors, that provided models for behavior, that rewarded the well behaved and punished those who strayed, and that formed the reference group against which one's own behavior was compared. That smaller areas within provinces were more similar to each other than they were to areas in other provinces, however, suggests that village networks linked communities in a larger provincial area. Marriage and migration were probably important in creating such links. As we have seen, most spouses were born in the same province, but they were often from different villages; marriage would have created a path among villages, as the outmarrying spouse returned to visit friends or relatives. Migrants, both temporary and permanent, maintained links with their communities of origin. In France, women who left their villages to work as domestic servants sometimes returned to marry or retire (McBride 1976, 10). The heterogeneity of provincial demographic behavior in the nineteenth century, however, suggests that the paths that connected villages with each other, with villages in other provinces, or with cities became more attenuated as distance increased.

CHAPTER 3

Limits to Demographic Diversity

A WORLD map of demographic behavior around 1870 would show western Europe in one color. The most distinctive feature was marriage behavior. In western Europe, women tended to marry relatively late and the proportion of spinsters was high, typically with fewer than half the women between the ages of fifteen and forty-nine married. In contrast, in most other parts of the world women typically married at a much younger age (under twenty) and few reached age fifty without having been married. In China in the early 1930s, the average age of marriage for women was less than eighteen, and over 99 percent of women aged forty-five to forty-nine years had been married (Barclay et al. 1976). In traditional Japan, as in China, virtually all women married (Cornell 1984).

Differences in marital fertility would be less evident on this map, but marital fertility may have been higher in western Europe than elsewhere, for pretransition levels were higher than in many noncontracepting populations in developing countries in the 1960s and 1970s. Western European levels of illegitimacy were probably least distinctive, though perhaps higher than elsewhere. There were more single women of reproductive age in Europe, and the definition of illegitimacy was particularly broad: "European society seems always to have classed the largest possible number of children as illegitimate" (Laslett 1980, 8). Thus, while from a western European perspective there was a great deal of local diversity, some options in the worldwide demographic repertory were not taken. Location in western Europe limited demographic diversity. That is, variation within western Europe was small compared to the differences between western Europe and the rest of the world.

In this chapter, I consider whether location in a particular country constrained demographic diversity still further. Was the same range of demographic behavior evident in each country, or did provinces in one country differ systematically from those in another? And if countries did differ, why were some countries more diverse than others?

COUNTRY LIMITS TO DEMOGRAPHIC DIVERSITY

We can begin exploring the limits to diversity by comparing actual to "possible" diversity. One approach to defining possible diversity would be to take the range from 0 to 1, since the indexes used here were constructed to fall between 0 and 1 (although as we shall see, marital fertility in a few Belgian arrondissements was above 1.00). This is unsatisfactory, however, because actual pretransition demographic behavior can be expected to be less diverse than this "possible" range; we would not expect to find provinces in which no women had children, or even provinces with very low fertility before the introduction of modern contraception, or provinces in which no women married.

A better comparison of actual to possible variation can be accomplished if we use the observed range of *country* medians to define possible diversity and then compare this to the actual diversity of provincial values within each country. To define possible diversity, we first establish the country median for each country by using the median province within that country (half the provinces have higher values, half lower values). This between-country range (the maximum country median—the minimum country median) can then be compared to the actual within-country range of provinces (the maximum province value within each country—the minimum province value within each country).

The country medians are shown at the bottom of table 3.1.[1] For marital fertility (I_g) the range of country medians is .290 (from France at .556 to Belgium at .846); the range of country medians for marriage (I_m) is .236 (from Ireland at .386 to Spain at .622). We can now compare the within-country range defined by the highest and lowest provincial values with the between-country range, defined by the highest and lowest country medians. For a few countries the range of provincial values is larger than the between-country range; for Germany, for example, the range for marital fertility (.369) is greater than the between-country range (.290). For most countries, however, the range of marital fertility is less than .290. If we consider marriage (I_m), where the difference between Ireland and Spain is .236, the range for individual countries is almost always smaller.

The within-country range of provincial values exaggerates diversity, because either the maximum or minimum provincial values may be suspect. But comparison of this actual within-country range with the "possible" between-country range shows the limits of diversity; for both marital fertility and marriage the actual within-country range is smaller than the "possible" range defined by country medians. This conclusion does not, however, hold for illegitimacy (I_h); in many countries, the range defined by the maximum country median (Germany) and the minimum (Ireland) is *smaller* than the within-country ranges.

In summary, although the within-country range is sensitive to error and may exaggerate the degree of variation, it shows both how different the provinces of Europe were and how similar. Considering all the countries of western Europe together and comparing them to the rest of the world, only a relatively

---

[1] As in chapter 2, the date is the first date for which the indexes used here can be calculated; it was given in table 2.1.

TABLE 3.1

Maximum, Minimum, and Range of Marital Fertility (I_g), Illegitimacy (I_h), and Marriage (I_m), by Country, First Date

	Marital Fertility I_g			Illegitimacy I_h			Marriage I_m		
	Max.	Min.	Range	Max.	Min.	Range	Max.	Min.	Range
Northwestern Europe									
Belgium	1.052	.488	.564	.093	.011	.082	.534	.348	.186
England and Wales	.761	.603	.158	.068	.022	.046	.556	.415	.141
France	.815	.348	.467	.100	.007	.093	.658	.388	.270
Germany	.942	.573	.369	.140	.012	.128	.549	.388	.161
Ireland	.782	.597	.185	.027	.004	.023	.529	.340	.189
Netherlands	.892	.717	.175	.035	.012	.023	.444	.319	.125
Scotland	.793	.701	.092	.098	.014	.084	.569	.295	.274
Switzerland	.990	.420	.570	.040	.006	.034	.552	.312	.240
Scandinavia									
Denmark	.760	.585	.175	.100	.024	.076	.493	.371	.122
Finland	.790	.597	.193	.082	.027	.055	.558	.434	.124
Norway	.869	.649	.220	.083	.014	.069	.514	.344	.170
Sweden	.826	.496	.330	.114	.032	.082	.491	.290	.201
Mediterranean									
Italy	.744	.628	.116	.068	.022	.046	.592	.517	.075
Portugal	.800	.552	.248	.137	.023	.114	.566	.354	.212
Spain	.824	.508	.316	.101	.007	.094	.691	.410	.281
Country medians	.846	.556	.290	.066	.011	.055	.622	.386	.236
	B	Fr		G	Ire		Sp	Ire	

small part of the available distribution was used; when we look at individual countries, despite their differences, they appear to be variants of a western European pattern.

A statistical technique, one-way analysis of variance, offers another approach to evaluating the importance of country location in accounting for demographic behavior. Because analysis of variance will be used several times in what follows, it is useful to explain it briefly.

Two statistics are used to summarize the analysis of variance, the R^2 and the F-value. The R^2 statistic gives the proportion of the total variation in province values that is "explained" by differences among countries. To understand this statistic, we must first define "total variation" and "explained variation."

The "total variation" is a measure of how observed values vary around the mean of all values. To be specific, 490 provinces are taken from 15 countries, in the analysis in table 3.2. The overall mean, M, of all 490 province values is calculated. Then, for the first province, the *difference* between that value and M is obtained. This difference tells us how far this particular province is from the overall mean. This type of *deviation from the mean* can be computed for each province. Although one might first think either the sum or the average of these deviations would be a good measure of variation among provinces, this is not the case. The sum of deviations from the mean is, by definition, equal to zero. Statisticians, therefore, *square* the deviations, so that a province that exceeds the mean by two and a province that is two less than the mean each are considered the same *distance*, or squared deviation, from the mean. The sum of the squared deviations is known as the *total variation*, or *total sum of squares*.

In a sense, the total sum of squares tells us how well, or how badly, we can predict the values for individual provinces when we predict that each one will be equal to the overall mean. We can then ask whether we would do better if we predicted that each province would be equal to the *mean for the country* in which that province is located; that is, does knowing country location for a particular province help us to predict its demographic behavior? To answer this, we calculate the deviation from its country's mean (where now there is a different mean for each of the fifteen countries considered) and then square it. The sum of these squared deviations is known alternatively as the "unexplained variation" or "error sum of squares" or "within-country sum of squares." It is the variation in province values that remains after we do our best to predict the provincial values from the country mean.

The total sum of squares can be split into two pieces: the "within-country

TABLE 3.2
One-way Analysis of Variance between Countries in Marital Fertility (I_g), Illegitimacy (I_h), and Marriage (I_m), All Provinces, First Date

	Marital Fertility (I_g)	Illegitimacy (I_h)	Marriage (I_m)
R²	.43	.39	.55
F-value[a]	26.1	21.1	42.1
Sum of squares			
Between country	2.56	.12	1.68
Within country	3.33	.19	1.36
Total	5.89	.31	3.04

Note: Because 15 countries and 490 provinces are in the analysis, there are 14 degrees of freedom for between-country variation and 475 for within-country (or error).

[a] All F-values are significant at the .0001 level or better.

sum of squares'' just calculated and the remainder, the ''between-country sum of squares,'' which is also known as the ''explained sum of squares'' because it is the amount of the original variation that is ''explained'' by the fact that countries differ in their mean values.

The statistic R^2 is the ratio of the explained sum of squares to the total sum of squares, or the *proportion* of the original variation that is explained by adopting the notion that countries have different means. Clearly, if there is no difference in means among countries, then R^2 will be zero, or close to it. If all province values cluster closely around their country means and these country means do differ, then R^2 will be close to one—we will get very close to the province value by predicting that it equals the mean for the country in which it is located.

The R^2s shown in table 3.2 are sizable: country location accounts for 55 percent of the variation in marriage (I_m), for 43 percent of the variation in marital fertility (I_g), and for 38 percent of the variation in illegitimacy (I_h).

The second statistic, the F-value, provides a measure of the extent to which country means vary over and above what would be expected if all actually had the same true mean, but differed by chance or measurement error in the observations we have at hand. We can consider the provinces of a country as a ''sample'' from all European provinces, so that we actually have fifteen such samples.[2] If all countries can be considered samples from a single pan-European population of provinces, there is a well-known statistical relationship between the variability of the country means and the variability of provinces within countries.

This relationship is expressed in the F-value, which is calculated from four quantities: the between-country sum of squares and the number of countries on the one hand, and the within-country sum of squares and the number of provinces on the other. The number of countries minus one (a quantity known as the between-country degrees of freedom) is divided into the between-country sum of squares to obtain the between-country mean square. Although it is

[2] ANOVA and some of the other analyses that follow use conventional statistical techniques and present measures (such as the F-value) of statistical significance. These tests and measures are based on the assumption that the data are a random sample from a larger population, a sample of which is being used to estimate the effects present in the larger population. The data used in this book are not a sample, but the whole population: all the births, all the married women, and so on. In this case, the measures lose their formal statistical meaning. They can, however, be used heuristically, in much the same way that measures such as the mean and the median are used to describe the central tendency in a body of data, and the standard deviation and the midspread are used to describe the amount of dispersion in those data. Thus, the F-value and levels of significance become not a measure of statistical significance in the formal sense, but a description of the relative orders of magnitude of between-country and within-country differences. Similarly, violation of the equal variance assumption of ANOVA vitiates measures of statistical significance, but not its descriptive value. (For further description of analysis of variance, see Wonnacott and Wonnacott [1984]).

beyond the scope of this discussion to provide even a heuristic proof, this mean square is an estimate of the variability of individual province values *if the hypothesis that all countries have the same mean is true*. The within-country mean square, which is the within-country sum of square divided by its degrees of freedom (number of provinces-number of countries), is also an estimate of the variability of individual provinces. The F-value is the ratio of the between-country mean square to the within-country mean square. Thus, an F-value close to one supports the hypothesis that the countries all have the same mean, i.e., that country is unimportant as a determinant of province values. But if knowing the country in which a province lies allows better prediction of the index for that country than one would find using the mean for all provinces as the predictor, the F-statistic will be large. The greater the F-value, the more important is country as an explanation for the differences we observe in province values.

The F-value is important for an additional reason: it is the quantity that is used to test whether R^2, the proportion of the total variation that is explained by country differences, is significantly different from zero (i.e., there is more variation than expected in country means). The F-values in table 3.2 are large, which shows that the variation across countries is substantial and significant—far larger than one would predict on the basis of the variation within countries.[3]

The finding that country location matters is substantively significant for two reasons. First, because provinces within a country were more like each other demographically than they were like provinces in other countries, country boundaries circumscribed a distinct and coherent social entity, at least as measured by its demography. Thus it is appropriate to take countries as units of analysis. Second, demographic diversity was constrained by national boundaries. At the beginning of the last quarter of the nineteenth century, national populations already showed some demographic homogeneity, although as we shall see in chapter 5 the importance of country boundaries for demographic behavior increased substantially between 1870 and 1960.

Country boundaries mattered most for marriage and least for illegitimacy (the R^2 is largest for I_m, smallest for I_h). This suggests that levels of marriage were more sensitive to determinants that operated over a geographically larger area than the province, whereas the determinants of illegitimacy appear to have been more local in scope or varied less among countries.

That country boundaries matter for demographic behavior is a statement about statistical aggregates, not about any particular group of provinces or any particular border. On the demographic map of western Europe, border prov-

---

[3] In a separate analysis France was excluded to see if its unusual marital fertility patterns might have biased the results. All F-values remained significant at the .0001 level. The R^2 dropped to .25 for I_g, stayed roughly constant for I_h at .39, and rose to .59 for I_m.

inces may be more like provinces on the other side of the border than like neighboring provinces in the same country. A comparison of the demography of the provinces of Alsace-Lorraine with its French neighbors and its German neighbors in the 1860s shows that the boundary that separated France from Germany was quite porous.

Alsace-Lorraine was then a part of France, as it had been on and off in the past, but its culture was German. The standard written language of Alsace-Lorraine was Hochdeutsch, the home languages were Germanic dialects (Stephens 1976, 341).[4] In the 1860s the levels of marital fertility and marriage in the three provinces of Alsace-Lorraine (Haut-Rhin, Bas-Rhin, and Moselle) were more like their German neighbors (Pfalz and Trier) than the contiguous French departments (Haute-Saône, Vosges, and Meurthe).[5] In general more French women than German women were married, and marital fertility was higher in Germany than in France. The average level of marriage (I_m) of the three provinces of Alsace-Lorraine was .42, of the three neighboring French departments .50, and of the two neighboring German administrative areas .47. Marital fertility was an average .72 in Alsace-Lorraine, .49 in the French neighbors, and .78 in the German neighbors. All three of the neighboring French provinces had a level of marital fertility that shows the fertility transition had begun (.600), while none of the provinces of Alsace-Lorraine or its German neighbors had marital fertility below .600. We can summarize by saying that with respect to marital fertility Alsace-Lorraine was much more like its German neighbors than its French neighbors; with respect to marriage, Alsace-Lorraine was even more German than the German provinces. If national boundaries had followed demographic boundaries, Alsace-Lorraine would have been included in Germany, not France.

Sources of Demographic Diversity

If there was an important role for others in the determination of demographic behavior—that is, if some of the sources of variation were social rather than individual—we would expect that the demographically most diverse countries were those in which local communities were more isolated from one another,

[4] There are more precise estimates of the proportion speaking French or German in Alsace-Lorraine at dates somewhat later than those used here, but they are of dubious accuracy. The German censuses in 1900, 1905, and 1910 show a vast majority German speaking, while the French censuses of Alsace-Lorraine in 1921 and 1926 show a vast majority French speaking (Tesnière 1928, 371–78; see especially the table on p. 373). A change between 1910 and 1921 of the magnitude indicated seems to me unlikely. Tesnière notes that the questions are different (the Germans asked mother tongue, the French asked usual language) but also notes other considerations, e.g., the ''régime d'oppression'' in Alsace-Lorraine before the war (Tesnière 1928, 374).

[5] The indexes for the French departments were measured in 1861 and for the German administrative areas in 1867. Two other German administrative areas touch Alsace-Lorraine (Karlsruhe and Freiburg), but no data are available for them in 1867.

where life was shaped largely by local institutions and local conventions. Conversely, we would expect that the demographically more homogeneous countries were those in which the degree of social integration across provinces was greater.

Let us explore this issue further by comparing the degree of diversity across countries. Which countries were the most diverse, which the least? Figure 3.1 permits us to make this comparison easily.

The boxplots depict the distribution of provincial values (from highest to lowest, for example) and show the degree to which they are either concentrated or spread out. In figure 3.1 the length of the box is the midspread, which includes the central 50 percent of the provincial values (and thus excludes the lowest 25 percent and the highest 25 percent of the provincial values). The top of the box is the upper quartile boundary; the bottom of the box is the lower quartile boundary. If the distribution of that central portion of provincial values is spread out, the box is long; if the distribution is compressed, the box is short. The horizontal bar within the box marks the median, and the dot marks the mean. (The values for the medians and midspreads are in appendix table A3.1.) The maximum and minimum country values are also shown on the boxplots as asterisks. The minimums for marital fertility are usually large cit-

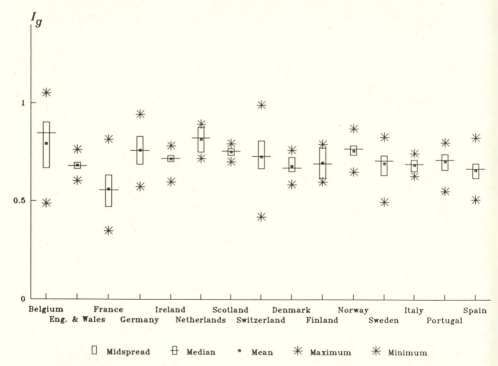

Figure 3.1a. Boxplots of Marital Fertility (I_g) within Each Country, First Date

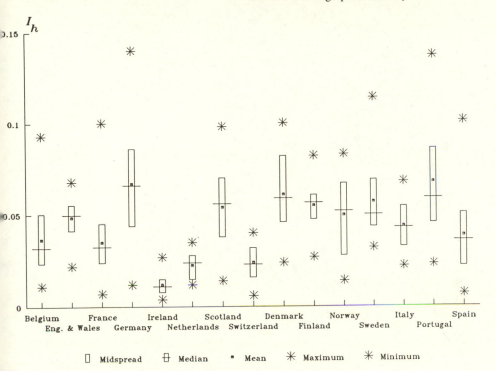

I_h

Figure 3.1b. Boxplots of Illegitimacy (I_h) within Each Country, First Date

ies, often capital cities: for example, Dublin, Geneva, Stockholm, Lisbon, and Barcelona. Illegitimacy is distinctive both in large cities and in some remote areas. For example, in Portugal the three highest provincial levels of illegitimacy were the provinces of Lisbon (the capital), and Bragança, and Vila Real (both in the northeast).[6]

The demographic homogeneity of England and Wales both before and during the transition has been remarked by others (Wrigley and Schofield 1983; Teitelbaum 1984; Woods and Hinde 1985; Coale and Treadway 1986) and is evident in marital fertility (figure 3.1a), illegitimacy (figure 3.1b), and marriage (figure 3.1c).

The least diverse countries with respect to marital fertility are those of the British Isles (England and Wales, Scotland, and Ireland) and Norway, whereas the least diverse with respect to marriage are Norway, Italy, England and Wales, and the Netherlands.[7] When we consider illegitimacy, England

[6] Examination of stem-and-leaf plots of the distribution of provincial values within each country shows them to be fairly symmetrical for I_g and I_m, although often a large city is unusual. The distribution of provincial values for I_h is more skewed.

[7] Cormac Ó'Gráda has argued that the Princeton European Fertility Project underestimated

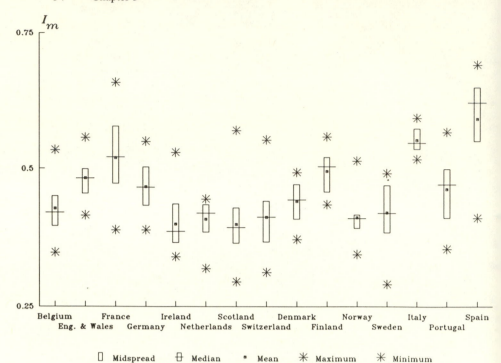

Figure 3.1c. Boxplots of Marriage (I_m) within Each Country, First Date

and Wales and Ireland are again quite homogeneous, along with Finland and the Netherlands. In contrast, Belgium, France, Germany, and Switzerland are relatively diverse on two out of the three measures. Note that the rankings on the three indexes can be quite different for the same country; the Netherlands, for example, is diverse with respect to marital fertility but not marriage or illegitimacy, whereas Portugal and Spain are quite diverse with respect to illegitimacy and marriage, but much less so with respect to marital fertility. (Appendix table A3.2 shows the rank order of the midspreads.)

What could account for these differences? I will first consider whether they might be due to relative underregistration in some provinces compared to others, or a statistical artifact, reflecting simply differences in the number of provinces within countries. I will then consider whether the greater demographic diversity in some countries might be caused by the early fertility decline that widened the demographic distance between the leaders in this process and the rest of the provinces. This issue was discussed in chapter 2 where the analysis

marital fertility in some Irish counties. Comparing his estimates for 1881 with those based on the project's would give a larger range and midspread than those shown here (Ó'Gráda 1988, 168–69). The midspread is still, however, one of the smallest in western Europe.

focused on all of the western European provinces together, but needs to be reconsidered for a comparison across countries. Next, I will examine the relation between demographic homogeneity or heterogeneity, on the one hand, and the size of the country and its population density on the other. I will conclude by showing that the differences appear to be long-standing and that the most diverse countries are those that were multicommunal, as indicated by the variety of languages and patois spoken by the inhabitants.

Differences in local recording practices might mean that births and marriages were fully recorded in some areas, but underregistered in others, thus biasing the measures of diversity. If the underregistration occurred in populations whose "true" levels of marital fertility, marriage, or illegitimacy were low, diversity would be exaggerated; if the underregistration occurred where the "true" levels were high, diversity would appear to be less than it should be had marriages and births been counted correctly.

Modern censuses and systems of vital registration are conducted by central statistical bureaus with uniform procedures for all parts of the country, but it is quite possible that in the nineteenth century local compliance differed. One might be especially suspicious a priori about local differences in recording in Germany. Although uniform regulations imposed some consistency after unification in 1871, the individual states maintained some autonomy in the collection and publication of vital statistics and census data (Knodel 1974, 23). In Switzerland, it was not until 1867 that the cantons agreed to standardize the compilation of vital events (F. van de Walle 1977). In Belgium, on the other hand, there are reasons for thinking that local differences in the accuracy of the data were relatively minor. Quetelet and his colleague Heuschling directed the census: "Both men undertook regular inspection trips all over the country, sometimes severely reprimanding the local authorities and clerks for the slightest deficiency in the vital statistics record" (Lesthaeghe 1977, 234).

One check on the accuracy of the marital fertility index is whether it rose between the first date for which it was calculated and the next. Rises in fertility might be genuine, but also might be due to improved birth registration. In all of the countries marital fertility (I_g) rose between the first and the subsequent dates in at least one province and sometimes in a substantial proportion (five out of eight provinces in Finland, sixteen out of thirty-three in Scotland, twenty-five out of forty-eight in Spain). Only in Italy and Finland were increases in marital fertility concentrated among the provinces with the lowest levels of marital fertility. In the other countries, the rises were no more likely to occur in low-fertility provinces (those in the bottom quarter of the distribution) than in high-fertility provinces (those in the top quarter of the distribution). Indeed, sometimes a rise in marital fertility was evident in provinces with quite high fertility (an I_g of over .800).[8]

---

[8] Knodel found that the twelve provinces with a suspiciously low proportion of stillbirths (in-

If these rises in marital fertility indicate faulty data, what is the magnitude of the possible error? The rises were usually quite small, rarely over 5 percent and usually less. In Belgium, Lesthaeghe examined data for births in 1846 and estimated that the maximum error in I_g was 7.5 percent and in I_m 3 percent (Lesthaeghe 1977, 249–50). It is reasonable to think this margin would have lessened by 1880, when the data used here begin.[9] In Finland, where fertility rose in five out of the eight provinces, the maximum increase was about 4 percent (calculations not shown). Because some rises in marital fertility were probably genuine (that is, they occurred for reasons other than improving registration), these figures suggest a rough upper bound to the pervasiveness and magnitude of errors in the data.

In summary, the provinces that appear to be affected by underregistration are few, and the likely magnitude of error is small. Only in Finland and Italy are rises in marital fertility evident in low-fertility provinces, biasing initial measurements of variation toward greater diversity; in other countries, rises in marital fertility occurred in high-fertility as well as low-fertility provinces. Thus, the errors probably do not greatly or systematically distort the picture of diversity. Equally important, they will not significantly affect the comparisons with 1960 in chapter 5.

For a few countries the indexes have been calculated for units that are either smaller or larger than the provinces used here. It was thus possible to compare relative diversity of the two sets of units, one with a smaller number of larger units and one with a larger number of smaller units. The differences are slight for both the range and the midspread (see appendix table A3.3). Only in Italy do the number and size of the units make a substantial difference; diversity in marriage in Italy would be almost twice as great if the smaller units were used, although Italy would still be relatively homogeneous compared to most other countries of western Europe. In general, however, the number and size of the units do not seem to substantially affect the measurement of diversity, especially when the midspread is used.

That several of the countries that appear most demographically heterogeneous are either French speaking or contain large French-speaking minorities raises the possibility that their demographic diversity is of recent origin, related to the earlier onset of the fertility transition in some provinces than in others. Since variation is expected to increase during a time of change, this might account for the relatively great diversity in France, Belgium, and Switzerland. This possibility cannot be ruled out, but the evidence does not point in that direction.

First, one of the most diverse countries is Germany, which did not have a

---

dicating failure to register all stillbirths and, perhaps, live births as well) were those with extremely high marital fertility rates (Knodel 1974, 27).

[9] In the 1846 Belgian census the tabulations were for provinces with boundaries different from those used from 1880 onwards.

significant French-speaking population. Second, it will be recalled that the analyses in this chapter and in chapter 2 are all done for the first date for which it is possible to calculate the indexes, in order to minimize the likelihood that early fertility decline in some provinces would affect the degree of demographic diversity. In the European Fertility Project, two indicators of the onset of the fertility transition were used: a 10 percent decline in I_g or an I_g of .600 or less. The former is significant because rarely was a decline of that magnitude reversed, the latter because levels that low are thought to be uncommon (though not unknown) without deliberate attempts to limit fertility within marriage. Belgium has five provinces and Spain six in which fertility decline appears to have preceded the first date at which the indexes could be calculated; the others either have no provinces or only one (usually a large city, often the capital) (see appendix table A3.4). Thus, since the midspreads exclude the lowest 25 percent of the provincial values, the comparison of demographic diversity using the midspread will not be biased by early fertility decline in some provinces.[10]

Third, even in France, where the fertility transition had begun in some areas around the time of the French Revolution but was not to begin in other areas until after 1870, there is reason to believe that demographic diversity was considerable before the fertility transition began. There were certainly large differences in local economies and social structures (see, for example, Bloch [1966]; Durand [1984]; Braudel [1988]).[11] Le Bras and Todd (1981) in their analysis of French historical series for a wide variety of political and anthropological measures, such as household structure, voting patterns, literacy, and suicide, also show considerable diversity in aspects of social life that presumably are not directly related to fertility, but express distinctive local communities. France, they say, contains not one people but a hundred, who differ in their conceptions of life and of death, in their kinship systems, in their attitudes toward work or violence (Le Bras and Todd 1981, 76).

[10] In Switzerland and Belgium, even though the midspread does not include provinces that had unambiguously begun the fertility transition, the French-speaking arrondissements usually had lower fertility than the German-speaking or Flemish-speaking arrondissements. In Spain, the early declining provinces were mostly in Catalonia, which had closer ties to France than most other Spanish provinces, as well as a distinctive language and earlier industrialization.

[11] Robert Muchembled represents a partial exception to the common emphasis on the diversity of prerevolutionary France. He argues that popular culture became more uniform during the seventeenth and eighteenth centuries, due in part to the penetration in state power, in part to the church, whose priests and missionaries took an identical message everywhere and worked for the religious unification of France just as the agents of the king worked for political unification, and in part to the dissemination of a uniform ideology through popular imagery and peddlers' literature (Muchembled 1985). The center's penetration of rural areas was incomplete, however, and when the ancien régime became sclerotic, a resurgence of popular "microcultures" continued into the first part of the nineteenth century; "The second quarter of the nineteenth century was . . . marked by the existence of solid microcultures within the rural world" (Muchembled 1985, 308).

David Weir has calculated I_g (marital fertility) for a national sample of forty villages for the period 1740–1790; the midspread is .157, virtually identical to the .159 midspread of French departments in 1831.[12] In France, an increase in marriage paralleled the decline in marital fertility, and thus, variation in marriage might also be of recent origin. But a comparison of the proportion single at age fifty for cohorts born in 1756 and cohorts born in the period 1796–1800 shows as much diversity among departmental levels in the earlier as in the later cohort, thus suggesting that diversity in marriage in France was not solely the consequence of early fertility decline (Watkins 1980). Thus, although some of the demographic diversity of Switzerland and Belgium may have been caused by early fertility decline in the French-speaking parts of these countries, this is not the case for Germany, and in France demographic diversity appears to be long-standing, preceding the onset of fertility decline.

We would be even more confident that the diversity among provinces reported here was not due to recent change in fertility and marriage if even earlier periods could be examined. Demographic information derived from the parish registers for England, France, and Germany for the eighteenth century do not permit a precise comparison because the parishes to which they refer are much smaller than the provinces, and the demographic measures that have been calculated are different. My analysis of age at first marriage and marital fertility rates at ages thirty to thirty-four using the figures reported for parishes in Flinn (1981, app. table 1, app. table 7) shows that England was demographically homogeneous in the eighteenth century, whereas France and Germany were far more diverse, results that are consistent with those based on provinces reported above.

The differences in demographic diversity among countries might be due to their sizes. Larger countries such as France and Germany, or those like Italy, Norway, and Sweden, which are narrow but extensive in a north-south direction, might encompass more variation in climate and soil type and thus, presumably, in modes of agricultural production, as historians of the *Annales* school have proposed. If demographic behavior is related to these factors, we would expect more diversity in large countries. Large countries also offer more space for settlement by people of different languages and different cultures. In an era when the technology was less developed than it is today, communication would have been more difficult and government more local in a large country than a smaller one (ceteris paribus). For the same reasons, small countries like Denmark, England, or the Netherlands might be expected to be more homogeneous.

Or, homogeneity might be a function of population density. Durkheim proposed that population density translates into "dynamic density"; as groups

---

[12] Calculated by David Weir from data reported in Weir (1983, 189, table 46).

come in more frequent and sustained contact with a wider range of other groups, the isolated homogeneity of each group would break down, and economic and cultural exchange would be stimulated (Durkheim 1964; Giddens 1971, 78). Similarly, Blau emphasizes the importance of contact for social integration: "the integration of individuals in a group requires direct associations among them" (Blau 1977, 85). In addition, greater population density probably means more indirect contact among individuals in different provinces, because denser populations can, ceteris paribus, better support communication infrastructures (e.g., a mail system).

If greater population density means more frequent and sustained contact, it is reasonable to expect that greater blending of demographic behavior might be a consequence. Thus, we might expect the countries that were the most densely settled to display the least amount of variation and those that were more sparsely settled to display the most.

Correlations (not shown) between the midspread of any of the indexes and either area or population density show that the signs of the correlation coefficients are in the expected direction (positive with area, negative with density); thus, countries that are larger and countries that are more sparsely settled are demographically more diverse, whereas the small, densely populated countries are demographically more homogeneous.[13] The correspondence, however, is weak; the correlation coefficients are small and not statistically significant, and the amount of variation left unexplained is large (at least 93 percent of the variation remains unexplained).[14]

The boxplots examined earlier showed that England and Wales, Scotland, and Ireland were the most homogeneous with respect to marital fertility and marriage; in general, these countries are still unusually homogeneous, even after area or population density are taken into account. Belgium, France, Germany, and Switzerland were the most heterogeneous when we looked at the boxplots and remain among the most heterogeneous in marital fertility even after area and population density are taken into account; with respect to marriage, France and Switzerland remain among the most diverse, but Belgium and Germany lose their distinctiveness.

[13] The area and total population were shown in table 2.1.

[14] To examine the relation between area, population density, and demographic diversity more closely, regression lines were fit relating the midspreads of each of the indexes either to area or to population density. Then the residuals from these regressions (that is, that part of the variation in the midspread that *cannot* be explained by area or population density, respectively) were plotted against each other (figures A3.2a–3.2c). Large positive residuals on both indexes, indicating more variation than could be predicted from the relation between either the midspread and area or the midspread and population density, are in the upper right-hand corner; large negative residuals, indicating more demographic homogeneity than expected, are in the lower left-hand corner. It is clear that countries tend to fall in either the upper right-hand quadrant or the lower left-hand quadrant.

Demographic Diversity and Linguistic Diversity

The correspondence between demographic diversity and linguistic diversity is striking. The demographically most diverse countries are, by and large, those that were multilingual in the latter part of the nineteenth century. By multilingual, I mean that there was more than one official national language or that some people were monolingual in a language other than the national language (or languages). I stretch the term "language" to include dialects that were incomprehensible, or comprehensible only with difficulty, to outsiders.[15]

Language is one of the most obvious signs of a distinct community. Language may be among the "gross actualities," like blood, race, locality, religion, or tradition (Geertz 1971, 655), or it may be a marker of other cultural differences, including ethnicity (Fishman 1977; Parsons 1975). The ethnic boundary, in turn,

> canalizes social life—it entails a frequently quite complex organization of behaviour and social relations. The identification of another person as a fellow member of an ethnic group implies a sharing of criteria for evaluation and judgement. It thus entails the assumption that the two are fundamentally "playing the same game." . . . On the other hand, a dichotomization of others as strangers, as members of another ethnic group, implies a recognition of limitations on shared understandings, differences in criteria for judgement of value and performance, and a restriction of interaction to sectors of assumed common understanding and mutual interest. (Barth 1969, 15)

Most relevant here is that a common language is a basis for interaction, the basis for a special bond between language and territory. Deutsch captures this with his distinction between the term "culture," which stresses the configuration of preferences or values, and the term "community," which stresses the aspects of communication (Deutsch 1966, 89). Inhabitants of the same country can be said to form distinct communities if they cannot communicate with each other because they speak different languages. Even when interaction is possible—when members of the group are bilingual, or when there is a lingua franca—a different mother tongue or a different accent may signify a different conception of the rules of the game, and may be experienced as a social boundary. In the Pays de Caux, in France, "people who lived in the Caux but did not speak the patois were not considered *cauchois(e)*, no matter how long they lived there" (Gullickson 1986, 11). Just as women would not have gossiped with those who spoke another language, they may also have felt that those across a social boundary marked by a distinctive ac-

---

[15] If two speeches can be traced back to a common language, they are dialects. However, when dialects diverge so far that they are no longer obviously related or they are mutually unintelligible, the term "language" is used (Sapir 1931). Dialects are characterized by differences of vocabulary and grammar as well as pronunciation (Trudgill 1983, 17).

cent were not subject to the same rules—of courtship or of breastfeeding, for example—as those within the same community.

While most western European countries had some monolingual minorities in their territorial populations, the proportions varied a great deal.[16] Because the midspread used to measure demographic diversity includes only the central portion of the distribution of provincial values, the demographically most diverse countries by this measure were generally those that were squarely bilingual or plurilingual, with substantial proportions speaking different languages; the demographically more homogeneous countries were generally those with a single dominant language, albeit often with small linguistic minorities.

The Scandinavian countries had small monolingual minority populations: Lapp speakers in the north of all countries except Denmark; German and Frisian speakers in Denmark; Swedish, Russian, and German speakers in Finland; Finnish speakers in Sweden.[17] Although historically many languages had been spoken in England (various Celtic languages, Anglo-Saxon dialects, Danish or Norwegian, and French [by the Normans]), by the eighteenth century only Welsh survived. In the Netherlands, Frisian was spoken in the single province of Friesland.[18]

Belgium, Switzerland, Germany, and France had much larger linguistic minorities. At the dates of the demographic analyses in this chapter, only Switzerland was officially multilingual (in French, German, and Italian).[19] In Switzerland in 1880, the mother tongue was German for 71.3 percent of the population, French for 21.4 percent, Italian for 5.7 percent and Romansch for 1.4 percent (McRae 1983, 50, table 6). Belgium became officially bilingual in 1898. In Belgium, the linguistic communities were of nearly equal size. In the 1880 census of Belgium, 42.6 percent of the population reported knowing French only, 47.5 percent Flemish only, and 8.1 percent reported knowing both French and Flemish (McRae 1986, 36, table 1).[20] The small proportion bilingual suggests little communication across the language boundary.

[16] The distribution of the population by language was sometimes a highly political issue in the nineteenth century as well as subsequently. Thus, often there is no official data (e.g., in Belgium after 1947) or the figures are questionable (e.g., the censuses of Alsace-Lorraine discussed earlier).

[17] There were nearly 340,000 Swedes in Finland in 1910, about 12 percent of a total population of nearly three million, as well as speakers of Russian, German, Estonian, and other languages (Tesnière 1928, 370). There were about 15,000 Finns in Sweden in 1870, out of total population of slightly over four million, as well as much smaller groups who spoke other languages (Tesnière 1928, 427). In Norway, some Danish was spoken, as well as several varieties of Norwegian. Norway will be discussed in more detail in chapter 6.

[18] Dutch and Frisian are closely akin linguistically, and their speakers are close also in tradition and outlook (Kloss 1968, 74).

[19] Romansch was added as a national but not an official language in 1938. Belgium became officially bilingual in 1898, Finland in 1919.

[20] The bilingual population was largely in Brussels, but also included the upper levels of Flem-

Without question, France was multilingual in the midnineteenth century. Breton, Basque, Flemish, and Italian were spoken, and some authors include Provençal, Corsican, and the Germanic dialects of Alsace-Lorraine as distinctive languages. Size estimates of the non-French-speaking population differ and will be considered in detail in chapter 7, but they support a conclusion that a substantial proportion of the population of France normally spoke either a language other than French or a dialect that would have been difficult for a French-speaker to understand.

With data aggregated at the level of the province it is not possible to know whether individuals who spoke a different language from others in the province behaved differently demographically. It is possible, however, to show a connection between language and demographic behavior for smaller communities than provincial populations. Paul Adams (1982) has analyzed fertility and marriage by canton (cantons are smaller than departments) in the department of the Pyrénées-Orientales. This department was formed in 1790 by the addition of three Languedocien cantons to the former province of Roussillon (which itself had only been part of France since 1659, and in which Catalan was spoken). In 1866 most of the cantons had high fertility and low proportions married; only the three Languedocien cantons were different, having the low fertility and high marriage of the rest of Languedoc. These distinctively different demographic regimes were in two regions "that were as economically and geographically alike as peas in a pod," suggesting that linguistic differences were associated with demographic differences (Adams 1982, 3). A supporting example comes from Switzerland, where an analysis based on units smaller than the canton showed more heterogeneity in marital fertility by language than by religion (F. van de Walle 1977).

Just as social exchange and interaction are surely hindered when individuals speak a different language, so also we expect less social exchange and interaction among villages or provinces when they are linguistically different. This does not mean, of course, that no significant differences remain among those who speak the same language; a common language is only one of the bases of social interaction. But it is necessary for direct interaction, and there is reason to believe that a common language reduces the salience of at least some other social divisions. For example, writing about migration from the countryside to the city of Nîmes in the nineteenth century, Leslie Moch says, "Regional dialect and attitudes may well have united the newcomer with the city as much as they alienated him or her" (Moch 1983, 24).

A comparison of linguistic diversity and demographic diversity supports this interpretation. It is clear that at the level of the country there was often (but not always) a correspondence between linguistic diversity and demo-

---

ish society. In addition, under 1 percent reported knowing only German (largely in the provinces of Liège and Luxembourg).

graphic diversity, and the analysis of variation among departments in France in chapter 7 will show that language was statistically significant in accounting for variation in demographic behavior in 1871.

There are some anomalies. I will consider first England and Wales and then Italy.

In this analysis the counties of England and Wales are considered together. In the 1880s, Welsh was the language of daily intercourse in northern and western Wales (Morgan 1981, 21); thus, we might have expected more demographic diversity.[21] That we do not find it may in part be due to the fact that in the Princeton European Fertility Project the demographic indexes were not calculated for the counties of Wales, but for two groupings of these counties (called North Wales and South Wales). But neither North nor South Wales was particularly distinctive demographically.[22] While the possible influence of economic and political integration in diminishing demographic diversity will be discussed at length later, it is interesting to note here that the economy of Wales seems to have been well integrated with that of England by the middle of the nineteenth century, with many English immigrants lured by industrial jobs in the south (Baines 1981; Hechter 1975). Braudel puts the economic integration of England and Wales even earlier, saying that Wales was already drawn into the London economic net by the sixteenth century (Braudel 1982, 40). In addition, Wales had been brought under the English crown in the fourteenth century. The possible influence of economic and political integration in diminishing demographic diversity will be discussed at length later.

Italy is particularly puzzling. There were deep differences in dialects and language, as well as other marked divisions that took geographical form (see Ascoli [1910] for the most complete discussion; see also Tesnière [1928]; Beales [1971]; Devoto [1978]; Procacci [1970]). When Garibaldi's troops went to the south, the peasants who cheered for "Italia" thought they were honoring Garibaldi's mistress (Beales 1971, 89). It is almost certain that the relevant community in Italy was much smaller than the province.[23]

[21] In 1901 30 percent of the Welsh population over age three spoke Welsh only (Williams 1982, 149, table 1.) Most of these speakers were concentrated in the counties of the north and west.

[22] If the two Welsh provinces were excluded, the midspread for I_g (marital fertility) would increase (.043 rather than .030); the midspread of I_m (marriage) would be virtually unchanged (.042 without Wales rather than .043 with Wales). When the counties of England and Wales are grouped into ten larger regions (e.g., the North Midlands, the Home counties, and the southeast), results of an analysis of variance show that Wales (North Wales, South Wales and Monmouthshire) is distinct. The overlap among the other regions, however, is sufficiently great so that region does not explain much of the variation among counties, unlike in France and Germany, where regional effects were quite large (Watkins, Casterline, and Pereira 1987).

[23] As noted earlier, however, Italy is still relatively homogeneous when the midspread is calculated for smaller units. Nonetheless, differences between nearby areas could be quite large: for example, I_m was .279 in Varallo, and .700 in Casale Monferrato, less than 40 miles south (Livi-Bacci 1977, 164). Finer measures of demographic behavior might show Italy to be more demo-

The unexpected lack of correspondence between linguistic diversity and demographic diversity in Italy calls attention to several important caveats. First, the number of countries considered here is small, only fifteen. If the countries were a sample, we would certainly be concerned about sample variability in such a small sample, and we should be no less concerned when we are dealing with a population (in this case, of countries) with only fifteen members. Second, the correspondence between linguistic diversity and demographic diversity has been singled out, but there are other dimensions along which societies are integrated or divided, such as religion, economics, and politics. Sometimes these coincided with linguistic divisions, as in Belgium, but sometimes they did not, as in Switzerland (both will be discussed at greater length in chapter 6).

Third, where we see linguistic diversity, it is reasonable to assume that language marks the boundaries between two societies, boundaries that also distinguish patterns of reproduction. The reverse assumption—that demographic homogeneity means a lack of cultural or social differences—is not tenable without knowing more about other elements of social integration, such as the degree of development of a national market or the penetration of the state. Where there were other bases for social integration we are on firmer ground in interpreting the demographic similarities as evidence of a community that stretched across provincial boundaries. Where such sources of social integration were largely absent, as apparently they were in Italy in the nineteenth century, the demographic homogeneity may be deceptive. (We shall see in chapter 5 that in Italy demographic diversity increased more during the demographic transition than in any other country, suggesting that underlying provincial differences had been masked at the earliest dates examined in this analysis.)

ENGLAND AND FRANCE

England was demographically far more homogeneous than France. John Stuart Mill observed that other kinds of homogeneity had increased in England and pointed out some of the processes that brought this about.

> The circumstances which surround different classes and individuals, and shape their characters, are daily becoming more assimilated. Formerly, different ranks, different neighborhoods, different trades and professions lived in what might be called different worlds; at present, to a great degree in the same. Comparatively speaking,

---

graphically diverse. It may be that more or less similar levels of nuptiality in Italy were the result of different combinations of age, and marriage, and spinsterhood. In Switzerland, for example, I_m was similar in French-speaking and German-speaking cantons. In the former, women married earlier than in the latter, but there were also more spinsters in the former than in the latter (van de Walle 1977).

they now read the same things, listen to the same things, see the same things, go to the same places, have their hopes and fears directed to the same objects, have the same rights and liberties, and the same means of asserting them. . . . And the assimilation is still proceeding. All the political changes of the age promote it, since they all tend to raise the low and to lower the high. Every extension of education promotes it, because education brings people under common influences and gives them access to the general stock of facts and sentiments. Improvement in the means of communication promotes it, by bringing the inhabitants of distant places into personal contact, and keeping up a rapid flow of changes of residence between one place and another. . . . A more powerful agency than even all these, in bringing about a general similarity among mankind, is the complete establishment . . . of the ascendancy of public opinion in the State. (Mill, [1859] 1956, 89)

By Mill's account, political changes, education, and communication should account for some of the differences in demographic diversity between France and England. Market integration should also promote some kinds of social integration. State formation is relevant because it provided common laws and common institutions, which could be expected to create a greater sense of national identity than there was in countries where a man from one province could not understand the governmental procedures of a neighboring province (Strayer 1971, cited in Tilly 1975, 43). Lastly, we would expect social integration to be greater in those countries with a more developed system of communications (e.g., the distribution of mail and newspapers) as well as those with higher levels of literacy.

The evidence suggests that in the midnineteenth century England was economically and politically more integrated than France, and that contact among the members of different provinces was also greater in England than in France. There is considerable disagreement about just when it can be said that either France or England had a national market, but it is generally agreed that this occurred earlier in England than in France. In England, data on the seasonality of weddings show that there was a national market in grains and pastoral products by the beginning of the eighteenth century (Kussmaul 1985); patterns in wheat prices show a national market by the end of the eighteenth century (Granger and Elliott 1967); the uniformity of costume, and particularly the spread of women's fashions, are signs that the English economy was a single unit in the eighteenth century (Braudel 1984, 367–68). In France, however, although there may have been large regional markets in grain, it would be premature to speak of a national market in the eighteenth century (Weir 1989). By the midnineteenth century, the market in wheat (the most typical agricultural product) was nearly national, but the labor market and the market in other products remained regional (Heffer, Mairesse, and Chanut 1986).[24]

[24] In France in 1800 the price of a hectolitre of wheat varied across regional markets from 11 francs to 46 francs, in 1817 from 26 francs to 81 francs, and in 1847 a difference still of 20 francs.

The greater integration of England's labor market in the midnineteenth century is also shown by migration figures, because much of the migration was a search for work. In France in 1861, 11.8 percent of the population was living outside the department of birth, in England, 21.9 percent, almost twice as many (McQuillan 1978, 168). In this movement of persons (temporary as well as permanent) London was relatively more important to England than Paris was to France; in 1851 10 percent of the English population resided in London, but less than 4 percent of the French lived in Paris (McQuillan 1978). Macfarlane goes so far as to say that "Any particular community in England in the past was probably no more isolated than a Chicago suburb or twentieth century Banbury" (Macfarlane 1977, 9).

In both countries in the nineteenth century the state intruded into local affairs largely via taxes, conscription, and the judiciary—all part of the centralization and coordination that define "stateness" (Tilly 1975). A list of national influences on local demographic history includes the Speenhamland system in England, the French provision of family allowances, legislation for the protection of individual health and welfare, the enclosure movement, the repeal of the corn laws, wars, civil wars, and rebellions (Eversley 1966, 29). States worked to define political identity, as well as "acceptable forms and images of social activity and individual and collective identity" (Corrigan and Sayer 1985, 3). The rapid growth in the number of state inspectors—likened to a "contagion"—acted as a "transmission belt" from the best examples of factories, prisons, schools, and so on, and "established and standardized a range of civic institutions that characterized cultural citizenship" (Corrigan and Sayer 1985, 125–26).

While both France and England are usually considered to be among the earliest nation states, England was unified much earlier than France (see, for example, Bloch 1966). Debate is considerable in the literature over the relative strength of the two states in the eighteenth and nineteenth centuries. From some perspectives, the English state is stronger, from others weaker. In the context of the discussion of demographic diversity, however, it is appropriate to emphasize the distinction between a mosaic state and a unitary state. The former tended to preserve earlier regional particularities, the latter to dissolve them (Strayer, cited in Tilly 1975, 42). France is an example of the former, England of the latter.

The consolidation of French territory occurred as the kings of France brought into the royal domain regions that had been ruled by other feudal lords, such as Brittany, Burgundy, and Languedoc. Although these regions were brought under the rule of the crown and the specialized bureaucracies of the state, many of them retained distinctive privileges (or burdens). Only with

---

After 1860, this price differential never reached 4 francs and remained generally between 2 and 3 (Price 1975, 72).

the French Revolution were these regional political particularities formally disavowed, and the regions dismembered into departments.[25] Despite the efforts of subsequent centralizing governments, however, the prerevolutionary regions retained an influence on market relations (e.g., Judt 1979) and on politics (Brustein 1988). In contrast, the Norman conquest effectively subjected the English to one legal system (Levine 1987, 11). Subsequently, the myth of the Norman yoke—that the Conquest deprived Anglo-Saxon inhabitants of England of their liberty and established the tyranny of an alien king and landlords—became a rallying cry of the revolution, stirring profound feelings of English patriotism: "Men fought for the liberties of *England*, for the birthrights of *Englishmen*" (Hill 1964, 67).

Lastly, Arthur Young noted on the eve of the French Revolution that England differed from France in its "circulation of intelligence."

> That universal circulation of intelligence, . . . which in England transmits the least vibration of feeling or alarm, with electric sensibility, from one end of the kingdom to another, and which unites in bands of connection men of similar interests and situations, has no existence in France. (Cited in Deutsch 1966, 99)

Literacy is relevant, for the literate could participate more fully in national life. Levels of literacy were only slightly higher in England than in France in the middle of the nineteenth century, but England was far more homogeneous in this respect. Using as a measure of literacy the percentage of spouses in each department who signed the marriage register, the standard deviation in France was .19, in England .08 (McQuillan 1978, 75).

The circulation of mail would facilitate interaction. Correspondence appears to have been far more extensive in England than in France. In a publication of 1673, Richard Blome examined the stages and post towns for the counties of England (Blome 1673). Using his data, I calculated that thirty-five of the forty-three counties had fewer than twenty post stops. A French government publication of 1815 permits a comparison with France more than a century later; then, seventy (out of eighty-six) departments had fewer than twenty post stops (*Le livre de poste*, 1816). The percentage of provinces with post stops is the same. However, nearly one hundred fifty years separates the two estimates, and the effective difference between England and France would be

[25] The French Low Countries (approximately the departments of Nord and Pas-de-Calais) are said to have a strong particularist spirit that has survived since the end of the Middle Ages. They were separated from other areas of France by different treatment of the *gabelle* and customs duties, as well as by a different judicial and religious organization (Souboul 1956, 32). Brittany, settled by the Celts in the Dark Ages, at the time of the revolution was ruled by the customs of Brittany rather than by the laws of France. Similarly, Provence had its own constitution before the revolution. "Roussillon constitutes in fact a part of Spain; the inhabitants are Spanish by language and customs, though they depend on the French Government" (Young [1792] 1929, 1:123).

even greater if one considers that the departments were more than three times as large in area as the English counties (see table 2.1).

The French document also gives the number of days that each place received mail. Departments that had unusually high marital fertility and low marriage in 1871 were those in which the delivery of mail was particularly infrequent. For each department, I multiplied the number of post offices times the number of days that each post office received mail in a week. In Isère, there were 125 mail deliveries per week, in Corsica two; marital fertility (I_g) and marriage (I_m) in Isère in 1831 were well within the midspread, whereas Corsica was among the departments with the most distinctive marital fertility and marriage.[26]

The comprehensiveness and frequency of mail delivery surely increased between the time that Blome examined post towns and the middle of the nineteenth century. One author recollects that when his mother was a child in Penzance (she was born in 1760), the area was relatively isolated; by 1790, letters were carried to Penzance six days a week. He writes, "one finds it difficult to believe that, after being brought into communication with the outside world on six days of the week, it can long have retained its pristine charm and simplicity" (Joyce 1893, 292). The introduction of the penny post in 1840 led to a fivefold increase in the number of letters by 1853 (Daunton 1985, 23, table 1.1).

Upper-middle- and middle-class English women (or at least some of them) corresponded with each other very frequently, writing to sisters, parents, and close female friends sometimes daily over many years; one woman wrote 268 letters in 1860, 398 in 1863, and 425 letters in 1864 (Jalland 1986, 3–4). Among the topics they wrote about were marriage and sex. One woman wrote, "Although it's very sad having a daughter who insists on marrying at 20, there is also a sadness if she refuses to marry at all"; another wrote of her physical passion for a man, "I wanted to eat my cake of sensation and thrill and have it also intact" (Jalland 1986, 80, 110). Although it seems unlikely that women lower in the social scale wrote as frequently, one contemporary observer, Harriet Martineau, expressed her pleasure that after the introduction of the penny post the poor could at last write to one another "as if they were all M.P's" (Robinson 1953, 153).

Gabriel Tarde emphasized the role of communications, and especially the newspaper, in creating a national public opinion.

The development of the mails by multiplying first public then private correspondence, the development of highways by multiplying new contacts between people,

---

[26] A comparison of "items of correspondence" per capita (Daunton 1985, 81) with demographic diversity for several countries (the United Kingdom, Germany, France, Italy, and Spain) at a later date (1900) shows that with the exception of Italy the order is completely regular. The demographically most homogeneous countries have the highest per capita mail; the demographically most diverse countries have the lowest.

the development of permanent armies by making soldiers from all the provinces fraternize with each other, and finally the development of the courts by drawing the aristocratic elite from all corners of the earth to the monarchical center of the nation—all had the effect of gradually developing the public mind. But it remained for the printing press to extend this great work to the fullest. . . . It was for the press, once it had reached the stage of newspaper, to make national, European, even cosmic, anything local which, despite its possible intrinsic interest, formerly would have remained unknown beyond a limited range. (Tarde, [1898] 1969, 303–04)

In the middle of the eighteenth century, the periodical press was concentrated in the capitals of both countries. There was some national distribution of periodicals and newspapers in both countries, but apparently far more in England than in France. In France, many departments had no newspaper in 1816 (Collins 1959, 13). In England, by the eighteenth century a well-articulated network extended throughout the country, with a socially more diverse readership than in France (Botein et al. 1981). It is significant that many of the newspapers and periodicals were national rather than local (Botein et al. 1981, 470) and that even in local papers most of the news for country papers was taken directly from newspapers and newsletters from London (Wiles 1965, 198, 202–03; Cranfield 1962, 70).[27] How these might have promoted a sense of belonging to the same community is nicely illustrated by an anecdote concerning Samuel Richardson (1689–1761).

When his story of *Pamela* first came out, some extracts got into the public papers, and used by that means to find their way down as far as Preston in Lancashire, where my aunt who told me the story then resided. One morning as she rose, the bells were set ringing and the flag was observed to fly from the great steeple. She rang her bell, and inquired the reasons of these rejoicings, when her maid came in bursting with joy, and said, "Why madam, poor Pamela's married at last; the news came down to us in the morning's paper." (Sutherland 1977, 69)

In summary, the comparison of diversity among countries shows that some were more diverse than others. Demographic diversity seems to be associated with linguistic diversity. A closer focus on England, one of the most homogeneous of countries, and France, one of the most diverse, suggests other sources of demographic differences.

DISCUSSION

On a worldwide demographic map around 1870, western Europe would be one color, an indication of commonalities across all of the provinces and their

---

[27] In England, foreign news was quite popular, with "a surprising amount of space . . . devoted to accounts of foreign politics and high diplomacy" (Cranfield 1962, 69). Foreign newspaper items were translated and printed in London and then copied by local printers (Wiles 1965, 201).

differences from regions in other parts of the world. If the focus were just on western Europe, however, the countries would be different shades of that color, and if the focus were on a single country, the colors of the provinces would be of different intensities and hues. A province's demographic behavior was constrained by its location in western Europe, as well as by its location in a particular country. It is easier to sketch a role for the local community in influencing demographic behavior than it is to account for either western European commonalities or distinctive national demographic patterns. Yet because the demographic map of western Europe around 1870 shows both western European commonalities and distinctive national demographic regimes, it is worth considering first what all western Europe had in common, and then what distinguished provinces within the same country from those in another.

Well before the nineteenth century, western Europe had an unusual degree of cultural homogeneity based on institutions that crossed national boundaries (Tilly 1975, 18). Western Europe was linked by the legacies of the Roman Empire, which provided a common set of legal rules and the idea of citizenship in a political entity (Rokkan 1975); by a courtly aristocracy that stretched across national boundaries (Elias 1982); by networks of trade and migration; and by the Catholic church. Of these, it seems likely that the European economy and the Catholic church were the most relevant for western European commonalities.

Market integration reduces local autarky and thus reduces the disparities in prices and wages. To the degree that demographic behavior was influenced by economic considerations, the demographic behavior most closely linked to prices and wages could be expected to be more uniform within market regions than across them. At least by the early modern period, western Europe can be treated as a unified economic system. Although there were, at any particular date, differences in the degree of development, and the location of the most advanced country varied from time to time, these were changes only within the same system (Jones 1988, 39).[28]

Western European economic integration is seen partly in the presence of coins brought to even the poorest local areas through itinerant merchants, town and village moneylenders, and village shopkeepers (Braudel 1984, 56); in the networks of trade that connected cities from Italy to the Baltic (Rokkan 1975); in the rise and fall in unison of prices (Braudel 1984, 75; Wallerstein 1974, 70). In addition to coins and goods, workers also moved around western Europe. In the seventeenth century, harvest migrations brought Germans from

---

[28] Scholars differ in dating the development of the European economy. Duby finds by the twelfth century "the formation across Latin Christendom of a single entity out of three geographical areas hitherto separated by profound economic disparities and now brought together by the multifarious links of trade" (Duby 1974, 263). Braudel dates it similarly to the period between the eleventh and thirteenth centuries (Braudel 1984, 82) but for Wallerstein the European economy is a later construction dating only from the sixteenth century (Wallerstein 1974, 67).

Westphalia to the Netherlands, French workers to Spain. In the nineteenth century, to construct railroads workers came from Ireland to England, from Poland to Prussia, from Italy to Bavaria, France, and Switzerland.

It is interesting to note a possible correspondence between the geographical limits of the European economy and the western European marriage pattern. In the seventeenth century, the eastern boundary of the European world economy ran east of Poland, excluding all of Muscovy (Braudel 1984, 26); Hajnal used an imaginary line drawn between Leningrad and Trieste to distinguish the late female marriage and high proportions of spinsters in western Europe from female marriage patterns elsewhere (Hajnal 1965). Moreover, Braudel also distinguished the economies of northern and southern Europe in medieval times, much as Smith distinguished a distinctive Mediterranean marriage pattern (Braudel 1984, 97; R. Smith 1981).

The sway of the Roman Catholic church was also roughly congruent with the area of the western European marriage pattern. Despite local differences in interpretation and the persistence of popular and sometimes unorthodox religious beliefs, from at least the twelfth century to the Protestant Reformation virtually everyone was a member of the Catholic church, participating in common religious rites and acknowledging—at least formally—a common set of beliefs. Church doctrine did not dictate the age of marriage, but it did establish that the consent of both spouses was necessary for a licit marriage (Sheehan 1978), and it did bestow a high value on sexual continence (Brown 1988). These doctrines were probably not irrelevant to the late female age of marriage and high proportions of spinsters; that they could be enforced in ecclesiastical courts might account for some of the homogeneity in western European marriage (R. Smith 1986). The influence of Catholic doctrines appears to survive the Protestant Reformation. Protestant spinsters in nineteenth century England did not claim the church as a vocation, but they justified their choice of celibacy in the religious rhetoric of purity and a noble calling (Watkins 1984).

Commonalities are seen in popular culture as well. Writing about the eighteenth century, Burke says, "Christianity had long been making European culture into more of a whole. The same festivals were celebrated all over Europe; the same major saints were venerated everywhere; similar kinds of religious drama were played" (Burke 1978, 54). One of the means by which European communities expressed their disapproval of inappropriate marriages, such as that between an old man and a young maid, was through the ritual called *charivari* in which village youths met noisily under the window of the offending couple and treated them to a boisterous serenade. Similar rituals often called by nearly the same term (albeit perhaps with different local meanings) are all over Europe: Gascony and the Basque provinces in France; Catalonia, Castile, and Galicia in Spain; Piedmont and Sardinia in Italy; Somerset and Yorkshire in England; Hesse and Mayence in Germany; and elsewhere (Fabre 1981, 430–34).

This brief summary of some sources of western European economic, political, and cultural integration suggests possible sources of demographic patterns common to western Europe. But there were also, as we have seen, distinctive national demographic regimes, as well as considerable local diversity within countries.

It seems likely that European unity was weakened by the Protestant Reformation and by the development of territorial states. The principle worked out during the troubled years after Luther tied religion to political territory: *cujius regio, cujius religio* became the rule. The peripheral states tended to be predominantly Protestant (Scandinavia, England) or predominantly Catholic (Italy, Portugal, Spain), with close links between church and state in both, although in the south the Catholic church retained its supranational character (Rokkan 1975). Countries in the center of western Europe were religiously mixed (Belgium, Germany, Netherlands, Switzerland). France was predominantly Catholic, but with considerable differences among its parts in the degree of devoutness (LeRoy Ladurie and Dumont 1971). The break with Rome also legitimized the use of the vernacular instead of Latin for worship as well as for state business (Rokkan 1975).

Roughly in tandem with the breakup of the Holy Roman Empire came the consolidation of territorial states. The comparison of England and France suggested the importance of the state for demographic behavior. It is not that the state directly intervened in demographic behavior, for other than setting minimum ages of marriage national governments did little in the nineteenth century that was explicitly aimed at influencing either marriage or childbearing (again, France is an exception). Rather, what seems to be relevant is the degree to which the provinces were integrated into a national political system. By 1870, state boundaries were, with few exceptions, as they would remain in the following century.

In some countries, however, territorial unification was quite recent, and in others state control was either weak or patchy, affecting some areas more than others. In general, the demographically most diverse countries around 1870 were the ones that had been most recently unified or incompletely unified. Switzerland was a confederation until 1848, when a federal constitution was adopted. In Switzerland, cantons formally retained far more autonomy than similar divisions in other western European countries. The Constitution of 1848 provided for uniform customs, postal services, military defense, law, and currency, but did not permit federal authorities to maintain executive agents in the cantons, and all federal measures were executed by the local authorities (Siegfried 1950, 139, 161). Germany was unified only in 1871, although some German states retained their earlier institutions even after unification (Orridge 1982, 63–64). Although Spain was unified fairly early, provincial privileges persisted, and in the late nineteenth century Spaniards were thought to be indifferent to participation in public affairs (Anderson and Anderson 1967). Again, there are important exceptions; Belgium, most of which was under common rule before it gained its independence from the Netherlands in 1830, was demographically diverse, and Italy, only recently unified, was demographically homogeneous.

Goods and people circulated within countries. In Germany, most of the migration until the twentieth century was rural-to-rural, and temporary (Hochstadt 1981). Others, such as construction workers and domestic servants, went to work in the city and then returned to their native provinces. Between 1740 and 1790, for example, Bordeaux increasingly attracted migrants from all over the southwest of France, mixing those of the city and the rural countryside (Poussou 1983). Marriage registers of this period show many marriages between those born in Bordeaux and immigrants, as well as marriages between immigrants and those residing in the countryside; in a radius of 30 or 40 kilometers, the villagers were not isolated from the city, nor the city dwellers from the countryside (Poussou 1983, 406–07). Similarly, in the mideighteenth century, ties between the immigrants to Lyon and their natal villages remained strong, with many returning to their villages after marriage (Garden 1970, 69). Thus, "by 1900, regions had long been bound together by their people who joined village with provincial capital and market town by webs of kin and friendship" (Moch 1988, 29). Because the development of national economies becomes most evident after 1870, discussion of this process will be postponed until chapter 6.

William McNeill has summarized these interrelated processes nicely.

As tax collectors, law courts, and other manifestations of central government reached down to affect the lives of more and more people in France and England, accompanying networks of communication also expanded their range, acting partly in harmony with and partly in opposition to the agents of political and administrative centralization. Market relations between town and country, and among merchants living in different towns, were perhaps the most important of these networks. By the eighteenth century even the poorest peasants living in remote and mountainous regions of France and England had become accustomed to selling at least a portion of their products in order to pay rents or taxes and be able to buy things they could not make for themselves. . . . As families and individuals entered the economic exchange network, they also exposed themselves to town-based cultural systems of value and meanings. Local differences tended to weaken; commonality across longer distances increased. (McNeill 1986, 39–40)

These large processes of national economic, political, and cultural integration appear to have constrained the variety of demographic behavior evident in western Europe around 1870. But compared to western Europe at a later date, it seems appropriate at this point to emphasize the local nature of demographic behavior.

Within each country, local diversity was striking. In the provinces with the highest marital fertility, women would have borne five or six more children than in provinces with the lowest marital fertility; in some, approximately two-thirds of the women of childbearing age were married, while in others less than a third were married. It is likely that even more diversity would be observed if it were possible to examine smaller units, such as villages, or finer measures of demographic behavior.

We usually think of demographic behavior as private and personal. The analyses in this chapter and in chapter 2 show, however, that there was a role for the community. The varieties of local demographic behavior support the claim of E. A. Wrigley that in the past fertility (and, this analysis shows, illegitimacy and marriage as well) was largely under social control (Wrigley 1978); the locus of that control seems to have been the local community in which most people lived for most of their years. It was these communities that determined whether sexual intercourse during courtship was acceptable and what would happen if the woman became pregnant, that set the prerequisites for marriage, and from whom young women learned how much breastfeeding was enough. Local communities were probably more integrated into national life than they had been in earlier centuries, but less so than they would be in 1960.

CHAPTER 4

The Fertility Transition

IN THE latter part of the nineteenth century, western Europe began what was to be a revolution in reproductive arrangements.[1] In 1870 married couples could expect to bear between seven and eight children, on average; by 1960 they could expect to bear between two and three. Not only the low fertility was new, but also the adoption of fertility control within marriage to prevent more children. In previous centuries, most couples continued childbearing until their physiological capacity to do so was exhausted or until one of the spouses died. In most European countries starting in the nineteenth century, couples relied on some mixture of abortion, abstinence, withdrawal, and contraception to stop reproduction. In the three decades between 1890 and 1920, most countries of Europe and most provinces within those countries began an irreversible change in reproductive behavior. The change was rapid and pervasive. By 1930 few areas of western Europe and few social groups had yet to adopt the new reproductive behavior. By 1960 fertility was low almost everywhere.

Much attention has been given to understanding why fertility fell. Most explanations have postulated lowered fertility as a response to altered economic circumstances that made children more costly to parents and less valuable as contributors to the family economy. Within that overarching model, researchers argued, the responses of couples were highly individual; people practiced fertility control, in David Levine's memorable phrase, "for their own reasons." It must have been the case, of course, that individuals did make decisions, and it seems likely that costs and benefits of children played some role in these decisions.

In this chapter, I will not attempt to provide new explanations for the fertility decline. I will ask instead what the pace and pervasiveness of the decline can tell us about the connections among the various populations of western Europe. The patterns of decline are not fully compatible with explanations that focus on isolated provinces, much less on isolated individuals deciding to practice fertility control "for their own reasons." Rather, the fertility transition seems in retrospect more like a popular movement. It is difficult to account for the pace and pervasiveness of the decline without assuming that fertility control within marriage was an innovation and that this innovation

[1] Parts of this chapter appeared earlier in Watkins (1987, 645–73).

spread along channels marked by personal networks that stretched beyond village, provincial, and national boundaries.

I begin by presenting the evidence that led to the conclusion that fertility control within marriage is an innovation. This will be followed by a description of the fertility decline that emphasizes not why the decline occurred, but how. I then focus more narrowly, asking what the two main variables of historical analysis—time and place—contribute to our understanding of the transition. I will first show that the importance of national boundaries, seen earlier in the greater variation between countries than within them, is also evident in country differences in the timing and pace of the fertility decline. I will then look at differences within countries, which suggest that those provinces that were somewhat isolated from the mainstream of national life lagged behind in the fertility transition.

NEW PATTERNS OF MARITAL FERTILITY

The view that the control of marital fertility was an innovation requires somewhat lengthy attention. It is critical for some current reinterpretations of the fertility transition (see, for example, Knodel and van de Walle [1986]; Coale [1986]; and Cleland and Wilson [1987]), as well as for the analyses in this book of the role of national and provincial communities in demographic behavior; in addition, the view of fertility control as an innovation has been quite controversial (see especially Blake [1985]).

We know about the pretransition past for western Europe primarily from parish registers and genealogies, some of which go back to the sixteenth century. Analyses of marital fertility rates provided by these sources lead to the conclusion that there is no persuasive evidence that couples deliberately and successfully attempted to stop childbearing once a desired number of children had been reached (Henry 1961; Knodel 1983; Bongaarts and Menken 1983; Wilson 1984; Coale 1986). Some individuals may have done so, but there were not enough successful controllers to affect aggregate measures noticeably.

Reproduction within marriage may be controlled either by successful attempts to stop childbearing, or by successful attempts to space births, or by both. It is considerably easier to measure and interpret stopping than it is to measure and interpret spacing. Stopping behavior is often measured by (1) steeper declines in the fertility rates of older women than would be expected on the basis of loss of reproductive capacity with age or (2) by an early age at the birth of the last child (Henry 1961). When stopping behavior is evident, deliberate motivation to limit childbearing is plausible. Deliberate spacing (lengthening or shortening the interval between one birth and the next to decrease or increase total family size) is more difficult to determine. Variation in birth intervals might be deliberate, but also might be due to other practices that in the absence of contraceptive intent can have the same effect as contraception. Much of the variation in birth intervals among women in developing countries who do not use contraception can be attributed to breastfeeding or to postpartum abstinence (Casterline et al. 1984; Caldwell and Caldwell 1977; Page and Lesthaeghe 1981).

Qualitative evidence also suggests that while couples may have attempted to avoid births when times were hard, neither deliberate spacing nor stopping were systematically practiced in western European pretransition populations to limit family size. Diaries, letters, and other sources show that while condoms and other means of fertility control were indeed known, references to their use were usually in the context of premarital or extramarital relations (E. van de Walle 1980; Knodel and van de Walle 1986).

There were indeed differences in marital fertility levels among economic groups in pretransition populations, but these are usually more evident in measures of fertility that include the effect of mortality and/or marriage than in marital fertility. Even when accounting for mortality and marriage, differentials in marital fertility remain. They are, however, only occasionally in accord with expectations based on the experience of couples with infant mortality or their economic characteristics. For example, before the transition began aggregate-level correlations between infant mortality rates and marital fertility in western Europe were weak (F. van de Walle 1986), and German parents who saw all their children survive to age five were not much more likely to stop childbearing than were parents whose children died (Knodel 1988).

Perhaps most critically, long-run fluctuations in economic circumstances are not closely paralleled by long-run fluctuations in marital fertility. In England, total fertility rates declined by about one-third between the midsixteenth and the late seventeenth century, after which marriage age declined again and fertility rose to even higher levels (Wrigley and Schofield 1981). As noted in chapter 2, changes in the real wage did affect marriage, but marital fertility remained surprisingly stable; the same combination of fluctuating proportions married, and stable marital fertility was evident in France before the transition (Wrigley and Schofield 1981; Wrigley and Schofield 1983; Weir 1984a).

Evidence from the few western European countries for which there is a long time-series of age-specific fertility rates for married women shows that the first stages of the fertility transition were marked by steep declines in fertility among older married women rather than younger women (Coale 1986; Coale and Treadway 1986). Because it is difficult to imagine alternative explanations for this pattern, it can be interpreted as evidence of deliberate fertility regulation within marriage. Such an interpretation is enhanced by considering that the early stages of the fertility decline were accomplished largely by the use of abortion, abstinence, and withdrawal. It seems sensible to think that couples would have been likely to turn to these only after they decided they had all the children they wanted, rather than using them to space children—in anticipation, as it were, of overshooting some target number.

It is these findings—the absence of evidence of stopping behavior before the transition, the failure to find expected relationships between levels of marital fertility and either economic circumstances or parental experience with infant mortality, the correspondence of stopping behavior with the onset of a sustained decline in marital fertility—that lead to the conclusion that the regulation of marital fertility was an innovation. The evidence is more persuasive with respect to stopping behavior, less so with respect to spacing.

The conclusion that deliberate regulation of marital fertility was not widespread in the past has been quite controversial. The empirical evidence for historical Europe is fragmentary and for developing countries where there are fuller records of what people say as well as what they do, only somewhat less incomplete. Thus much depends on interpretation, imagination, and preconceptions.

Challenges to the view that marital fertility control was an innovation are based on alternative interpretations of variations in levels of marital fertility as well as on qualitative evidence suggesting motivation for fewer children or knowledge of effective techniques (Himes [1936] 1970; Seccombe 1983; McLaren 1984). Ansley Coale set out three preconditions for control of marital fertility: control must be within the calculus of conscious choice, couples must perceive reduced childbearing to be advantageous, and effective methods must be available (Coale 1973).

It seems likely that these preconditions would have been met, at least by some, in the past. It is hard to believe that family strategies of production would not imply family strategies of reproduction as well (Levine 1977). Perhaps even harder to believe is that the control of marital fertility was not always within the calculus of conscious choice, for this suggests that pretransition populations blundered through reproduction. Accounts of risk-averse peasants (see Scott [1976]) make it seem likely that they did plan births, especially in the view of modern analysts who consider fertility control central to a well-ordered life and who give economic motives primacy in many domains besides reproduction.

But knowledge, motive, and the calculus of conscious choice need not go together. In Thailand, focus group interviews showed that women whose childbearing was largely completed before the advent of family planning programs complained about too many children, but said traditional herbs were ineffective, abortions dangerous, abstinence unacceptable, and withdrawal unknown to most (Knodel, Napaporn, and Pramualratana 1984). In interviews with African women in Bobo-Dioulasso, Francine van de Walle found that some women wanted fewer children but did not know any effective planning methods, while others knew of contraceptive techniques but thought the number of children was up to God or wanted as many children as possible (van de Walle and van de Walle 1985).

We need not crudely summarize these responses as fatalistic and so reject them. Pierre Bourdieu offers an alternative based on his fieldwork in Kabylia, Morocco:

> in the extreme case . . . the natural and social world appears as self-evident. This experience we shall call *doxa*, so as to distinguish it from an orthodox or heterodox belief implying awareness and recognition of the possibility of different or antagonistic beliefs. (Bourdieu 1977b, 164)

That childbearing began with menarche or with marriage and continued to menopause may have been self-evident: perhaps the possibility of different patterns was not recognized; perhaps unregulated marital fertility was part of the *doxa* of the community.

Reproduction was not unregulated in the past. In the aggregate and over the long run community controls of reproduction were effective. In western Europe until the middle of the eighteenth century and elsewhere until the twentieth century growth rates were modest at best. Even in high-mortality populations both overall fertility and marital fertility were below the maximum possible (Bongaarts 1978) and usually below the maximum observed in a few populations. But what looks like control at the societal level does not look like control when we focus on the fertility of individual married women. We do not find evidence of deliberate attempts to reach a target number of children.

THE PACE AND UBIQUITY OF THE FERTILITY TRANSITION

In western Europe, the earliest sustained fertility transitions at the national level occurred in France. The French fertility transition was evident in the early nineteenth century, but marital fertility had begun to drop among rural French women even earlier.[2] The last western European countries to experience the onset of the decline were Italy (1913), Portugal (1916), Spain (1920), and Ireland (1922) (Coale and Treadway 1986, table 2.1).

Unlike the previous chapters, where the aim was to analyze diversity before the fertility transition, in this chapter and those that follow the emphasis will be on comparisons between 1960 and the past. For the time periods covered to be as close to equal as possible, in this and subsequent chapters the analyses will be at four dates (approximately 1870, 1900, 1930, and 1960) unless otherwise indicated. To ensure that the comparisons over time are based on the same number of provinces at each date, provinces were omitted from the anal-

---

[2] Coale and Treadway (1986) estimate the date of the 10 percent decline in marital fertility as 1827. David Weir has shown widespread declines in marital fertility among rural French women in the late eighteenth century, apparently associated with the French Revolution (Weir 1983).

yses if data were not available for each of the four dates.[3] The countries, dates, number of provinces in each country, and the specific provinces omitted are given in appendix table A4.1.

Figure 4.1 shows the magnitude and timing of the decline using the median of western European provinces. In 1870 median provincial marital fertility (I_g) was .70. By 1930 it had fallen to .35, a decline of 50 percent, and by 1960 to .33. Although there were differences among countries (and, within countries, among provinces) in the timing of the onset and in the pace of the fertility declines, by 1930 fertility decline had begun in all countries and was well on its way in most. By 1960 marital fertility was low (under .40) in virtually all of the provinces of western Europe. Compared to the centuries of apparent stability in marital fertility in the pretransition period, the transition in marital fertility appears quite rapid.

The pace of the fertility decline was due to its pervasiveness. That fertility decline was ubiquitous in western Europe can be examined by erasing national

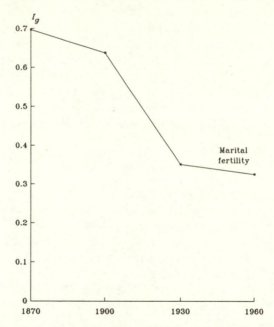

Figure 4.1. Trends in Marital Fertility (I_g) 1870–1960, Median Western European Province

[3] Although national and provincial boundaries remained rather stable over the period 1870–1960, some were redrawn. Thus, for example, the departments of Alsace-Lorraine are in France at some dates, and in Germany at others. If provinces that are present at one date but not at another were atypical, measures of diversity would be affected. Thus, they are excluded, as are provinces for which data are missing in 1870, 1900, 1930, or 1960.

boundaries from the demographic map of western Europe and considering all the provinces together: first the timing of the onset of the transition, then the direction of change in the provinces, and lastly social group differences in the timing of the decline. Subsequently, the fertility transition in individual countries will be examined.

The date of a 10-percent decline in marital fertility (I_g) is conventionally used to mark the onset of the fertility decline, since after marital fertility had fallen by that amount its subsequent decline was almost invariably monotonic (Knodel and van de Walle 1986). The timing of the onset of the fertility transition was quite compressed. If the departments of France are omitted, 59 percent of the provinces experienced a 10-percent decline in marital fertility in the three decades between 1890 and 1920 (Coale and Treadway 1986). Figure 4.2 makes the compression in timing quite vivid.

We also see the widespread nature of the fertility decline, as well as marriage and illegitimacy, when we examine the direction of change in all of the western European provinces by time period. Figure 4.3 presents, for three discrete time periods of three decades each, the number of provinces in which the index was lower at the second date than at the first, and the number of provinces in which it was higher. In the first two periods, fertility fell in almost all the provinces; the last, which includes the postwar baby boom, is less uni-

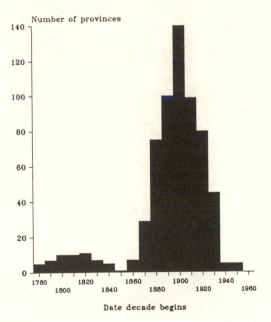

Figure 4.2. Distribution by Decade of Provinces of Europe Experiencing 10-percent Decline in Marital Fertility (I_g). *Source*: Coale and Treadway (1986, fig. 2.2, p. 38).

Figure 4.3. Number of Provinces in Which Index Fell or Rose, by Index and Period, 1870–1960, All Provinces of Western Europe

form. Overall, in only eight of the provinces is marital fertility higher in 1960 than in 1870, and seven of these are French departments with very low marital fertility in 1870. (The data are shown later, in appendix table A5.1.)

The pervasiveness of the fertility decline is even more impressive if we examine social groups. Fertility decline was usually evident first in urban areas and among the more educated and latest among rural farmers; the statistical correlations are modest, but in the expected direction (Watkins 1986). What is striking, however, is the rapidity with which other groups adopted the new behavior. Urban provinces were leaders, but rural provinces followed within a few decades, well before they became equally urban (Sharlin 1986); in Denmark, only in one province was that lag greater than fifteen years (Mathiessen 1985). In Prussia, the fertility rates of agricultural workers were higher than those of workers in three other large occupational groups between 1882 and 1907, but fertility declined in all four occupational groups during those years (Knodel 1974, 115.) In the Belgian city of Verviers, once fertility control spread outside the small wealthy elite, it affected almost all occupations equally among couples where the women were born from 1826 to 1835 (Alter 1988, 187–89). In Switzerland, all social groups participated in the fertility decline by 1906–1910 (Wrong 1980).

The fertility decline has the characteristics of a social movement, a popular revolution. Not only were the declines pervasive and rapid, affecting most provinces and most social groups by 1930, but they were accomplished with contraceptive methods that were difficult to use successfully and in the face of opposition from leaders of important groups in the society.

The early stages of the fertility decline were accomplished by some mix of abortion, abstinence, and withdrawal, all of which are presumably harder to use with consistent success than modern coitus-independent methods. The spread of family planning programs was not important in accounting for the onset of fertility decline in Europe. There were few private or public agencies for the dissemination of contraceptive information or techniques before the 1930s, when marital fertility had already declined there by about 40 percent. Nor do the mass media seem to have been particularly important in most countries; contraception, abortion, and issues of family size were rarely mentioned in the mass media as late as the 1950s (Freedman 1987, 72).

The church, the medical profession, labor unions, and women's groups (with few exceptions) spoke up against contraception (Soloway 1982; Mc-Laren 1983) but with little apparent effect on declining fertility rates. Indeed, if there was any effect it was probably to hasten the declines by spreading the news that fertility control within marriage was possible, and that others were doing it (see, for example, the argument by Banks [1954] on the effect of publicity given to the Bradlaugh-Besant trial in England).

Once the fertility decline had started, the decline continued monotonically almost everywhere.[4] The irreversibility—indeed, what might be called the ir-resistibility—of fertility control is evident in the modest effects of pronatalist policies in Germany and in Italy during the 1930s. In western Europe, fertility decline has continued during periods of prosperity (the 1920s) and periods of depression (the 1930s), during periods of worry about population explosion, and periods of worry about population stagnation. Only the baby boom has been an interruption: a period of earlier marriage and more rapid births, in which having a third or fourth child rather than stopping at two seems in ret-rospect like a fad. During the baby boom, most social groups participated in the rise in fertility, just as they had participated in the earlier decline.

DIFFUSION

Much of the interest in fertility decline has been in determining the circum-stances under which it has occurred. "Why did fertility fall?" has been the dominant question in historical examinations of fertility, as well as most con-temporary ones. Because they were formulated in the period after World War II, when accounting for fertility decline seemed particularly important given the rapid rates of population growth in the Third World, most theories of the demographic transition stressed the centrality and adaptability of individuals making cost-benefit calculations about the value of another child. In the past, it was thought, these calculations dictated many children; when socioeco-nomic circumstances changed, couples adapted to the changes, and their new calculations dictated fertility control. Most versions were not as starkly deter-ministic or as spare as this brief summary suggests, and as research progressed other characteristics of individuals, such as their ideological stances, were taken into account (see, for example, Lesthaeghe and Wilson 1986). But even when the fertility measures used to test these theories were based on informa-tion about aggregates rather than individuals (as they were in the Prince-ton project), it was the characteristics of individuals that were thought to mat-ter, rather than their membership in groups, their communities, and their net-works. Aggregation was seen as a problem rather than a source of insights into social integration.

It is hard to account for the pace and pervasiveness of the fertility declines without calling on diffusion. It is true that the socioeconomic characteristics of provinces are clearly, if weakly, correlated with the onset of fertility de-cline; whether or not a province was urban, literate, and/or industrial helps distinguish between the leaders and the laggards (Watkins 1986). Ideational change also seems to have been important. People in provinces that challenged traditional political ideologies by voting for socialists and anarchists were gen-

---

[4] Again, France is an exception. In some departments fertility fell, then rose, then fell again (E. van de Walle 1974; Wrigley 1985).

erally among the first to adopt the new fertility behavior in their private lives (Lesthaeghe and Wilson 1986). More generally, when we examine fertility differentials at any given time we often find typical patterns: rural fertility was higher than urban, Catholic fertility higher than Protestant, the fertility of the illiterate higher than the fertility of the literate.

However, when we examine fertility differences by the same categories a few years later, we find that fertility has fallen in all categories, even though the relative ranking of the categories often remains the same. A particularly striking example of this is shown in the parallel decline in fertility among religious groups in the Netherlands. When religious groups are compared at the same date, Catholic fertility is almost always higher than the fertility of Protestants and Jews. Less often noticed, however, is that Catholic fertility was declining at approximately the same rate. This is evident in figure 4.4, taken from F. van Poppel's (1985) analysis of fertility decline in the Netherlands. The close parallel holds even when the population is categorized by social group of the husband as well as by the religious denomination of the woman, as in figure 4.5.

That certain socioeconomic or ideational characteristics of individuals are associated with lower (or higher) fertility at any point during the fertility decline is a widespread finding in empirical research. And it is likely that the list of relevant factors will be added to, or subtracted from, as research goes on. The pervasiveness of the declines suggests, however, that it is unlikely that interpreting cross-sectional differentials as evidence for differentials in the costs and benefits of children to their parents will provide a complete account of the decline. This approach is inadequate, I suggest, because it does not account for the rapidity with which fertility decline among the illiterate followed that among the literate, or the rapidity with which fertility decline among rural populations followed that among urban, and so on, or the rapidity with which declines in legitimate fertility followed those in illegitimate fertility.

It is also inadequate because it does not account for the evidence that language differences affected the timing of the onset of the decline (Coale 1973; Anderson 1986; Watkins 1986). The early declining provinces outside France were often French speaking or contiguous to France, e.g., the canton of Vaud in Switzerland and the Walloon provinces in Belgium, or Catalonia in Spain. Within Belgium, the language border acted as a brake to fertility decline, separating early-declining Walloon villages from nearby late-declining Flemish villages similar in socioeconomic characteristics (Lesthaeghe 1977, 111–14); in Spain, the pattern of marital fertility rates in 1911 followed linguistic and historical boundaries (Leasure 1963); in the French department of the Pyrénées-Orientales, as we have seen, the three Languedocian-speaking cantons differed demographically from the Catalan cantons (Adams 1982); and in the Loire low marital fertility in the period 1851–1891 was associated with lin-

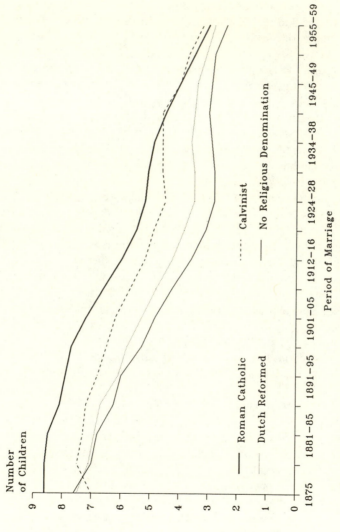

Figure 4.4. Average Number of Children per Marriage in the Netherlands by Period of Marriage and Religious Denomination of the Woman (Marriage Contracted before the Woman Was Age 25). *Source*: van Poppel (1983, fig. 3, p. 12A).

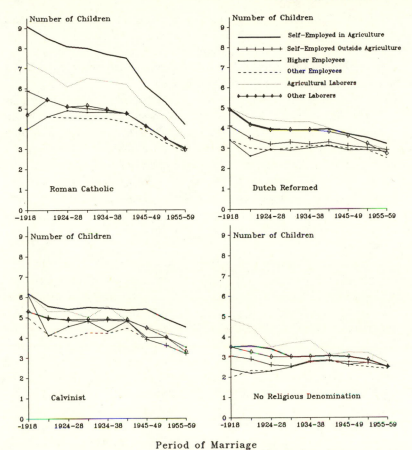

Figure 4.5. Average Number of Children per Marriage in the Netherlands by Period of Marriage, Social Group of the Husband, and Religious Denomination of the Woman (Marriage Contracted before the Woman Was Age 25). *Source*: van Poppel (1985, fig. 3, p. 357).

guistic differences between the northern and southern parts of the department (Lehning 1984).

Rather, the parallel declines point to networks that connect social groups to each other. Because the data used in most analyses of the European fertility decline, as well as in this one, are aggregate, we glimpse these networks only indirectly. We see patterns of fertility decline that are consistent with such networks and not consistent with a view of isolated individuals making fertility decisions at what has been called "fertility-relevant bedtimes."

To get a picture of how these networks might have worked, we can turn to research on the diffusion of innovations in contemporary populations. A review by Everett Rogers (1983) of more than 900 empirical studies provides the basis for a set of generalizations about diffusion. An innovation typically enters a local community either through the mass media (that is, a central source), or through innovators who are characterized by more frequent contacts with those outside the local social system.

The innovation then spreads, more or less rapidly, within the social system, but stops at its borders: "the social system constitutes a boundary within which an innovation diffuses" (Rogers 1983, 24). Mass media and innovators are typically important in introducing new information to the community, but friends, relatives, and neighbors dominate in determining whether or not that information will be acted upon. For example, a study in Taiwan showed that the number of potential acceptors of family planning who subsequently adopted contraception after an action program was directly related to the number of friends, relatives, and neighbors already using family planning (Freedman 1987, 72).

The important elements of interpersonal relations are spatial and social distance. In one contemporary study, married women in a Korean village were interviewed to determine the role of interpersonal networks in the diffusion of family planning innovations. Even in this small village, spatial location was an important predictor of who talked with whom, as was social similarity. A particularly interesting finding of this research was "unplanned diffusion." Although the study divided the population into an experimental group that was subject to information spread via posters about family planning and a control group that was not, the investigators found that interpersonal relations of some in the study group spread beyond the boundaries of the treatment area to individuals beyond that area. A general conclusion of the diffusion studies is that spatial and social distance were the main determinants of who talked to whom (Rogers 1983, 83; see also p. 300).

Diffusion is harder to trace for past populations. Angus McLaren, however, has shown how an abortifacient spread in England in the late nineteenth and early twentieth centuries (McLaren 1988). After an outbreak of lead poisoning in Sheffield from contamination of the water supply, the local women noted that those who were pregnant had aborted, and they reasoned that lead could be used to induce miscarriages. A lead compound, diachylon, that was used on cuts and sores was readily available. Its use as an abortifacient spread northward among the thickly populated manufacturing populations rather than to the more sparsely inhabited east, west, or south. The physicians who described it in a 1906 *Lancet* article noted that diachylon was a home remedy, whose efficacy was passed on by word of mouth, "like any of the other 'household remedies' or 'cures' which every woman knows" (Hall and Ransom 1906, 510). "Hence its slow progress, for the women of this class do not travel farther than to and from their nearest market town or center" (Hall and

Ransom 1906, 511). Eventually, however, diachylon was distributed commercially as "Mrs. Seagrave's Pills" (McLaren 1988).

While analyses of fertility differentials by occupation are usually used to test hypotheses of the value of children to different socioeconomic groups, a recent study of occupational differences in England based on the 1911 census (Szreter 1983) provides some evidence that it is the degree of interaction among those in different occupations that may be relevant.

> It appears to be the case that those occupations which entailed a closer contact, indeed any actual contact, with the wealthy and highly educated parts of the nation, all recorded lower fertility levels than other occupations lacking such physical and social proximity, no matter what their comparative income levels, working conditions, skill attributions, or positions of authority over others. (Szreter 1983, 307)[5]

The most direct evidence of the role of conversation—this time men's conversations—comes from an analysis of fertility decline in a village in Sicily (Schneider and Schneider 1984). Marital fertility declined among the artisans in the interwar period. Interviews with elderly survivors of this period led the authors to conclude that the method used was coitus interruptus, which the men called "reverse gear." They talked about it in workshops, as well as in a club to which many belonged. In these conversations, they compared the Sicilians unfavorably to the French: the French, they said, "can pick up a glass of water, drink half of it, and put it down again, in contrast to the Sicilians, who cannot but finish the whole thing" (Schneider and Schneider 1984, 260).

Postulating diffusion as a mechanism of fertility decline in western Europe has been troubling. It is not clear just what it was that was diffusing: new techniques, new family size ideals, or the legitimacy of controlling marital fertility. Nor is it clear whether diffusion was more rapid or intense among women or men. Some analysts find diffusion difficult to accept because it implies a sort of cultural imperialism in the most private of personal behaviors, others because it implies that the lower classes were aping the middle or upper classes. Perhaps an even greater barrier is the picture that emerges of fertility change in those groups for whom the motivation for smaller families has apparently not changed—that is, they are no more literate, or less agricultural, and so on, than they had been before—but who, nonetheless, begin to practice fertility control within marriage. We must continue to assume, I think, that smaller families were attractive to those who adopted fertility control even though neither our theories nor our measures tell us much about why. Because, however, the pattern of fertility change among provinces in western Europe is consistent with many of the generalizations about the process of diffusion based on observation of individuals in contemporary studies, it deserves more focused examination in future research.

---

[5] Szreter cautions that his findings are not a generalizable explanation for the fertility decline.

Conjoining the patterns of fertility decline in western Europe with the generalizations based on diffusion studies elsewhere also suggests rethinking the standard interpretation of the socioeconomic variables that have been prominent in accounts of fertility decline. Granovetter (1973) has proposed that innovations are likely to enter a community via weak ties. When ties between individuals are strong—when they see and talk to each other frequently—they are likely to know the same things. It is those who are connected only by weak ties that are likely to bring in innovations. In general, analysts of the European fertility decline have interpreted urbanization, industrial occupations, and education as measures of the value of children, or as evidence of new habits of mind that make new behavior more acceptable. But city life and schools, as well as factory work, can also be interpreted as locations in which weak ties are likely to be more widespread than they are in a village community. Thus, the consistent effect of these variables may not be because they are measures of the relative value of children or new habits of mind, but rather because they are sites of concentrated weak ties.

TIME AND PLACE

We have seen that the fertility transition was a western European phenomenon affecting virtually all provinces and social groups in a rather short period of time, and I have argued that the patterns of fertility decline suggest diffusion along networks that linked members of the same community as well as networks that connected communities to each other. The emphasis on the importance of spatial and social distance in the diffusion studies summarized above leads us to expect that we would find differences among countries in the timing and pace of the fertility decline, as well as differences within each country. I will treat these in order.

Countries differed in the timing and pace of the fertility transition (figure 4.6). The earlier fertility decline in France is evident, as is the later fertility decline in Ireland. The Mediterranean countries have patterns very similar to each other, but the decline is later and slower than in the countries of Northwestern Europe or Scandinavia. Countries in eastern and central Europe (which are not shown here) in general had an even later decline. Differences in the timing of the onset of the decline were greater in multilingual countries than in others. All of the provinces of Switzerland experienced a 10 percent decline in marital fertility (I_g) in seventy years, and in Germany in thirty-three years. In England and Denmark, in contrast, the process was more rapid: Denmark in twenty-five years, England in sixteen.

We can think of influences on the timing and pace of the fertility decline within a single country as the combination of two sets of factors, one that represents influences that affected all the provinces within a country, and one that represents the characteristics of individual provinces. The relative impor-

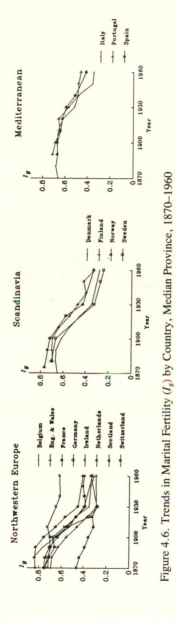

Figure 4.6. Trends in Marital Fertility (I_g) by Country, Median Province, 1870–1960

tance of each of these sets of factors can be evaluated by comparing the effect of date alone, of province alone, and of both together on variation in marital fertility. In table 4.1 date and province together account for a considerable proportion of the variation in marital fertility over the century: the R^2s in Model 3 are quite high. That the R^2 for the model with province and date together (Model 3) is significantly greater than for either the model with province alone (Model 1) or date alone (Model 2) shows that each has a significant effect in accounting for variation in marital fertility. It is evident that date, representing national influences on the long-term decline in fertility, makes a larger contribution than provincial location in every country except France. Thus, we can again conclude that although provincial differences are important, national influences predominate in accounting for the fertility decline. In this analysis, only four dates (1870, 1900, 1930, and 1960) were used; another analysis (not shown), which included all dates for which the indexes were available, gives quite similar results.

TABLE 4.1
Proportion of Variation in Marital Fertility (I_g) Accounted for (R^2) in Models That Include (1) Province Alone, (2) Date Alone, or (3) Both

	(1) *Province*	*(2)* *Date*	*(3)* *Both*	*Number of* *Provinces*
Northwestern Europe				
Belgium	.25	.69	.92	41
England and Wales	.02	.97	.98	45
France	.57	.41	.80	87
Germany	.21	.82	.97	66
Ireland	.27	.56	.79	31
Netherlands	.16	.86	.95	11
Scotland	.06	.94	.98	33
Switzerland	.37	.58	.94	25
Scandinavia				
Denmark	.12	.90	.98	19
Finland	.17	.82	.93	8
Norway	.06	.92	.96	20
Sweden	.06	.89	.96	25
Mediterranean				
Italy	.21	.64	.84	16
Portugal	.36	.54	.86	21
Spain	.35	.66	.90	48

Note: The observations are for each province at four dates (1870, 1900, 1930, and 1960). For Germany, observations in 1960 are omitted. The number of observations equals four times the number of provinces in the country given in appendix table A4.1.

The importance of national factors can also be seen by examining the direction of change in each country. Within each country, provinces generally moved in the same direction at the same time (figure 4.7). The change is so comprehensive that the story is unlikely to have been very different had even smaller units been examined. For example, in England and Wales in 1891 very few of the approximately 600 small registration districts had an I_g below .50; by 1911, few did not (Woods 1987). The sweep of change across provinces within a country shown in the province-level fertility declines suggests factors that affect all provinces in the country at roughly the same time. Fertility change was like not only a popular movement, but a national popular movement.

If national-level influences were relevant, as the pervasiveness of the fertility decline across provinces within the same country and the strong effect of date suggest, we would expect that these national influences would tend to make marital fertility increasingly similar across provinces. We would thus expect the amount of decline across provinces to vary according to the initial level of fertility. That is, we would expect fertility decline to be greater in provinces where fertility was initially high than in provinces where fertility was initially low. This can be examined by correlating the level of fertility at one date with the percent change (the absolute amount of change divided by the initial level) over the next three decades (see table 4.2). At the end of the nineteenth century there was little relation between level and percentage change, but by the last three-decade period (1930–1960) there was, in most countries, a high degree of association between the level of marital fertility in 1930 and the percentage change between 1930 and 1960. The increase in the degree of association over time and the fact that the correlations between the level in 1930 and the amount of change between 1930 and 1960 are usually positive (the higher the level in 1930, the greater the subsequent fall) suggest that national factors that tended to make provinces more and more similar may have become increasingly important.

Despite the apparent effect of influences operating at the national level, provincial characteristics mattered for the timing and pace of the fertility decline. Local communities were not impervious to outside forces, as the sweep of change across all provinces within a country suggests, but their responses seem to have taken different forms and intensities in interaction with distinctive local traditions. Striking differences in the timing of the onset of fertility decline in nearby Baden villages show just how important local differences could be (Knodel 1988, 289), and, as noted earlier, provincial differences in literacy, urbanization, and economic development played a modest role in accounting for the timing of that onset. Moreover, these provincial particularities systematically seem to have favored either higher or lower fertility over the short run. If provinces are ranked according to their level of fertility (from high to low) at 1870, 1900, 1930, and 1960, the correlation between their rank order at one date and at the next subsequent date is rather high, usually posi-

Figure 4.7a. Number of Provinces in Which Marital Fertility (I_g) Fell of Rose by Country and Period, Northwestern Europe, 1870–1960

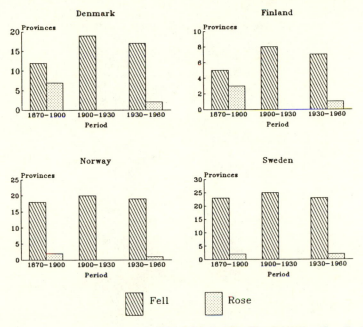

Figure 4.7b. Number of Provinces in Which Marital Fertility (I_g) Fell or Rose by Country and Period, Scandinavia, 1870–1960

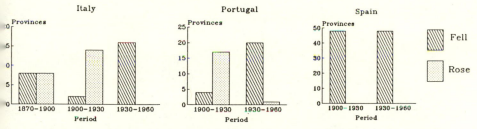

Figure 4.7c. Number of Provinces in Which Marital Fertility (I_g) Fell or Rose by Country and Period, Mediterranean, 1870–1960

tive, and usually statistically significant (table 4.3). Over the short run (e.g., from 1870 to 1900, 1900 to 1930, or 1930 to 1960) most provinces that have relatively high marital fertility at one date have relatively high marital fertility at the next. Over the long run (1870–1960), however, the rank order switched substantially so that most of the correlation coefficients are not significant. And in some countries (Ireland, Norway) the movement of some provinces from relatively high levels of marital fertility to relatively low levels means that even though the short-run correlations are positive, the long-run correla-

TABLE 4.2

Correlations between Provincial Level and Percentage Change in Marital Fertility (I_g) by Country and by Period

	Correlations		
	Level in 1870 and percentage change 1870–1900	Level in 1900 and percentage change 1900–1930	Level in 1930 and percentage change 1930–1960
Northwestern Europe			
Belgium	− .76***	.14	.87***
England and Wales	.02	− .06	.91***
France	.18*	.65***	.74***
Germany	− .25**	− .35***	—
Ireland	.44**	.04	.35*
Netherlands	− .13	− .20	.89***
Scotland	.03	− .16	.80***
Switzerland	− .30	− .54***	.86***
Scandinavia			
Denmark	− .39	− .59***	.88***
Finland	.77**	.004	.69*
Norway	.72***	− .58***	.79***
Sweden	− .56***	− .18	.89***
Mediterranean			
Italy	− .02	− .25	− .20
Portugal	.32	− .01	− .39*
Spain	− .22	− .50***	.70***

Note: Probability values (probability of observed coefficient when true correlation is zero): *p<.10, **p<.05, ***p<.01. The percentage change is the absolute amount of change divided by the level at the beginning of the period.

tions are negative; for example, Roscommon in Ireland has the second highest fertility in 1871, but by 1961 it ranks twenty-ninth. Over the short run, then, local circumstances seemed to favor persistently high or persistently low fertility; over the long run there is little evidence of enduring provincial preferences.

We can gain another perspective on the importance of provincial characteristics by examining the characteristics of the provinces that in 1960 remained outside the national pattern. These provinces are defined using a combination of the distribution of provincial values from high to low and the trend. If the distribution is divided into quartiles, both the top and the bottom quartile can be considered unusual. Because, however, marital fertility continued to fall

ABLE 4.3

ank Order Correlations of Province Values of Marital Fertility (I_g), by Country and Period

| | Correlation of I_g measured in | | | |
	1870 and 1960	1870 and 1900	1900 and 1930	1930 and 1960
orthwestern Europe				
elgium	.53	.94	.87	.90
ngland and Wales	.12[d]	.63	.45	.43
rance	.19[d]	.86	.71	.84
ermany[a]	—	.87	.83	—
eland	− .02[d]	.28[d]	.65	.42
etherlands	− .03[d]	.50[d]	.80	.73
cotland	.31[d]	.62	.76	.74
witzerland	.71	.89	.88	.92
andinavia				
enmark	.50	.71	.91	.90
nland	.21[d]	.83	.21[d]	.95
orway	− .12[d]	.30[d]	.66	.71
weden	.18[d]	.96	.76	.50
editerranean				
aly	.10[d]	.52	.44[d]	.94
ortugal[b]	.72	.56	.51	.85
pain[c]	.19[d]	.86	.83	.42
l provinces	.21	.80	.70	.76

[a] Germany 1960 is omitted because provincial boundaries changed.
[b] Portugal 1870–1960 is 1890–1960.
[c] Spain 1870–1960 is 1887–1960.
[d] Not significant at the .05 level.

after 1960, those provinces outside the national pattern are defined simply as the *top* quartile of the distribution of marital fertility (I_g) in 1960.

The full results will not be presented, for they are easy to summarize. The provinces that were outside the national pattern in 1960 were usually geographically contiguous to each other, but distant from the nation's capital geographically and socially. These provinces were also often either at the borders of the country or in mountainous regions, and they were often provinces in which populations previously had spoken a language that differed from that of the majority.

Belgium is a good example (figure 4.8). Seven arrondissements are in the top quartile of I_g (Maaseik, Bastogne, Tongeren, Neufchâteau, Tielt, Diksmuide, and Marche). These provinces fall roughly into three clusters of con-

Figure 4.8. Map of Top Quartile, Marital Fertility (I_g), Belgium, 1960

tiguous arrondissements that had high marital fertility in 1960: one in the northwest corner of Flanders, one on the eastern border of Flanders, and one in eastern Wallonia, next to the border with Luxemburg. These arrondissements are about as far from the capital of Brussels as it is possible to be.

In Denmark (figure 4.9) almost all of the demographically distant provinces are in the west, far from Copenhagen. In England and Wales (figure 4.10) one cluster of counties with high marital fertility is in the northwest, far from London, but another cluster is in the south, rather close to the capital.

Given the role that language plays in accounting for demographic diversity in the pretransition period and its association with the timing of the onset of the fertility transition, it seems likely that provinces that were traditionally distinctive linguistically may also have been demographically distinctive in 1960. In Scotland, counties with relatively high levels of marital fertility in 1960 were found predominantly in a band of counties in the far northwest, including the highland counties and the islands off the coast.[6] These are the counties where Gaelic was widespread in the nineteenth century and where the

---

[6] The Scottish Highlands consists of the western parts of Sutherland, Ross and Cromarty, Inverness, and Argyll; the islands are Orkney, Shetland, and parts of Caithness.

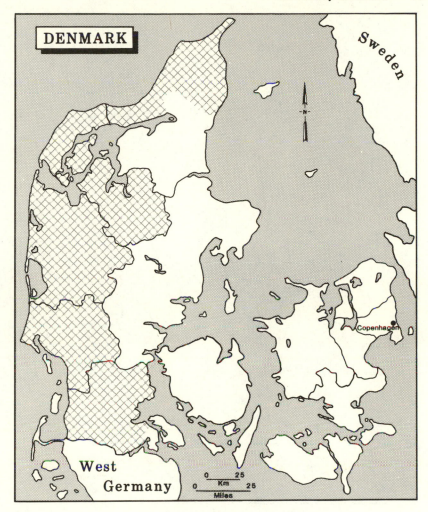

Figure 4.9. Map of Top Quartile, Marital Fertility (I_g), Denmark, 1960

few that continued to speak Gaelic in 1961 were largely concentrated.[7] Marital fertility was high in these counties in 1871 (table 4.4); in 1961, while the absolute levels were lower, with one exception (Sutherland) they were higher in the rank order than they had been earlier.

The pattern is similar in the Netherlands. The province of Friesland is

---

[7] Only 477 are enumerated in the 1871 census as speaking only Gaelic; 1.8 percent of the population could speak both Gaelic and English; the rest spoke only English. Gaelic speaking was most widespread in the Highland counties and in the islands off the Western Coast (Stephens 1976, 51–77).

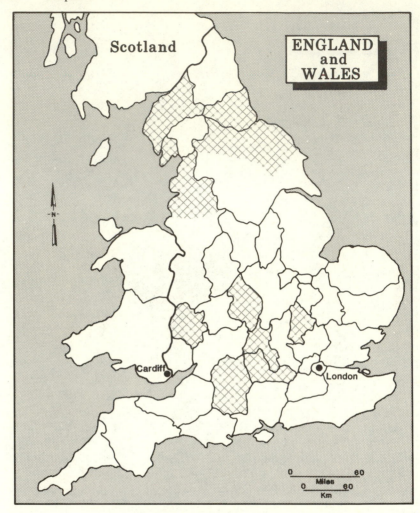

Figure 4.10. Map of Top Quartile, Marital Fertility (I_g), England and Wales, 1960

unique in the Netherlands in having its own language, which in some respects is more like English than like Dutch (Stephens 1976, 567). By 1960 the inhabitants of Friesland were bilingual, but since 1937 the government has allowed the teaching of local dialects during school hours, and Frisian was admitted to the educational system.[8] In 1859 marital fertility in Friesland was the lowest of all the provinces of the Netherlands; in 1961 its I_g was the third highest. What appears to account for this shift is the switch from breastfeeding

---

[8] In 1975 no secondary schools used Frisian as a teaching language and very few had Frisian as a subject (Stephens 1976, 573).

TABLE 4.4
Rank Order of Marital Fertility (I_g) in the Highland and
Island Counties of Scotland in 1871 and 1961

	Marital Fertility (I_g)	
	1871	1961
Sutherland	7	7
Ross and Cromarty	15	1
Inverness	11	4
Argyll	14	12
Caithness	5	3
Orkney	30	20
Shetland	26	8

Note: Scotland's 33 counties are ranked from 1 = highest I_g to 33 = lowest I_g.

to contraception as the predominant influence on marital fertility. Breastfeeding in Friesland was of particularly extended duration, accounting for the relatively low fertility in 1859; its distinctive language, however, probably isolated it somewhat from the networks through which the innovations in reproductive practices diffused, thus accounting for its relatively high fertility in 1960.

We might expect the provinces of Sweden and Finland in which Lapp speakers are concentrated to be demographically distinctive. In both countries, all school instruction has been in the national language since the nineteenth century. In Sweden there has been a Lapp newspaper since 1919, but it deals in Swedish with such matters of special Lapp interest as problems connected with reindeer breeding and news from other Scandinavian Lapp communities (Stephens 1976, 689). In provinces where the Lappish language was spoken (Norbotten, Västerbotten, and Jämtland in Sweden, Oulu, Vaasa, Kuopio, and Lappi in Finland) marital fertility was among the highest both in 1880 and in 1960.

In most of these examples, the number of counties with a distinctive linguistic tradition is relatively small, making it difficult to draw firm conclusions. Nor can their demographic distance be attributed solely to their linguistic differences, because these counties were isolated in many ways. For example, the Scottish Highlands

are characterized by problems in inaccessibility, social isolation and the lack of a threshold population large enough to attract even the most basic services and facilities. The whole western coast of the Scottish Highlands . . . contains no resident dentist, solicitor, estate agent or optician and no hospital, health centre, pharmacy or secondary school. As a result, there is considerable dependency on the east coast towns, involving car journeys of three hours or more for all but the most basic services. (Johnston and Doornkamp 1982, 307)

The general correspondence between demographic distance and linguistic distance (a correspondence that will be explored in more detail for France in chapter 7) is yet another indication that personal networks mattered for the fertility transition and continued to matter in 1960.

CONCLUSIONS

The control of fertility within marriage by stopping childbearing appears to be something new in western Europe. There is little evidence of this behavior before the late eighteenth century in France and before the last quarter of the nineteenth century in the other parts of western Europe; by 1930, in contrast, the fertility decline had begun almost everywhere, and in most countries and most provinces low levels of fertility suggest widespread family limitation.

Although it was not the purpose of this chapter to study the determinants of fertility decline, the ubiquity and pace of the fertility decline in western Europe are difficult to reconcile fully with a view of isolated individuals engaged in fertility calculations "for their own reasons." Socioeconomic circumstances measured at the province level clearly mattered in accounting for the earlier onset of the fertility transition in some provinces more than in others, and ideational factors are probably important (Lesthaeghe and Wilson 1986; Lesthaeghe 1983; Caldwell 1976). But neither accounts well for the virtually parallel declines among provinces within a country or among social groups that shared the same territory.

Without data on individuals and their circumstances, it is not possible to trace the process of diffusion precisely, nor is it possible to exclude alternative explanations. The individuals and their networks are invisible, glimpsed here in studies from contemporary societies as well as a few historical examples such as the adoption of an abortifacient by women in late nineteenth century Sheffield, England, its subsequent spread to nearby local communities, and eventual evolution into a commercially distributed product. But even though the networks are invisible, the parallel declines of countries, provinces within a single country, and social groups suggest that the geographical and social distances in the late nineteenth and early twentieth centuries might not have been as great as is usually thought.

If it is correct to say that "the social system constitutes a boundary within which an innovation diffuses" (Rogers 1983, 24), then tracing the diffusion of fertility control should provide a way to determine the boundaries of social systems. Fertility declined all over western Europe in a relatively brief time, evidence that western Europe was a social system. There is also reason to believe that location in a particular country influenced the timing and the pace of the fertility decline. Rural areas were integrated with urban ones, for example, by migration and by economic exchange. People came from the countryside to the city and often returned again; rural and urban fertility change may have been so close in timing because they were the same people (Moch 1988). City, provincial, and social group boundaries seem to have been relatively porous, linguistic boundaries and national boundaries (which often, of course, coincided by 1960) somewhat less so. Those provinces that were demographically distinctive in 1960—that is, their fertility was relatively high—were generally geographically distant as well, and there is some indication that they were isolated in other ways from the main currents of national life.

Fertility differences during the transition would appear to be studied fruitfully as a way of tracking spatial and social distance. Catholic fertility is usually higher than that of Protestants. Catholicism might be interpreted in a specific context as a proxy for the costs and benefits of children (e.g., perhaps Catholics were disproportionately farmers), or the differentials might be interpreted as indicating the influence of church doctrines about contraception on Catholics. But the time series presented earlier for three religious groups in the Netherlands shows that it is not that Dutch Catholics did not adopt fertility control. Rather, they were somewhat later in adopting this new behavior than other groups, and since their lateness was not compensated for by a relatively rapid diffusion compared to the other groups, the differentials persisted. The differences in timing suggest a degree of isolation from the main currents of national life, just as the examination of provinces outside the national pattern in 1960 suggested that these were areas that were both geographically and socially distant. But the parallel declines can be interpreted as evidence that Dutch Catholics were members of a larger national community, and thus that we might examine fruitfully the connections among Catholics and other religious groups. More generally, findings of parallel declines in fertility among provincial and social groups within the same country suggest attention to the national as well as to the local community.

The use of contraception is a private act, but one that members of a society were, so to speak, performing together. The accounts that individuals give— to survey takers in modern times or to each other in the past—may be phrased in individual terms, but the differences among countries in the timing and pace of the decline and the pervasiveness of fertility change within countries suggest that it was not only individual characteristics, or even the local, face-to-face communities that mattered for fertility decline, but the national networks that linked local communities together.

CHAPTER 5

Demographic Nationalism

WHAT HAPPENED to demographic diversity during and after the transition? In this chapter, I first consider what we would expect to happen on theoretical grounds. I then examine what did happen, looking first at the whole period from 1870 to 1960 and then focusing on 1960 in an analysis similar to that presented in chapter 3 for 1870.

During a period of change, we expect variation to increase. Some provinces are likely to adopt new behavior earlier than others, thus making differences among provinces greater than they were before the change began. Because the timing of the changes in level differed for marital fertility, illegitimacy, and marriage, we can expect the periods of greatest variation to differ as well.

Demographic diversity *after* the period of substantial and rapid change in demographic behavior is over, however, is of greatest interest here. Do we expect demographic variation to be the same as it was before, greater, or less?

Neither demographic transition theory nor the literature on the diffusion of innovations provides a basis for predictions about heterogeneity after the transition. Demographic transition theory predicts a change in the levels of mortality and fertility, but change in level does not imply a change in variation; levels could change while the amount of diversity remained stable, increased, or decreased. If demographic change were predominantly the result of innovation diffusion, we would expect variation to increase as some adopt the innovation while others do not. But because the entire population may not adopt the innovation, there are no grounds for predicting whether diversity will be greater or less than it was before the process began.

Convergence theory offers a basis for expecting a reduction in demographic differences among *countries*.[1] It does not speak to demographic variables, except to predict that modern societies will have low mortality and fertility and that family structures are likely to be nuclear rather than extended.[2] But expectations about demographic behavior follow easily because some of the de-

---

[1] Ian Weinberg traces the ideas expressed by convergence theory back to the eighteenth century *philosophes*, as well as to theorists such as Marx and Spencer who were persuaded that "industrial societies had common destinations, despite their origins" (Weinberg 1976, 335). The debate on convergence was particularly lively from the mid-1950s to the mid-1970s, when it was often cast in the context of comparisons among industrial countries with different political systems, particularly the USSR and the United States, or of predictions about the future of developing countries.

[2] William Goode, for example, has argued for a close fit between industrial structures and the nuclear family household (Goode 1970).

terminants of demographic behavior specified in demographic transition theory are just those that are emphasized in convergence theory.

The core of the argument, presented most clearly by Marion Levy, is that there is relatively little flexibility in many social structures in relatively modernized societies (Levy 1966). The least flexible of these structures, and the ones to which convergence theorists gave the greatest attention, are those most closely linked to the new modes of production. But it is not only in the workplace that one can expect to find similarities. Because of the close functional interdependence of social systems, structural constraints are imposed not only on the economy but elsewhere as well (Moore 1965, 11–12). To the extent that an industrial system is functionally integrated, involvement in industrial work and a market economy leads to involvement in a variety of other groups and novel social structures—" 'broadening spheres' of social activity extending outward from the work place" (Feldman and Moore 1960, 62). The likelihood of increasing similarities among countries is enhanced by high levels of borrowing—not only of scientific and technological advances, but also of social programs. In addition, normative changes have been thought to be relevant in inducing convergence. For example, Alex Inkeles emphasizes the diffusion from centers of cultural influence of new conceptions of morality, autonomy, and self-fulfillment (Inkeles 1981, 55).

Others have been either hostile to predictions of convergence, or more moderate, distinguishing between social structures that are likely to become more uniform, those where old patterns are likely to persist, and those that are expected to diverge. Those who doubt that convergence will occur criticize the theory because of its technological determinism, because it is not sufficiently respectful of traditions, and because it lacks historical specificity. Wilbert Moore is cautious, noting that the weight of the evidence favors those who hold a less deterministic view of the social order at a given time, who emphasize preindustrial differences among societies, and who predict different rates and routes of change (Moore 1965, 13). In particular, he notes that multicommunal states, characterized by diversity in ethnicity, in language, in religion, or caste may have virtually no common value system (Moore 1979). In addition, family behavior might be particularly resistant to the forces pressing for convergence (Levy 1966).

The predictions of convergence theorists have to do with similarities *among* modern countries. There are also reasons for expecting diminished demographic diversity *within* modern countries. First, the circumstances in which provincial populations lived in 1960, especially their economic circumstances, could be expected to be more similar than they were in 1870. Part of the process of economic growth is the unification of national markets (Williamson 1965). The associated extension of transportation and communications encourages the development of national rather than subnational institutions and, hence, results in nationally orchestrated programs to deal with various economic problems (Deutsch 1966). If demographic behavior responds to economic circumstances, then the unification of national markets that produces greater uniformity in these circumstances would predict greater demographic uniformity as well.

A second basis for expecting demographic diversity within countries to diminish between 1870 and 1960 was an increase in social integration.

> A modern society is not just a complex of modern institutions. It is a mode of integration of the whole society. It is a mode of relationship between the center and the periphery of the society. Modern society entails the inclusion of the mass of the population into the society in the sense that both elite and mass regard themselves as members of the society and, as such, of approximately equal dignity. It involves a greater participation by the masses in the values of the society, a more active role in the making of society-wide decisions, and a greater prominence in the consideration of the elite. This process of integration into a single society is the problem of macrosociology. (Shils 1963, 21)

Increased integration would result from deliberate attempts by states to mobilize the citizenry for political purposes. In addition, labor mobility and the proliferation of semipublic and private national organizations such as labor unions and the Girl Guides would have brought inhabitants of the different provinces into direct contact with each other. Citizens would also be brought together through the media, which showed those in different parts of the country what the other inhabitants of the nation were like.

Let us summarize the expectations of changes in demographic diversity outlined above. First, the combination of demographic transition theory with convergence theory leads us to expect *less* diversity among the *countries* of western Europe in 1960 than in 1870, a sort of demographic internationalism. The logic does not predict the particular forms of demographic arrangements—marriage may be early or late, cohabitation widespread or rare—nor that differences in levels will disappear—Sweden and France may become more alike without becoming identical. But the logic of the argument does predict that the more ''modern'' the countries are the more similar they will be.[3]

Second, there are reasons to expect that the differences among provinces *within* a country should diminish, a sort of demographic nationalism. The expansion of capitalism and the proliferation of the functions of national states would be expected to reduce disparities in the circumstances in which provincial populations lived. In addition, the spread of personal networks beyond the local community would heighten the sense of membership in a national community. This does not mean that differences between Cornwall and Kent, or

---

[3] Often the term ''convergence'' means that the extremes at both ends move toward the middle. This is not the sense in which it is used here. Here the term will only mean a reduction in variation.

between Corsica and the Nord, would not remain, just that they would be likely to be smaller in 1960 than they were in 1870.

There are several qualifications to the predictions of reduced demographic diversity based on convergence theory and mobilization theory. Particularly relevant is the emphasis of critics of convergence theory on the historical traditions of different countries as well as on the historical traditions of provinces within countries. In chapter 3, we found that, in general, greater demographic diversity characterized the multilingual states; thus, although we might expect this diversity to diminish by 1960, we would expect that these states would continue to be more diverse, that provinces would not be as similar as in those countries that showed signs of higher levels of social integration before the transitions began.

The predictions of convergence also need to be qualified for those countries for which it is reasonable to believe that the demographic transition is not yet over because we expect higher diversity during the transition than before or after. But how do we tell when the transition is over? Specifying the end of the demographic transition is not easy: When has fertility fallen as far as it ever will? It is easy to make the argument circular: if there is less diversity, it is over; if there is greater diversity, it is not. There are no satisfactory answers. Least unsatisfactory, I think, is to say that the fertility transition is over when fertility has fallen so that the national average is close to the average for Northwestern Europe in 1960, which was between two and three children per couple. Thus, if fertility is above that level in 1960, and if it subsequently falls, we can conclude that the transition is not yet over.

The analysis in this chapter compares 1870 and 1960. While measures are also presented for 1900 and 1930 as well, the fact that demographic diversity is expected to increase during a time of change suggests the difficulty of interpreting differences among countries or provinces at these intermediate dates. It is obviously inappropriate to reify either 1870 or 1960, because data are often not available before 1870 or after 1960, or even for 1880 or 1950. But 1870 and 1960 do roughly encompass a period of great demographic change as well as social and economic transformations. The year 1870 is chosen because in most countries this date precedes the onset of the fertility transition, and because data are available to calculate the indexes for most of the provinces at this date. Although there will be some discussion of 1970 in the next chapter, the analysis ends in 1960 because subsequently there were major changes in marriage and, it has been argued, more generally in the family systems of western European countries (see, for example, Bourgeois-Pichat 1981). These changes also affect the calculation of the indexes, compromising comparison with 1870.[4] As in chapter 4, data for 1870 (or the nearest

---

[4] The increase in cohabitation after 1960 made designation of marital status less consistent than it had been earlier; a different classification of births by marital status may have been used in the

subsequent date for which data are available), 1900, 1930, and 1960 are used and provinces for which data are missing at these dates are omitted, so that comparisons are based on the same provinces.[5] For rhetorical ease, I will use "1870" or "1960" when referring to analyses that include all countries or all provinces, but will retain more precise dates (e.g., 1871) when referring to the analysis of a specific country. Germany will be omitted from some analyses because boundary changes following World War II distort before-and-after comparisons of provincial variation.

VARIATION DURING THE TRANSITIONS

Since chapter 4 focused only on the transition in marital fertility, it is useful to begin by reviewing the changes in levels in illegitimacy and marriage.

The overall changes for the median of western European provinces are shown in figure 5.1 (the changes in marital fertility, shown earlier in chapter 4, are included for comparison). The change in illegitimacy preceded the transition in marital fertility (although this is hard to see in the figure), whereas the large shifts in marriage occurred later.

The median of the provinces in each country is shown in figure 5.2. Although the timing and magnitude of the change varied in details, the similarities in the direction of change during this period is again evidence of a common western European demographic system. Comparing 1870 to 1960, in each country marital fertility fell, the proportions married increased, and illegitimacy fell. Between 1870 and 1930, illegitimacy fell in most countries and then rose in some between 1930 and 1960. Declines in marital fertility were relatively slight between 1870 and 1900, steepest between 1900 and 1930. For most countries the greatest period of marriage change was the last, between 1930 and 1960.

The transition in marital fertility in the Mediterranean countries and in Ireland lagged behind that in the other countries of Northwestern Europe and Scandinavia. In Ireland, Italy, Portugal, and Spain marital fertility was lower in 1960 than it had been earlier, but still higher than elsewhere. Marriage be-

registration of births and the classification of the marital status of the parents in the census. Increases in divorce and a reduction in remarriage rates were accompanied by large increases in the proportion of births occurring to couples not formally married (Coale and Treadway 1986, 77–79). In addition, many countries did not publish the requisite tabulations in the census to calculate the demographic indexes for 1970 and 1980, or province boundaries changed.

[5] Note that the pretransition dates used in this chapter may differ slightly from those used in chapters 2 and 3. These earlier chapters used measures of variation based on indexes calculated for the first date for which it was possible to calculate them, in order to avoid as much as possible any effects of the fertility transition on the measures of variation. In this chapter, where the focus is on a comparison between 1870 and 1960, it is important that the time period and number of provinces be consistent for all countries. A comparison of the midspread at the first date (appendix table A3.1) and at 1870 (appendix table A5.4) shows that the differences are slight.

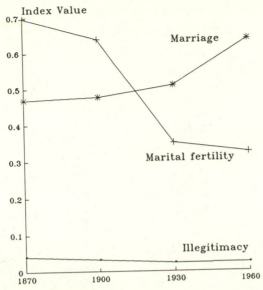

Figure 5.1. Trends in Marital Fertility (I_g), Illegitimacy (I_h), and Marriage (I_m), Median Western European Provinces, 1870–1960

gan to rise in several countries between 1870 and 1900, while it fell in others; only between 1930 and 1960 were the trends uniform across all countries. Changes in illegitimacy were even more irregular across countries.

The importance of country location for change in demographic behavior can be expressed more formally by considering an analysis of variance that includes a term for the importance of country, a term for the importance of date, and a term for the interaction between the two. We saw earlier (table 4.1) that date was far more important than *provincial* location in accounting for demographic variation in marital fertility within countries over the whole period. Here (table 5.1) we compare the effects of date—representing influences that are common to all of western Europe—and *country* location—representing influences particular to each country. Again date is more important than place (country location) in accounting for variation in marital fertility over the whole period; date also dominates place in understanding changes in marriage. For illegitimacy, however, place is more important than date. It is likely that the effect of date varies by country (or vice versa). The interaction term (country × date) tests this assumption. The interaction term is important (table 5.1), particularly in accounting for variation in marriage (including the interaction term raises the R^2 more for marriage than for marital fertility or illegitimacy).

At the level of the province, the sweep of change in marriage (I_m) is almost as comprehensive as that shown for marital fertility in chapter 4 (appendix table A5.1 contains these totals). In only 46 of the provinces (excluding

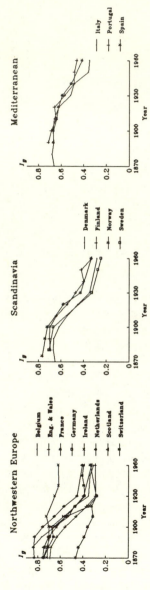

Figure 5.2a. Trends in Marital Fertility (I_g) by Country, Median Province, 1870–1960

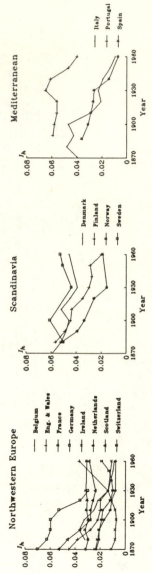

Figure 5.2b. Trends in Illegitimacy (I_h) by Country, Median Province, 1870–1960

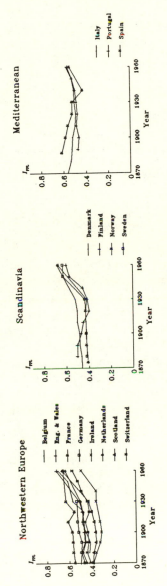

Figure 5.2c. Trends in Marriage (I_m) by Country, Median Province, 1870–1960

TABLE 5.1

Proportion of Variation in Indexes Accounted for (R^2) in Models That Include
(1) Country Alone, (2) Date Alone, (3) Both Country and Date, and (4) Country-Date
Interaction

	I_g	I_h	I_m
Models with			
Country	.18	.31	.28
Date	.53	.10	.34
Country and Date	.71	.41	.62
Country, Date, and Country × Date	.81	.49	.78

Note: There are fifteen countries and four dates (1870, 1900, 1930, and 1960) in the analysis. In every case, inclusion of additional variables in the model raises the R^2 significantly.

Germany) was the proportion married *lower* in 1960 than it was in 1870, and more than half of these were in northern Spain, which since 1870 had moved closer to the western European marriage pattern as the countries of western Europe began to abandon it (Cachinero-Sánchez 1982). Changes in illegitimacy were somewhat less uniform, but illegitimacy was lower in 78 percent of the provinces; a third of the exceptions were in France and over half in France and Ireland combined. As one might expect from considering the importance of country location in table 5.1, the direction of change was even more similar when we consider the provinces within each country. Levels of marital fertility, illegitimacy, and marriage changed more or less in unison.

The unison is only more or less, however. Because some provinces led and others lagged, within-country variation increased after 1870. Although this increase in variation occurred in all countries, the timing and the magnitude of the increase differed by country. Illustrative examples are England and Wales, one of the more homogeneous regions; Denmark, a "typical" country; and Italy, where the fertility transition occurred late (see appendix tables A5.2a–c for the midspreads for all countries).

Let us begin with marital fertility (I_g), shown in figure 5.3a. (The boxplots were described in chapter 2.) In all three countries variation increased until 1930; by 1960 it had decreased in England and Wales and Denmark, but not in Italy. Although the scales are somewhat different for the three countries, the greater homogeneity of England and Wales and the greater heterogeneity of Switzerland that characterized them before the transition are also evident during the transition; variation increased more in Denmark than in England and Wales. In Italy, which had been surprisingly homogeneous in the latter part of the nineteenth century, variation increased enormously, and in 1961 was about five times greater than it had been in 1871.

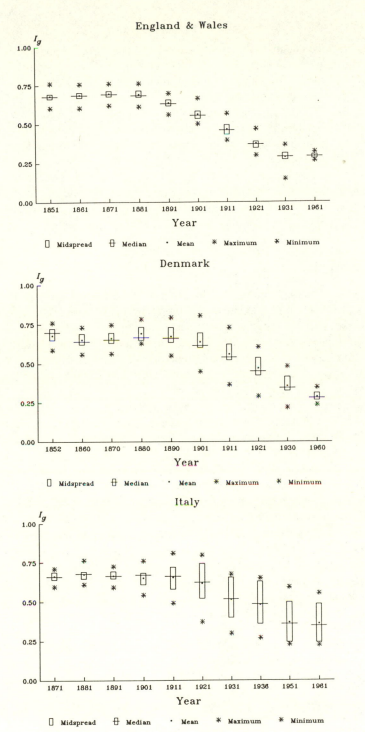

Figure 5.3a. Boxplots of Marital Fertility (I_g), England and Wales, Denmark, and Italy

In all three countries illegitimacy declined between 1870 and 1930; it subsequently increased in England and Wales and Denmark but continued to fall
in Italy (figure 5.3b). Declines in illegitimacy often preceded those in marital
fertility, which may account in part for the considerable diversity in illegitimacy in 1871. In England and Wales the declines in level were roughly paralleled by declines in variation, while the post-1930 increase in illegitimacy
was greater in some areas than in others, which led to an increase in the size
of the box (compared to 1930).

When we turn to marriage (figure 5.3c), we see again that the homogeneity
of England persists throughout the transition with relatively little change in
variation. Italy's initial homogeneity was again replaced by much greater heterogeneity throughout the transition, and in 1961 it was still quite diverse.

AFTER THE TRANSITION

By 1960 demographic diversity had diminished in western Europe. As I will
show, there was less variation across all provinces, less variation among countries, and, particularly striking, less variation within countries.

Before proceeding, a methodological digression is in order. Comparison of
variation may be influenced by differences in the level of the index; thus, we
might expect to account for at least some of the decline in the midspread of I_g
simply by noting that the median has fallen. In addition, we might expect that
when the median is near either the upper or lower boundary (i.e., near either
1 or 0), variation might be reduced because as the province values approach
either a ceiling or a floor, they could be jammed together.

The relation between the median and the midspread is not, in these data,
very close.[6] Although, as we shall see, the midspread for marital fertility was
smaller in 1961, when the median was low, than it was in 1871, when the
median was high, during the early stages of the transition (while the median
was falling) the midspread increased. In addition, and more significantly, we
shall see that as the median level of marriage increased, the midspread decreased. Thus, *both* the fall in marital fertility *and* the rise in marriage were
accompanied, over the long run, by a decrease in variation.

The second problem, location on the scale between 0 to 1, arises when the
numbers approach a boundary; for example, a province cannot have negative
fertility nor can more than 100 percent of the women be married. It seems
reasonable, then, that a midspread that is near the lower boundary ought to be
evaluated differently than a midspread that is near the middle of the distribution. Location on the scale is not a serious problem when the object is to
compare variation in either marital fertility or marriage over time, because

---

[6] Inspections of scatter plots of the median and midspread also showed little consistent relation
between them.

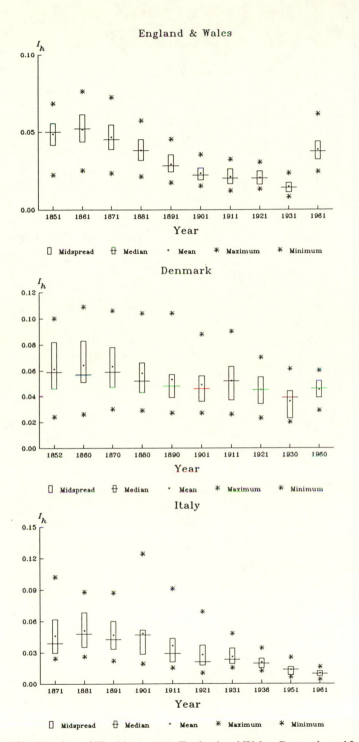

Figure 5.3b. Boxplots of Illegitimacy (I_h), England and Wales, Denmark, and Italy

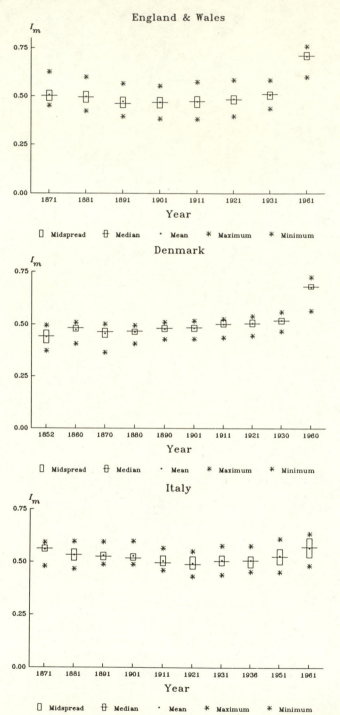

Figure 5.3c. Boxplots of Marriage (I_m), England and Wales, Denmark, and Italy

neither in 1870 nor in 1960 were many values close to either 0 or 1 (that is, few were either above .80 or below .20).[7] Location on the scale is, however, an issue in the comparison of illegitimacy over time and in the comparison of variation in illegitimacy with variation in marital fertility and marriage.

There is no single best measure to correct these problems. A variety of appropriate measures intended to be less dependent on location within the range from 0 to 1 were calculated, and all gave quite similar results. The logit transformation, which "stretches out the tails of the distribution" so that approaching the boundary is less of a constraint, will be presented here.[8]

The change when all provinces are considered together is shown in table 5.2. The midspread decreased very little between 1870 and 1960. The conclusion that variation in marital fertility (I_g) and marriage (I_m) across all western European provinces diminished only slightly is not affected by using the transformed measure. It is affected, however, for illegitimacy, for which the values are small. The midspread of the logit shows variation in illegitimacy, relative to its level, to be greater in 1960 than in 1870.

TABLE 5.2
Median, Midspread, and Midspread of the Logit of Marital Fertility (I_g), Illegitimacy (I_h), and Marriage (I_m) for All Provinces in 1870 and 1960

Measures	Median		Midspread		Midspread of Logit	
	1870	1960	1870	1960	1870	1960
I_g	.70	.33	.12	.10	.57	.46
I_h	.04	.02	.04	.03	.91	1.18
I_m	.47	.64	.11	.10	.46	.43

[7] In addition, the distributions are not very skewed to the high-fertility end in 1960, as we might expect if variation in marital fertility were constrained by a lower but not an upper boundary (and vice versa for marriage).

[8] The logit is defined as the log of the index divided by 1 − the index (ln (index/1 − index)). A simple example will demonstrate how the logit transformation affects calculations of variation. Consider the difference between two numbers near the boundary (say .01 and .02) and two numbers in the middle of the distribution (say .51 and .52). The absolute difference between them is the same (.01); thus, if each pair of numbers were actually quartile boundaries, the midspread of both would be the same. The difference between the logit of .01 and the logit of .02 is .07, whereas the difference between the logit of .51 and the logit of .52 is .013, a much smaller number. Thus, although in absolute terms the difference in the two midspreads would be the same, the logit transformation makes a midspread that is near zero *larger* than a midspread that is at a higher location on the scale.

A third issue concerns changes in the age distribution, which affects these measures slightly. Standardizing the age distribution would affect the magnitude of the changes slightly, but not the direction; standardizing the age distribution would make the decline in variation appear even larger, especially for I_g.

The reduction in variation in marital fertility and marriage is small, but it is meaningful. Consider, for example, marital fertility (I_g). Given the contraceptive techniques available in 1870, the clustering at the higher end of the distribution seemed reasonable; it would have been hard for populations in 1870 to achieve very low marital fertility. By 1960 the constraints imposed by contraceptive technology were much less (though not as slight as they were to be after the widespread introduction of the pill, the intrauterine device, and legal abortion). Yet despite the expansion of *possible* variation in marital fertility, the distribution is even more tightly clustered than it was earlier.

Diversity across all provinces could have decreased either because the countries became more similar to one another or because the provinces within a country became more alike. As we have seen, there are reasons to expect each.

We can use analysis of variance first to examine the importance of country location over time and then to distinguish between the two possible sources of greater homogeneity. The R^2 increases over time (table 5.3). We can interpret this to mean that in 1870 country boundaries already tended to enclose national demographic regimes and that they became increasingly important over the century. In 1870 national boundaries were of approximately equal importance for marital fertility and for marriage; in 1960 the R^2 was larger for marriage than for either marital fertility or illegitimacy.

The R^2 could have increased either because the countries became more different from each other or because there was greater homogeneity within countries, or both, but with a larger drop in within-country variation. As we have seen, there are reasons to expect each. Examination of the sums of squares permits us to distinguish between the two sources of variation. The between-country sum of squares shows what happened to differences between countries. For both marital fertility (I_g) and marriage (I_m) the between-country sum of squares increased after 1870; for a while, the countries became more different from one another.[9] In 1960, however, the between-country sum of squares was less than it had been in 1870. In accord with the expectations of convergence theorists, in 1960 the countries were more similar to one another than they had been at any previous date. The within-country sum of squares shows what happened to variation within countries. This increased temporarily for marital fertility, but by 1960 was less than it had been in 1870. For marriage, the within-country sum of squares decreased steadily across the four dates. Illegitimacy followed a slightly different course, with no difference in the between-country sum of squares and a steady decline in the within-country sum of squares.[10]

---

[9] The actual dates (i.e., 1870, 1930) should not be given much significance. If data were available at intervening dates, variation might peak at 1920 or 1940 rather than 1930.

[10] We might expect the results to differ if the Mediterranean countries were excluded. The transition occurred later there, which would be reflected in large between-country differences. In addition, the unusually large increase in variation during the transition in the Mediterranean countries would lead us to expect that the within-country sum of squares would be particularly large

TABLE 5.3

One-way Analysis of Variance between Countries in Marital Fertility (I_g),
Illegitimacy (I_h), and Marriage (I_m) in 1870, 1900, 1930, and 1960

	1870	1900	1930	1960
Marital fertility (I_g)				
R²	.57	.57	.64	.68
F-value[a]	41.79	43.00	55.81	68.21
Sum of squares				
Between country	4.25	5.37	5.52	3.09
Within country	3.26	3.99	3.16	1.45
Total	7.51	9.36	8.68	4.54
Degrees of freedom				
Between country	13	13	13	13
Within country	416	416	416	416
Total	429	429	429	429
Illegitimacy (I_h)				
R²	.37	.39	.47	.57
F-value[a]	18.44	20.72	28.32	42.63
Sum of squares				
Between country	.08	.08	.08	.08
Within country	.15	.12	.09	.06
Total	.23	.20	.17	.14
Degrees of freedom				
Between country	13	13	13	13
Within country	416	416	416	416
Total	429	429	429	429
Marriage (I_m)				
R²	.59	.67	.76	.75
F-value[a]	45.68	64.68	98.74	94.81
Sum of squares				
Between country	1.95	2.37	2.76	1.67
Within country	1.36	1.17	0.89	0.56
Total	3.31	3.54	3.65	2.23
Degrees of freedom				
Between country	13	13	13	13
Within country	416	416	416	416
Total	429	429	429	429

Note: This table uses all provinces with data available at the date. This analysis omits Germany.

[a] All F-values are significant at the .0001 level or better.

To summarize, when 1960 and 1870 are compared between-country variation did diminish (except for illegitimacy), but within-country variation decreased even more. Country location was statistically more important in accounting for demographic behavior in 1960 than in 1870 largely because the provinces within a country had become increasingly similar. It is this finding that gives statistical meaning to the term "demographic nationalism." Because variation is expected to increase during a time of change, it would be inappropriate to speculate on other causes of this increase; it is the comparison between variation in 1870 and in 1960 that is of interest here. I will discuss later, however, what might have led to the lesser variation in 1960 than in 1870.

Analysis of variance is a statement about aggregates, about all provinces and all boundaries, rather than about any particular provinces on any particular boundary. We would like to know, for example, what happened in the Basque region: Did the border that separated the French Basque provinces from the Spanish Basque provinces become more evident as well? We can say more about which boundaries matter more, which less, by looking at sets of contiguous provinces first on one side of a national boundary and then on the other and comparing within-country differences to between-country differences.

In this analysis, sets of provinces that touched the same border were identified. First, all pairwise differences between provinces on opposite sides of the boundary were calculated, squared, and added; this formed the numerator. Then all pairwise differences between provinces on the same side of the boundary were calculated, squared, and added; this formed the denominator. The ratio was calculated twice for each boundary. The numerators in each case (the cross-boundary sums of squares), are identical, but the denominators (the within-country sums of squares) differ depending on the country. If a boundary becomes more important, we would expect that in 1960 the average difference among provinces on the same side of the border (for example, all the provinces in Spain that touched the French border or all the provinces in France that touched the Spanish border) would be less than the average difference among provinces on opposite sides of the border (that is, the average difference between Spanish and French border provinces). In 1870, in contrast, the average differences among provinces on each side of the border (all the French border provinces or all the Spanish border provinces) should not be much different from the average difference among provinces on opposite sides of the border.

The results of this analysis are shown in table 5.4. Following each country is a list of the countries with which it shares a border (Germany is excluded).

in these countries. Excluding the Mediterranean countries from the analysis changes the numerical results somewhat, but not the overall findings (appendix table A5.3). Both the within-country and the between-country sums of squares were less than they had been in 1870, with the reduction in variation within countries greater than the reduction in variation between them.

TABLE 5.4
Cross-boundary Analysis of Marital Fertility (I_g) and Marriage (I_m) in 1870 and 1960

	Marital Fertility (I_g) Ratio[a]		Illegitimacy (I_h) Ratio[a]		Marriage (I_m) Ratio[a]	
	1870	1960	1870	1960	1870	1960
Belgium						
+ France[b]	3.82	5.56	4.00	25.00	12.00	3.00
+ Netherlands	.53	1.89	.78	.25	1.35	2.33
England and Wales						
+ Scotland	30.00	5.00	.20	70.00	4.00	15.00
France						
+ Belgium	1.62	8.33	2.67	16.67	2.00	15.00
+ Italy	1.38	5.71	.50	15.00	2.50	.60
+ Spain	.83	6.67	3.00	25.00	4.20	10.00
+ Switzerland	.92	11.67	1.00	10.00	.75	3.75
Netherlands						
+ Belgium	10.00	8.50	77.78	12.50	2.00	7.00
Scotland						
+ England and Wales	1.50	.50	.40	.70	40.00	17.14
Switzerland						
+ France	.57	.64	.50	10.00	3.00	5.00
+ Italy	1.00	1.23	2.00	12.50	106.67	5.00
Norway						
+ Sweden	.42	8.00	2.00	10.00	6.00	12.00
Sweden						
+ Norway	1.67	13.33	.67	2.50	1.50	3.00
Italy						
+ France	275.00	200.00	11.11	300.00	25.00	.67
+ Switzerland	50.00	5.25	.20	12.50	53.33	25.00
Portugal						
+ Spain	1.50	4.00	3.00	25.00	7.00	.67
Spain						
+ Portugal	3.75	9.00	30.00	50.00	2.00	2.50
+ France	4.67	2.00	1.00	55.55	5.25	1.00

[a] The ratio is the average of the sum of the squared difference between contiguous provinces on opposite sides of the border to the average of the sum of the squared difference between contiguous provinces on the underlined country's side of the border.

[b] "+" is used as an abbreviation for "border with."

The ratio shows the importance of that particular border: the larger the ratio, the more the border matters for demographic behavior.

The overall picture is much as we have seen earlier. In general, at each particular border the ratio of between-country to within-country differences increased, just as it did when we considered all provinces and all countries. Thus, country borders tend to be places of discontinuity between demographic behavior in one country and that in another. There are, however, many exceptions as well as many inconsistencies (changes in the opposite direction in marital fertility and in marriage). The boundary between England and Wales and Scotland becomes less important for marital fertility (whether seen from the English side or from Scotland), but the results are inconsistent for marriage (stronger boundaries in 1960 when seen from the English side, weaker when seen from the Scottish side). When we look at the French-Spanish border (largely the Basque area) for both I_g and I_m, we see that from the point of view of Spain the Spanish-French boundary became less, not more, important; from the point of view of France, however, the boundary became more important. Because the number of provinces is small (sometimes no more than three provinces in a country touch a particular border), random fluctuations can be expected to be large, and one should be quite cautious about interpreting changes along any particular border. In general, however, most borders were more evident in 1960 than in 1870.

In chapter 2 the analysis of the provinces of Alsace-Lorraine showed little correspondence between the political boundary that separated France and Germany and the demographic boundary. The three departments of Alsace-Lorraine, though included in France at the time, were nonetheless more like their German neighbors than they were like contiguous French departments.

Alsace-Lorraine was part of Germany between 1871 and the end of World War I, and then became part of France once again. The Alsatian dialect remained the most widespread means of communication, but children went to French schools and learned French. By the 1960s only old people and children under six remained dialectical monolingualists (Tabouret-Keller 1968).[11]

The provinces of Alsace-Lorraine were less distinctive in 1960 than they had been earlier. In part, this was due to the increased similarity between French and German demographic behavior; by 1960 the median French and German provinces were much more like each other. In addition, the provinces of Alsace-Lorraine became much less distinctive when compared to other French provinces. In 1861 they had among the highest levels of marital fertility and the lowest levels of marriage in all the French departments. By 1961 they were more like other provinces of France. Marital fertility in Moselle was still relatively high (tenth highest out of ninety departments), but Bas-Rhin

---

[11] The linguistic situation is complicated now because German is heard in Alsace-Lorraine on German television (Tabouret-Keller 1968).

and Haut-Rhin were relatively low (twenty-seventh highest and forty-third highest).

The effect of national borders can also be examined by comparing France with the United Kingdom (England, Wales, Scotland, and Northern Ireland) in table 5.5. France has no internal boundaries; the U.K. has borders of varying political significance, but with considerable (though again, presumably, varying) interchange across these borders. The first interesting comparison is among England, England and Wales, and the U.K.; variation in both I_g and I_m decreased in all three, but with a greater decline for the U.K. than for either England or England and Wales. Membership in the U.K., in other words, appears to be increasingly relevant for demographic behavior. The second interesting comparison is between the U.K. and France. Variation in marital fertility and marriage decreased in both, but the reduction in diversity was greater for marital fertility in France and for marriage in the U.K. It is likely, however, that the early fertility decline in France exaggerates the diversity in marital fertility in 1871. Thus, it is reasonable to conclude that by 1960 the U.K. was demographically much like a single country; indeed, with respect to marital fertility it was less diverse than was France.

Now let us look more closely at variation within each country. The comparison between 1870 and 1960 can be summarized by a simple ratio of the midspread in 1960 to the midspread in 1870. If the ratio is greater than 1, variation was greater at the later date than at the earlier, and if the ratio is less than 1, variation had diminished. The results can be appreciated best by show-

TABLE 5.5

Midspread of Marital Fertility (I_g) and Marriage (I_m) for England, England and Wales, the United Kingdom, and France in 1871 and 1961

	Midspread	
	1871	*1961*
Marital Fertility (I_g)		
England (no Wales)	.033	.021
England and Wales	.036	.022
United Kingdom	.062	.037
France	.180	.059
Marriage (I_m)		
England (no Wales)	.049	.036
England and Wales	.038	.036
United Kingdom	.115	.059
France	.059	.048

ing these ratios graphically and separately for Northwestern Europe, Scandinavia, and the Mediterranean in figures 5.4a, 5.4b, and 5.4c. (The medians and several alternative measures of variation are shown in appendix tables A5.2a, A5.2b, and A5.2c.)

In most countries, variation was less in 1960 than in 1870.[12] This generalization holds least well for the three countries of the Mediterranean, where the transition was later than in the rest of western Europe, and somewhat better for the countries of Scandinavia. In the Mediterranean countries, Italy—where variation was surprisingly little in 1870—is again quite unusual. The midspread is five times larger for marital fertility (I_g), three times larger for marriage (I_m). In Scandinavia, Norway is the most unusual, with greater diversity in marital fertility and marriage in 1960 than earlier.[13]

The midspread decreased in almost all of the eight countries of Northwestern Europe, often by 25 to 50 percent. The exceptions are Ireland (which includes both the counties of Eire and of Northern Ireland), where variation in marital fertility was greater in 1960, and Belgium, where variation in marriage was greater in 1960. In Switzerland, the midspread is approximately identical at the two dates for marital fertility, but decreased for marriage. The exceptions will be discussed in detail later.

The comparison of midspreads emphasizes the degree of change, rather than the absolute amount of variation in either year. Examination of the values of the midspreads (shown in appendix tables A5.4a, A5.4b, and A5.4c) shows that although variation has decreased in most countries, the countries that were most diverse in 1870—Belgium, France, Switzerland—were still among the most diverse in 1960, whereas England and Wales, Ireland, and Scotland again appear among the less diverse countries.

It is tempting to try to account for the diminished variation in marital fertility by speculating that only small families are compatible with the structures of modern society. If this is the case, however, it would seem to be only part of the explanation. Marriage is usually *less* diverse than marital fertility; only Belgium and England and Wales (and Scotland, where the values of the midspread of I_g and I_m are equal) are exceptions.

Until now, we have ignored mortality. We might expect reductions in variation in mortality, especially infant mortality, to be particularly large. It is reasonable to believe that parents in western Europe wanted their children to

[12] This statement holds not only for the midspread, but for other measures of variation (the standard deviation, the coefficient of variation, and the midspread of the logit). The standard deviation and the midspread of the logit are shown in appendix tables A5.4a, A5.4b, and A5.4c.

[13] An analysis of variance (not shown) that tested whether location in Northwestern Europe, Scandinavia, or the Mediterranean accounted for provincial variation in each of the four years (1870, 1900, 1930, and 1960) showed that the F-values were significant at the .0001 level. However, the R^2s were small, suggesting that the differences between the three regions are not of substantive importance.

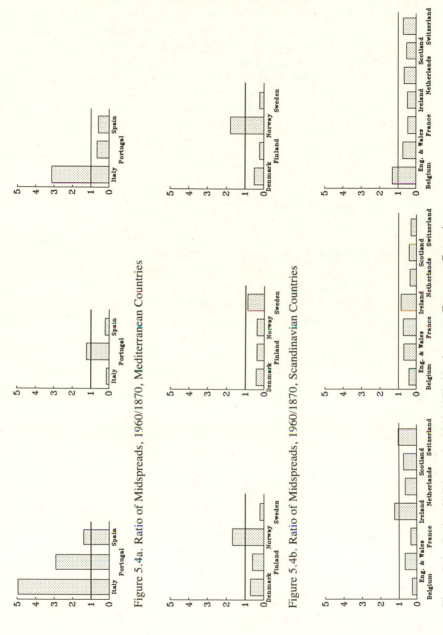

Marital Fertility (I_g)   Illegitimacy (I_h)   Proportions Married (I_m)

Figure 5.4a. Ratio of Midspreads, 1960/1870, Mediterranean Countries

Figure 5.4b. Ratio of Midspreads, 1960/1870, Scandinavian Countries

Figure 5.4c. Ratio of Midspreads, 1960/1870, Northwestern European Countries

live, in 1870 and in 1960, and that those desires were fairly uniform across provinces. What changed, however, was the ability to keep children alive.

In 1870 major declines in infant mortality had not begun in most countries (F. van de Walle 1986). Local environmental conditions (e.g., whether the water was clean or dirty) were particularly important in accounting for levels of infant mortality in the nineteenth century, as were group differences in childcare practices (e.g., the age at which children were weaned or the type of supplementary foods given) (Preston 1985). By 1960 public health measures such as the installation of clean water systems and campaigns for clean milk as well as improvements in preventative and curative medicine made lower infant mortality far more achievable. Public health policy was largely set at the national level, and knowledge about "best practice" was disseminated among national (as well as international) associations of health care professionals. By 1960 infant mortality could be expected to vary more across income groups than across provinces within a country.

Unlike the typical picture for marital fertility and marriage, the midspread of the infant mortality rates steadily decreased rather than first increasing and then decreasing (table 5.6). Variation did not disappear. But compared to the nineteenth century, there was very little variation in 1960.[14]

The reduction in variation in marriage in 1960 and earlier appears even more significant when it is compared to variation in infant mortality. It is reasonable to believe that parental desires about infant survival were more uniform across provinces than were notions about the proper age to marry. In addition, intervention to reduce mortality and to diminish discrepancies between high- and low-mortality provinces were seen as appropriate functions of the state in a way that state intervention in marriage (other than setting a minimum age) was not.

---

[14] Note that the reduction in variation in infant mortality might have played a role in reducing variation in marital fertility. Because the measure of marital fertility used here is based on live births (rather than surviving children), the reduction in infant mortality would affect variation in marital fertility through its interruption of breastfeeding and thus a quicker return to ovulation. Areas with relatively high infant mortality had relatively high marital fertility, thus contributing to the high degree of variation in marital fertility that was evident in 1870. The decline in variation in infant mortality, therefore, would act to decrease variation in marital fertility in 1960. In addition, both infant mortality and marital fertility are affected by the duration and extent of breastfeeding. Thus, a reduction in provincial differences in breastfeeding such as occurred in Germany (Kintner 1985) would reduce provincial differences in both.

It seems that national boundaries are important for mortality as well as for the other demographic indexes. In an analysis of mortality using expectation of life at birth for the 1970s, van Poppel says, for example, that the Spanish provinces bordering on Portugal "have an expectation of life that bears no relation at all to that of Portugal" (van Poppel 1981, 342). In his analysis, the most diverse countries with respect to mortality are France, Italy, Spain, Portugal, and Norway, the least diverse are England, Sweden, the Netherlands, and Belgium/Luxembourg (in that order). With the exception of Belgium, the order is quite similar to that of these countries on I_g and I_m.

TABLE 5.6
Measures of Location and Variation in Infant Mortality Rates
in Selected Countries in 1870, 1900, 1930, and 1960

	1870	1900	1930	1960
Northwestern Europe				
England and Wales (45)				
Median	.14	.13	—	.02
Midspread	.03	.04	—	.003
Midspread of the logit	.25	.35	—	.15
France (85)				
Median	.18	.13	.08	.02
Midspread	.04	.03	.02	.004
Midspread of the logit	.27	.27	.27	.20
Netherlands (11)				
Median	.16	.13	.05	.02
Midspread	.07	.04	.01	.003
Midspread of the logit	.52	.35	.21	.15
Switzerland (25)				
Median	.22	.13	.05	.02
Midspread	.06	.02	.01	.006
Midspread of the logit	.35	.18	.21	.31
Scandinavia				
Denmark (19)				
Median	.12	.11	.08	.02
Midspread	.03	.03	.01	.002
Midspread of the logit	.28	.31	.14	.10
Norway (rural) (18)				
Median	.09	.09	.05	.02
Midspread	.02	.01	.01	.007
Midspread of the logit	.24	.12	.21	.36

In the middle of the nineteenth century, Quetelet commented on the greater homogeneity across Belgium in the proportions married than in mortality. "One can say," he wrote, "that the Belgian people pay their tribute to marriage with greater regularity than they do to death; one does not, however, consider whether to die in the same way as one considers whether to marry" (Quetelet 1848, 66). The results of a comparison of variation in marriage and in infant mortality in 1960 (table 5.7) are mixed. (Because of the very low level of infant mortality, the logit is used for this comparison.) As in nineteenth-century Belgium, marriage is more uniform than infant mortality in

TABLE 5.7
Midspread of the Logit of Infant Mortality Rates and Marriage (I_m),
Selected Countries in 1960

| | Midspread of the Logit | |
	Infant Mortality Rate	Marriage (I_m)
Northwestern Europe		
England and Wales	.15	.18
France	.20	.22
Netherlands	.15	.15
Switzerland	.31	.22
Scandinavia		
Denmark	.10	.10
Sweden	.36	.08

Switzerland and Sweden, but infant mortality is more uniform than marriage in England and Wales, the Netherlands, France, and Denmark.

Until now, we have focused on demographic differentials among groups defined by geographical location. It would be of considerable interest to examine changes in variation in fertility or marriage among groups defined by class or occupation. Such an analysis is not possible for the time span covered here, because by the first date that comprehensive data are available for the social groups by country, the fertility transition already had begun among the aristocracies and in some urban populations and probably some of the higher socioeconomic groups as well (Livi-Bacci 1986; Sharlin 1986). We would thus be comparing variation in fertility in 1960 with a time when we expect variation to be high, and we would almost certainly find that class differentials had diminished.

The pattern of change in provincial variation need not be the same as that of class variation; in England, geographic differentials during the transition were modest, but class differentials in marital fertility widened and then contracted (Glass 1938). On the other hand, the reduction of regional differentials indirectly suggests that the same process may reduce differences among social classes: "If the differences between the various parts of the country are breaking down, there is no reason to believe that the social classes are impervious to similar influences" (Glass 1938, 33–34).

Dennis Wrong, surveying information available in 1956 on class differentials in fertility, concluded that the general pattern was for an increase in such differentials up to about World War I (Wrong 1980, 265). At that time, fertility differentials were probably greater than at any time before or since. (The

Mediterranean countries were not included in his survey.) Subsequently, class differentials in fertility diminished. During the baby boom they diminished even further due to larger rises among the low-fertility groups than among the higher-fertility groups (Wrong 1980, 282).

There were national differences in the timing of the contraction of class differentials. In France, class differentials were relatively stable in the 1920s and 1930s, and manual-nonmanual differentials remained relatively stable between 1910 and 1946 (Wrong 1980, 277). The contraction of class fertility differentials proceeded furthest in the interwar years in Scandinavia and in Germany. It is possible that the earlier convergence in the Scandinavian countries was due to the earlier development of powerful trade unions and cooperatives that favored reduction of economic inequalities and elected reformist socialist governments by large majorities (Wrong 1980, 277, 287–88). In Switzerland fertility decline had begun in the upper- and middle-class areas of Zurich, and the differentials continued to be large until World War I (Mayer 1952). By the 1930s, however, the workers had nearly caught up with the others, and the differential had almost disappeared (Mayer 1952, 110). Religious differentials also appeared to have narrowed in Switzerland, as they did in Germany (Mayer 1952, 111; Chamie 1981).

A set of surveys in western Europe in the mid-1970s permits us to examine variation in fertility for several socioeconomic categories.[15] The differentials are rarely more than half a child (table 5.8).[16] Even when potentially more extreme categories (not shown) are chosen, the absolute variation is small. For example, in France persons with strong religious feeling had 2.3 children, those with weak religious feeling had 1.2; wives with incomplete elementary schooling who were not currently working had 2.9 children, whereas wives with postsecondary education, who were working currently, had 1.6 children; those who currently lived in a village had 2.2 children, whereas those who lived in a city had 1.8 children (Jones 1982, table 2, table 4, table 11).

Large and small are obviously matters of degree. A one-child difference is a small absolute difference, but a large difference relative to the mean when

[15] The surveys were conducted by the United Nations Economic Commission for Europe between 1975 and 1979. The respondents were large national samples of currently married women fifteen to forty-five years old in their first marriages. Problems with comparability are generally minor, but are greater for the definition of socioeconomic categories than for demographic behavior. For a more detailed description of the surveys, see Berent (1982) and Jones (1982).

[16] The measure of fertility is the average number of births per married woman by the time of the survey date, standardized by duration of marriage. The socioeconomic categories used were meant to represent the wife's background (rural-urban residence); her current characteristics (educational level of respondent and her husband, sociooccupational status of husband, wife's religion and intensity of religious feeling); the couple's living standards (total family income, husband's and wife's income, number of rooms in the household); and the respondent's employment. For a more detailed discussion, see Jones (1982).

TABLE 5.8

Average Number of Live Births, by Socioeconomic Characteristics, Selected Countries around 1975

Country	Residence[a]		Religion[b]		Wife's Education[c]		Husband's Occupation[d]		Husband's Income[e]	
	(R)	(U)	(C)	(N)	(EI)	(PS)	(Agr)	(NMWOA)	(VL)	(VH)
Northwestern Europe										
Belgium (Flemish)	1.9	1.8	1.8	1.5	1.8	1.9	2.2	1.8	1.7	2.0
France	2.2	1.9	2.0	2.0	2.5	1.7	2.0	1.8	2.2	1.8
Great Britain	—	—	2.1	1.7	2.2	1.7	2.0	1.7	—	—
Scandinavia										
Denmark	2.2	1.9	—	—	2.2	1.9	—	—	2.2	1.9
Finland	2.1	1.7	—	—	2.0	1.6	2.1	1.8	1.6	1.8
Norway	2.2	1.9	—	—	2.4	1.9	2.3	1.9	1.9	2.0
Mediterranean										
Italy	2.0	1.9	2.0	1.5	2.5	1.5	2.3	1.9	—	—
Spain	2.5	2.4	2.4	2.5	2.6	2.4	2.6	2.4	—	—

Source: The data for achieved fertility come from Elise Jones (1982, tables 2, 4).

Note: Fertility is the average number of live births per married woman, standardized for marital duration.

[a] Residence is current residence; the two categories are Rural and Urban.

[b] The two categories presented for religion are Catholic or None.

[c] For Wife's Education the category EI includes both those who have not completed elementary school and those who have completed only elementary school, except in France, Italy, and Spain where the category includes only those who have not completed elementary school; PS means some postsecondary education.

[d] Under Husband's Occupation, Agr indicates agricultural workers, and NMWOA indicates nonmanual workers outside agriculture.

[e] Husband's income is either Very Low (VL) or Very High (VH); these are the bottom and the top quintiles of the income distribution for each national sample, respectively.

the mean is low. Yet a one-child difference *seems* so large, I think, precisely because it is unusual to have more than three children in modern times. In the nineteenth century, the difference between couples that had seven children and those that had four may have been perceived as a smaller difference than the difference between two children and three children appears today.

A 1985 Honda advertisement illustrates the point nicely. The headline says, "Not All Families Have 1.8 Children." The ad goes on to say, in effect, that "We know that some of you have large families, so we've designed a car for you." The car is pictured, and next to it are three children—a child of about three and twins in strollers. Honda's advertising company seems to believe that in the U.S. these days three children comprise a large family; by showing the younger two as twins, it also implies that choosing three children is unlikely.

The fertility surveys of the 1970s also asked respondents how many children they *expected* to bear. The answer was presumably some mixture of their previous childbearing experience and their family size ideals.[17] Interestingly, within countries there is even less variation among individuals in expected than in achieved fertility; the standard deviations and the coefficients of variation are consistently larger for the latter than for the former.

In 1870 family size desires may have been more uniform than could be achieved, given what appears to have been a reluctance to use contraception within marriage and the kinds of contraception available. This may also have been the case in the 1970s. Norman Ryder has argued that research into fertility intentions (of modern populations) suggests that variations in the number of children a woman has is due more to the efficacy of fertility regulation than to variation in intentions (Ryder 1974, 79). We would thus expect that continued increases in the proportion of the population using effective contraception would result in an even greater contraction of provincial differences in marital fertility in the future.

The narrow range of variation around both average expected and achieved fertility can be interpreted as representing a widespread national consensus about the proper number of children to have, about what is too few and what is too many. These surveys are based on individuals, but their responses are hidden behind means and standard deviations. To try to bridge the gap between individuals and the notion of a national consensus, consider a middle-aged Lancashire housewife interviewed in 1945 whose words are quoted by David Levine to illustrate the internalized application of community morality.

---

[17] The exact form of the question varied. In Finland and Italy, the question referred to additional number of children expected in the future; in Belgium, Denmark, Great Britain, the Netherlands, and Norway, it referred to the total expected number of children; in France it referred to the additional number of wanted children; and in Spain to the number additionally intended (Berent 1982, 8).

> My own opinion is that people wish to have a small family on account of public opinion which has now hardened into custom. It is customary—and has been so during the last twenty-five years or so—to have two children and no more if you can avoid it. A family of five or six children loses in prestige and, some think, in respectability. It is on behalf of their children that parents feel this most keenly. (Levine 1985, 202)

There is other evidence to support the interpretation of the reduction of variation in demographic behavior as the expression of a national consensus among all classes. A set of comparable surveys sponsored by UNESCO in 1948 included questions that have been used to evaluate the strength of identification with compatriots compared to identification with class members in another country (Buchanan and Cantril 1972). The surveys attempted to compare national identification with class identification. Substantial proportions of respondents identified with class members in another country, but in every country except the Netherlands a higher proportion identified with countrymen not of their own class than with members of their own class in another country. The survey was taken in 1948, shortly after the end of the war. Wartime propaganda emphasized fighting for national defense and may account for some of the identification with compatriots.

The results of these studies of national identification are quite consistent with the findings that national boundaries became increasingly important for demographic behavior. In the nineteenth century the demographic diversity suggests that the communities in which demographic behavior was determined were largely local. The reduction in provincial demographic diversity between 1870 and 1960, the relatively small variation across classes within a country, and the fairly small differences among individuals in either achieved or expected fertility in the 1970s suggest a national consensus about the appropriate age of marriage and the appropriate number of children in a family.

This interpretation is, however, incomplete and still unsatisfactory, for several reasons. First, the aggregate data for provinces is quite far from individuals, except for the 1970s surveys. Second, the greater identification with nation rather than class seems far from demographic behavior, although the small class differentials in fertility are consistent with the findings of the UNESCO surveys. Third, if the reduction in demographic diversity shows the creation of a national consensus on age of marriage, or ideal family size, we would expect this to be evident on all of the demographic measures. This is not the case: in some countries demographic diversity diminished on some indexes but not on others. Fourth, it may be that such a consensus on marital fertility existed in the past but was not achievable given the variability in infant mortality and the contraceptive techniques available and acceptable then and that what we see in the modern period is simply the result of a greater ability to translate desires into outcomes. The comparatively greater uniformity in *marriage* than in marital fertility, however, suggests that mortality decline and technological improvements are not the whole story. Fifth, it may be that were we able to measure national identification along other dimensions in the nineteenth century, it would have been as high as in more recent surveys. This is unlikely to be the case; there are many reasons to believe that national integration would have increased over the last century, reasons that will be discussed in the next chapter.

CHAPTER 6

Languages, Markets, States, and Nations

LANGUAGES AND NATIONAL COMMUNITIES

THE STRONGEST support for viewing the reduction in demographic diversity within countries as evidence for increased social integration within national boundaries comes from an examination of parallel changes in linguistic diversity. Direct interaction with others outside the provincial community depends on a shared language. In addition, those who speak the same language are more likely to be taken as models for behavior, and their praise or condemnation be taken seriously, than those whose distinctive language marks them as members of another community.

Between 1870 and 1960 linguistic homogeneity increased in most of the countries of western Europe. France is perhaps the best example. Writing of a walking trip in Lower Brittany in 1882, Maupassant said "for often during a whole week, while roaming through the villages, one does not meet a single person who knows a word of French" (quoted in Weber 1976, 76). By the 1920s that had changed dramatically. A schoolteacher from a village in the department of Vosges wrote in 1910 that only two or three children spoke nothing but patois when they first came to school; these children, he wrote, came from the mountains and were raised by their grandparents (Bloch 1921, 5). Brittany—the departments of which retained high fertility and late marriage until the very end of the nineteenth century—appears to have persisted longest in maintaining its own language. Even there, however, the children were monolingual in French by the interwar period. In 1987 a well-known champion of Breton said to a *New York Times* reporter, "But now we have reached the state where speaking your own language in your own land makes you a marginal person. . . . When I speak Breton to my kids in Rennes people look at me as if I were a strange animal" (Markham 1987).

Today, distinctive local accents, phrases, or vocabulary characterize some areas of France, but few do not speak French at all, and the overwhelming majority of French people do not know any language other than French (Rickard 1974, 127). Even in Corsica—which in 1960 had the highest marital fertility of any French department—in 1980 all children went to school in French, and only 10 percent of the schoolchildren were studying Corsican as a second language (Zeldin 1982, 30).

As in France, in most other countries over the past century a single language came to dominate regional languages. To measure linguistic change, it would be desirable to have two different measures: change in the proportion who can speak—or usually speak—the official language (or languages) and change in mother tongue. The former is a measure of the expansion of a lingua franca, the ability to communicate across linguistic boundaries, whereas the latter permits us to trace the persistence of linguistic differences (presumably associated with other cultural differences) even in the presence of a lingua franca.

It is clear that mother-tongue diversity declined. In table 6.1, taken from the work of Lieberson, Dalto, and Marsden (1981), we see two measures of the decline: the largest proportion of the population with the same mother tongue (where possible, mother tongue was the language first learned in childhood); and the probability that randomly paired members of a nation will have different mother tongues (Greenberg's A). The A-index ranges from 0 (everyone has the same mother tongue) to 1 (everyone has a different mother tongue).

A few countries have a very low value for the index of mother-tongue diversity in both 1930 (usually the first date for which the A-index was calculated) and 1960: Denmark, Germany, Italy, the Netherlands, Norway, Portugal, Sweden, and the United Kingdom. In all of these the A-index is .10 or less at both dates, with more than 95 percent of the population claiming a single language as their mother tongue. The list includes countries that were relatively homogeneous demographically in 1960 (Denmark, Sweden) and countries that were relatively diverse demographically in 1960 (Italy); it also includes Norway, where demographic diversity increased over time.

The more interesting figures are for countries with large linguistic minorities in the nineteenth century: Belgium, Finland, France, Germany, Spain, and Switzerland. Belgium, Switzerland, and Finland were the only officially multilingual countries in western Europe in 1960. In Belgium there are three official languages (French, Flemish, and German), in Switzerland four (French, German, Romansch, and Italian) and in Finland two (Finnish and Swedish). In Belgium, Switzerland, and Spain mother-tongue diversity declined, but they can still be considered multilingual; significantly fewer inhabitants shared the same mother tongue than in the other countries. Finland, however, can no longer be considered de facto multilingual. Even though Swedish remains an official second language, the proportion claiming it as a first language declined by 50 percent (from 14.3 percent of the population to 7.4 percent) between 1880 and 1960; of these, about half are monolingual in Swedish (Stephens 1976, 281). In the other countries (France, Germany) Lieberson's figures show that mother-tongue diversity decreased slightly.

The estimates of mother-tongue diversity are almost certainly underestimates of what we really want to measure: the change in the degree to which members of the national community can communicate with each other. In the first place, in most countries the measures only go back to 1930; presumably, a longer time series would show more change. Second, by 1960 these estimates included guestworkers; it is their inclusion that probably explains why the decrease in mother-tongue diversity in France between 1931 and 1961 is

TABLE 6.1
Mother-tongue Diversity, by Country around 1960

Nation	Year	A-Index[a]	Proportion Speaking Most Prevalent Tongue
Belgium	1910	.549	.516
	1920	.543	.512
	1930	.540	.510
	1960	.555	.500
Denmark	1930	.041	.979
	1960	.060	.970
Finland	1865	.246	.857
	1880	.253	.852
	1890	.241	.861
	1900	.231	.867
	1910	.212	.880
	1920	.201	.887
	1930	.190	.894
	1940	.180	.900
	1950	.163	.911
	1960	.141	.924
France	1931	.265	.854
	1960	.260	.860
Germany	1910	.150	.920
	1933	.018	.991
	1960	.000	.993
Italy	1931	.061	.969
	1960	.020	.990
Netherlands	1930	.043	.978
	1960	.100	.950
Norway	1930	.039	.980
	1950	.006	.997
Portugal	1930	.008	.996
	1960	.000	1.000
Spain	1930	.508	.661
	1960	.445	.730
Sweden	1930	.018	.991
	1960	.040	.980
Switzerland	1880	.442	.714
	1888	.440	.714

TABLE 6.1 (*cont.*)

Nation	Year	A-Index[a]	Proportion Speaking Most Prevalent Tongue
Switzerland	1900	.460	.698
	1910	.471	.692
	1920	.448	.709
	1930	.438	.719
	1941	.427	.726
	1950	.435	.721
	1960	.474	.694
	1970	.531	.649
United Kingdom	1930	.050	.973
	1960	.040	.980

Source: Stanley Lieberson, Guy Dalto, and Mary Ellen Marsden (1981, 50–52, table 1).

[a] The A-index is the probability that randomly paired individuals will have *different* mother-tongues. The index ranges from 0 (everyone has the same mother-tongue) to 1 (everyone has a different mother-tongue).

so small. In addition, the guestworkers are predominantly male. If language statistics were available only for adult women—those who generate the birth and marriage statistics that are the basis of the demographic indexes used there and speak the majority language—we would probably see less linguistic diversity. Lastly, mother-tongue diversity is of vastly different significance in the absence of a widely used lingua franca as compared to its significance in its presence (Fishman 1968, 67). Most of those who now claim a nonstandard language as a mother tongue speak the standard language as well (Trudgill 1983, 142–44). They can thus participate fully in exchanges with inhabitants of other provinces.

Belgium and Switzerland are particularly interesting, because demographic diversity increased in Belgium (for marriage and illegitimacy) but not in Switzerland. Let us consider just Flemish and French speakers in Belgium and German and French speakers in Switzerland. In both countries, the proportions claiming these different languages as mother tongues have remained relatively stable, but the proportion who are bilingual is larger in Switzerland than in Belgium. In Belgium in 1930, 80.48 percent of the population was monolingual in either French or Flemish; in 1947, the most recent language census, 75.95 percent were monolingual in either French or Flemish. The proportion speaking both languages (the bilinguals) rose, from 6 percent in 1866, 12.9 percent in 1930, to 15.6 percent in 1947 (*Annuaire Statistique*, Belgium, 1964, 160).[1]

[1] There were small shifts in the proportion speaking German only, German combined with either French or Flemish, or all three, i.e., trilingual (*Annuaire Statistique* 1964, 160).

Estimates are less certain for Switzerland, which, although it has unusually good language statistics in other respects, does not have them for bilingualism.[2] Since 1888 the degree of language homogeneity within each linguistic area has been high (McRae 1983, 55, table 8).[3] In a survey taken in 1972, about 60 percent of the population of Switzerland could speak a language other than their own mother tongue (McRae 1983, 68, table 16). Another survey, taken in 1973, showed that 65 percent of German-Swiss knew French, and 52 percent of French-Swiss knew German (McRae 1983, 67). It is not possible to estimate whether this is an increase since 1870. It is significant that there is a greater degree of bilingualism in Switzerland than in Belgium; this corresponds to the lesser demographic diversity in Switzerland than in Belgium.

Why did national languages take over? Pierre-Jakez Hélias, in his autobiography *The Horse of Pride: Life in a Breton Village* (1978) suggests an answer. Returning from his first weeks at school in French, just after World War I, he complained to his parents.

> "But you, my own parents, never speak French. Nobody in town or in the country speaks French, except for poor Madam Poirier."
>
> "We don't need to," said my parents, "but *you* will need to. . . . *You* will need to speak French all the time."
>
> "But what happened?"
>
> "It's the world that has changed, from one generation to another." (Hélias 1978, 145)

The relevant changes in the world were, I think, of two different sorts. First was the insistence by the state that schoolchildren be taught in the standard language, and second was the increased interaction with people outside the local community.

Schools were clearly important in accounting for the domination of a standard language. By the end of the nineteenth century, states imposed obligatory schooling on the majority of school-age children and controlled both teaching and curricula (Katznelson and Weir 1985). With few exceptions, the institution of universal compulsory schooling was associated with an insistence by the state that this be in the official language rather than in dialect or patois. Linguistic markets were integrated under the sponsorship of the state (Bourdieu 1977a). Universal and compulsory schooling in the standard language, argues de Swaan, was promoted primarily by metropolitan elites, particularly

---

[2] McRae thinks the language figures can be considered accurate from 1880 on, when the census began to list the language of each individual rather than the language of the household or commune. Initially the census question asked for "mother tongue"; since 1910 there have been slight variations of "language in which one thinks" and understands best (McRae 1983, 49).

[3] While there has been some dilution of linguistic homogeneity in the German Swiss areas, this probably stems more from an influx of foreign workers than from the migration of other Swiss (McRae 1983, 55).

state bureaucrats with an interest in unmediated communication with citizens in all parts of the country, and economic entrepreneurs (de Swaan 1988).

Although France was as or more insistent than other countries on the use of public institutions to promote the use of French and its identification of language with citizenship, even without schools or state development, economic growth, by promoting interaction beyond the local community, would have encouraged learning a common language. A standard language, or at least a lingua franca, is an advantage for those involved in the dense networks of commercial exchange in a modern economy.

As with the diffusion of fertility control considered earlier, we can see this more clearly in contemporary countries. For example, Swahili spread "spontaneously" for economic reasons in spite of the indifference, even hostility, of the educational establishment (Cooper 1982, 9–10). Similarly, an analysis of the spread of English overseas shows that it is closely linked to changes in the intensity and nature of commercial interaction (Lieberson 1982, 44). A weak intensity of communication is associated with a great variety of languages, and vice versa (Laponce 1987, 60).

Hélias' grandfather consoled him for the miseries of learning French by emphasizing the expansion of opportunities associated with French. "With French, you can go everywhere. With only Breton, you're tied to a short rope, like a cow to a post. You have to graze around your tether, and the meadow grass is never plentiful" (Hélias 1978, 135). Similarly, Harald Eidheim, who studied Lapp communities in Norway, reports that although most of the Lapps he studied were bilingual, they were bothered by not being fully proficient in Norwegian. The Lapps thought it necessary and right to speak Norwegian to children. " 'They shall not have the same handicaps as we have had,' they say" (Eidheim 1969, 46). Many families had made the decision to prevent their children from learning Lappish (Eidheim 1969, 55). The basis for their dilemma, he concluded, is that "in order to achieve the material and social goods they appreciate, and to share in the opportunities available in the society, people have to get rid of, or cover up, those social characteristics which Norwegians take as signs of Lappishness" (Eidheim 1969, 45). In Ireland in the decades following the famine, the Gaelic language was increasingly abandoned. "Its eradication was the achievement of ambitious parents as much as of English-speaking schoolteachers" (Foster 1988, 340).

The insistence by the French state on French as the language of schooling may have been more emphatic than in other countries, but linguistic diversity diminished almost everywhere. Although the key to understanding linguistic change often lies outside individuals—for example, in structural changes in the economy, or in the education of children in an imposed language—it is, like the fertility transition, the outcome of many individual actions. It is the summation of microphenomena—"the foreign language one decides to learn at school, the friendships one makes thanks to this second language, the voyages and the marriages, these millions of small events and the millions of daily decisions they involve, [which] contribute every day to the pressure toward the unilingualism of sovereign states, and the bilingualism of subordinate elites'' (Laponce 1987, 200)—that in the end result in language change.

Despite the decline in linguistic diversity, and even in countries that are not officially bilingual, languages other than the standard language do remain as mother tongues. Examples are Welsh or Celtic in the United Kingdom, French in Italy, Danish in West Germany, Dutch in France, Lappish in Norway, Sweden, and Finland, Frisian in Germany and Holland, Basque and Catalonian in Spain and France, and Breton in France. In some cases this is due to the relative isolation of these areas. A study of east Sutherland, Scotland, shows the inhabitants lagged behind their neighbors in switching from Gaelic to English (Dorian 1980); in the previous chapter, it was suggested that the Highland counties (including Sutherland) retained high marital fertility in 1961 in part because of their relative isolation.

Local languages can be used to signify a local or ethnic solidarity; in a modern village in Transylvania, the Romanians complained to the anthropologist Katherine Verdery that while the German minority could understand Romanian, they gossiped among themselves in German. ''Gossip informs the ranking and re-ranking of every household, an activity in which many Romanian women spend a good deal of time. It infuriates them that [the Germans] manage so successfully to insulate themselves from this merciless process'' (Verdery 1985, 66).

Once the local language is lost, it is difficult to revive. Even where there are movements for ethnic revival, and even when these movements emphasize, as they often do, the preservation of a distinctive language, where the language has been effectively lost the activists have not insisted that it become obligatory in the school system or a requirement for party activity. The national party of Wales (Plaid Cymru) has promised that learning language will not be compulsory; the resuscitation of the language is not a prominent element of the Scottish nationalist movement; support for adoption of the Irish vernacular in the postindependence period is modest (Connor 1977, 37–38). Among the Bretons and the Welsh, ''linguistic rivalry rarely goes beyond the level of disputes regarding the appropriate medium for elementary schooling'' (Kirk 1946, 235). In Ireland, ''Revival of the national language and reunification of the country remain formal goals of both [Fine Gael and Fianna Fail] parties, but it seems reasonably clear that the bulk of opinion on each side regards both as unrealistic in the present circumstances'' (Rumpf and Hepburn 1977, 220). The Basques, among the most militantly nationalistic elements in Spain, display less interest than other groups either in using their own language in everyday conversation or in having it taught in the schools (Connor 1977, 37–38).

National boundaries between countries would be even more evident on linguistic maps of western Europe in 1960 than they were in the nineteenth century, just as national boundaries would be even more evident on demographic maps of western Europe.[4] The decline in local languages and the decline in the importance of the province for demographic behavior both indicate the decline in the importance of local communities, or, put another way, the expansion of community from local to national. Second languages have sometimes persisted, as have dialect differences within the standard languages. What is important, however, is that by 1960 almost all of the inhabitants of one province in a country could understand the inhabitants of another province in the same country. Similarly, demographic differences have remained despite the reduction in demographic diversity that indicates a more widespread consensus about appropriate demographic behavior. Local communities remain important both for language and for demographic behavior, but local communities seem less important for both than they did in the nineteenth century.

ECONOMIC INTEGRATION, STATE FORMATION, AND NATION BUILDING

What might account for the increased importance of national boundaries for demographic behavior? I think it is possible to distinguish three processes that would produce greater demographic uniformity: market integration, state formation, and nation building. Market integration, state formation and nation building are like "distant thunder"; they are public and institutional, apparently far removed from birth and marriage. We cannot interrogate individuals; and indeed, even if we could, it is unlikely that they could be articulate about the influence of these processes on their private lives. Nor can we enter each of the provinces one by one. But an examination of the parallels between these processes and demographic behavior suggests links between them. The discussion that follows is based on the secondary literature on these topics. I have summarized below what I think is most suggestive of connections between these macrolevel societal changes and the demographic behavior of provincial populations.

It is hardly necessary to argue that modern demographic behavior is responsive to economic circumstances. A vast literature attempts to account for the decline in fertility by calling on economic development or industrialization. Usually, economic indicators are used as measures of the costs and benefits of children. To try to account for decreasing demographic diversity, however, I think it is more pertinent to examine changes in geographical economic inequality and the integration of national markets.

Most analysts expect regional inequalities to increase during the early stages

---

[4] Supporting this is the finding that the German language has developed differently in different German-speaking countries, including East and West Germany after World War II (Clyne 1984, 26).

of industrialization and then to decrease. A comprehensive empirical analysis by Williamson (1965) shows that this was indeed the case in western Europe.[5] Most studies of market integration are less comparative, focusing rather on prices within a single country and often emphasizing the effect of improved transportation, particularly railroads, on prices (see, for example, Price 1975; Tipton 1976; and O'Brien 1983), but the results are similar.

Since market integration will be discussed at some length, it is important to point out that there are two levels of markets to consider: the between-country market (western Europe) and the within-country market. Although economic exchange across both provincial and country boundaries in the nineteenth century was considerable, it is indisputable that there was far more of both in 1960 than in 1870. The increase in interregional (within-country) exchange, however, seems to have been greater than the increase in between-country exchange. Particularly after 1870, western European economic integration was overbalanced by state-driven moves towards national economic autarky (Pollard 1981). In the late nineteenth century and on into the twentieth, national economies were defined by tariff walls, the removal of internal customs barriers, and other policies and programs, such as the payment of national subsidies.

Since World War I, most states "ruthlessly" followed their own interests in regulating both immigration and emigration (Bade 1980, 376). Somewhat paradoxically, pan-European events played a role in defining national economies. During the depression, international flows of both labor and capital were severely restricted (Kenwood and Lougheed 1983, 249). Both world wars vastly enhanced the powers of the nation states over their own economies (even in nonbelligerent Sweden) (Heckscher 1954). There would almost certainly have been more national market integration even without war, but there was almost certainly more yet as a result of the mobilization of the civilian economy in wartime.

How might the decline in provincial economic inequality and the increase in national market integration affect demographic behavior? First, to the degree that economic circumstances affect demographic behavior, we would expect the decline in provincial economic inequality to result in reduced demographic inequality. If marriages and children are indeed like consumer durables, it would not be surprising that provincial populations bought similar family packages.

There is some evidence for this. The gross rankings on demographic diversity (using the demographic indexes of this study) and Williamson's measures

---

[5] Most of the series of economic indicators upon which Williamson based this conclusion are not long enough for us to be confident that they represent regional economic inequalities before industrialization, but in France, where an agricultural wage series begins in 1862, regional variation was less in 1953 than in 1862 (Williamson 1965, 29–30). In England regional wage differentials declined after the 1860s (Hunt 1973; O'Grada 1981; O'Brien and Engerman 1981).

of economic inequality for several of the same countries in the 1950s are not identical, but they are close.[6] Generally the Mediterranean countries are most diverse both in income and demography. Income inequality tends to be least in the Northwestern European countries (Netherlands, France) compared to the others, while demographic inequality tends to be least in the Scandinavian countries. The major discrepancy is the Netherlands, which has the least income inequality but is one of the most demographically heterogeneous in this subset of countries. The number of countries for which a comparison of demographic and economic diversity is possible is too small to permit firm conclusions, but the comparison does suggest that economic diversity and demographic diversity, while not completely congruent, are related.

A second aspect of the growth of national markets is the wider exchange of goods, capital, and labor.

> The expansion of a modern economic center has the consequence of breaking down local economic boundaries and incorporating labor and capital in larger and larger exchange networks. As modernization proceeds, individuals and firms whose fates were weakly connected in the premodern economy come to stand in many of the same relations to events in the center and to events characterizing the entire economy. Disturbances created in one sector of a modern economy have consequences throughout the economy to a much greater extent than was the case in earlier economies. Consequently, modern economic units are adapted less to local conditions and more to center events. (Hannan 1979, 265)

In chapter 3, I suggested that where demographic behavior was responsive to economic circumstances (for example, the timing of marriage), the weakness of national market integration in the pretransition period would have meant that some areas experienced prosperity (and thus earlier marriage) at the same time that others experienced hardship (and thus later marriage). Assuming that marriage remained linked to economic circumstances, economic shocks in the modern period would, as Hannan argues, be more likely to be felt all over the country.

In addition, national labor market integration would encourage more internal migration, and thus increase the possibility of direct interaction among those from different provinces within the same country. France provides a good example. By 1910 railroads had reached the most distant and inaccessible towns (Pinchemel 1969, 222). Presumably as a consequence, the increase was much greater in long-distance than in short-distance migration. An analysis of migration in France found that probability of short-distance migration

---

[6] Williamson uses the same provinces for Sweden, Finland, Netherlands, Norway, and Spain as those used here. For France and Italy, Williamson uses larger (and thus fewer) regions. Williamson's measure of regional economic inequality is a weighted coefficient of variation that measures the dispersion of the regional income per capita levels relative to the national average while each regional deviation is weighted by its share in the national population (Williamson 1965).

(from one department to an adjacent department) multiplied about 1.5 times between 1891 and 1956, but long-distance migration (from one department to another at least 600 kilometers away) increased fivefold (Courgeau 1970, 85).

The development of improved transport made a greater difference for the migration of women than of men; in France, they rarely accompanied male migrants in the first half of the century, but increasingly moved as workers (many as domestic servants) or as wives (Chatelain 1977).[7] Parish records of marriage for a valley in Spain that permit tracing migration from about 1600 to the present suggest a long tradition of male outmigration, seen in indications that men either died away from home or married women from the outside. The local women, however, seem not to have gone beyond neighboring villages for work until the last quarter of the nineteenth century, when their range expanded to neighboring valleys and then, after 1920, to a range beyond the western part of the province (Santander) (Christian 1972, 38). Moch writes that examination of marriage records for three French villages

> provide an extraordinary picture of the broadening of geographic horizons for women in the last half of the nineteenth century. Marriage records attest to women's legendary eagerness to leave the mountains and rural life succinctly expressed in the proverb from Western Languedoc: Goats ascend, girls descend. The women of the *belle epoque* simply went further than their mothers. (Moch 1983, 68)

It would have been easier to descend if they spoke French, and there is some evidence that women were more eager to learn French than were men. Brun writes of a small, rural village he visited frequently that at the cafes, in the square, and at work the men "called to each other, exchanged small talk and discussed" in Provençal; the women of the same generation, in their small gossip and lacemaking circles, chattered in French, and even spoke French to infants in arms (Brun 1927, 164–67).[8] This is consistent with other studies that show that women are more likely to use standard speech than men (Fishman 1985).

Once the women came down the mountainside, they were more likely to marry someone from a different province than would have been the case earlier (Watkins 1980). In the department of Loir-et-Cher, for example, 12.8 percent of the marriages between 1870 and 1877 involved one spouse from Loir-et-Cher and one from another department; from 1946 to 1954, 28.2 percent fell in this category (Sutter 1958; Sutter and Tabah 1955). Marrying away did

---

[7] In France at the turn of the century more females than males were living outside their departments of origin (Tugault 1973).

[8] Bourdieu, in a subtle analysis of the economics of linguistic exchanges in terms of class and power, offers an interpretation consistent with this finding. From the standpoint of men of the dominated classes, he writes, identifying with the dominant class in speech entails a repudiation of masculinity; women, however, can identify with the dominant culture more easily, without such a transformation being seen as a change in social and sexual identity (Bourdieu 1977a, 661).

not necessarily rupture the relations between the individual and his or her family. The temporary migrants of the late eighteenth and nineteenth centuries forged links between their new residences and their old, much as migrants did in the twentieth century. Writing about contemporary France, Laurence Wylie notes that virtually everyone in the village of Chanzeaux has relatives, close friends, neighbors, and landlords who are emigrants, and it is through them that the village gains ''intimate and personal contact with the 'New France,' which in many other respects has bypassed the small villages'' (Wylie 1966, 183).

Lastly, and more speculatively, the distribution of goods across all of the national territory would have meant that people in one part of the country could eat the same foods, wear the same clothes, and buy the same cars as those in another. Consider, for example, Michael Miller's history of the Bon Marché, the large French department store, between 1869 and 1920. It disseminated advertisements and pictures that showed people in the provinces what a proper bourgeois family (i.e., the Parisian upper–middle class) looked like—how it furnished its house, what its well-cared-for children wore. To advertise its winter season in 1894, 1,500,000 catalogs were mailed, of which half (740,000) went to the provinces (and 260,000 abroad) (Miller 1981, 61–62). The Bon Marché had a thriving mail-order business, as did other department stores. The department store ''made the culture of consumption a national one''; through the Bon Marché, Paris and the countryside became more alike (Miller 1981, 165).

The result would have been that when individuals encountered someone from another province within the same country he or she would have appeared, at least outwardly, to be more like themselves than would have been the case in the nineteenth century. This in turn would have, I think, facilitated interaction: it is reasonable to assume that people are more likely to feel that they have something in common with those who dress the same, to gossip with them, and to take their examples and their models seriously.[9]

The state's role went beyond shaping national economies. State functions expanded enormously, increasing what Braudel has called its '''diabolical' power of penetration'' (Braudel 1984, 51). In the nineteenth century, the state became more extensive and more intrusive than it had been earlier. In The Eighteenth Brumaire, Marx wrote:

> Every common interest was straightway severed from society, counterpoised to it as a higher, general interest, snatched from the activity of society's members themselves, and made an object of government activity, from a bridge, a schoolhouse,

[9] Perhaps in the same spirit, in 1963 the Committee for the Restoration of the Irish Language recommended that Irish speakers should be able to recognize each other by a distinctive badge to be worn on their clothing (Laponce 1987, 28).

and the communal property of a village community to the railways, the national wealth, and the national university of France. (quoted in Grew 1984, 89)

Governments rarely implemented policies explicitly intended to affect either fertility or marriage (fascist Italy and Germany were obvious exceptions, as were the pronatalist policies of France). The most direct link between state expansion and demographic behavior is through the expansion of social rights. If, as has been argued, children were valuable as a source of social security, then the implementation of community welfare programs would have decreased their value in this respect.

The last quarter of the nineteenth century and the first quarter of the twentieth saw the "collectivization of providence"; social welfare became collective, compulsory, and nationwide (de Swaan 1988). In France, for example, public assistance had been supported almost entirely from local funds, but during the Third Republic (1870–1940) these responsibilities were increasingly interpreted as national obligations (Weiss 1983). Although diffusion of public welfare programs and policies across countries was considerable (Meyer and Hannan 1979), these programs probably were perceived by citizens as national programs, social rights that belonged to them as citizens of a particular country. Welfare programs created a bond between the citizen and the state, a transfer bond that tied individuals as contributors and potential or actual claimants to national, public agencies (de Swaan 1988, 159–60). During the depression expanded welfare schemes must have further increased people's perceptions that not only their prosperity but their survival was directly linked to national policies, thus enhancing the consciousness of interdependence within the national community and enlarging the distance to communities on the other side of the border (Pollard 1981, 74).

Thus, national welfare programs may have directly affected demographic behavior by substituting the support of the national community for the support of the family; they also, however, were a sign of a growing sense of a national community, with shared obligations for members of the nation-state. In a recursive fashion, the increased dependence on other members of the national community would have heightened the sense of connection with other citizens.

The state acted in other, less direct, ways that may have promoted the sense of belonging to a national community. For example, the size of the state bureaucracy increased everywhere (Anderson and Anderson 1967), as did the number of points at which individuals came in contact with state bureaucrats, either face-to-face or via the paper trails of licenses, forms, regulations, and permissions. The state became far more visible in daily life. In predominantly Catholic countries in the nineteenth century (and presumably earlier) probably a high proportion of an individual's contacts with an extraprovincial institution were with the church. By the middle of the twentieth century, in some respects the bureaucracy had supplanted the church as a social institution (Anderson and Anderson 1967, 166). What is relevant is that parish priests represented an international institution, whereas the networks of state bureaucrats stopped at the national borders.

Now let us turn to nation building. Mass identification with a nation almost certainly grew in the nineteenth century (Tilly 1975; Hobsbawm 1987, 146; A. D. Smith 1986). Nation building includes the insistence by the state that everyone be able to communicate in the official language (or languages), the promotion of national identity by building statues to national heroes, and the invention of national traditions such as coronation rituals and anthems (Agulhon 1981; Hobsbawm and Ranger 1983). During the two world wars, the group that was living and dying together was seen to be the nation, which heightened intergroup solidarity (Simmel 1955). The creation by the state of the home front as an integral part of the war effort brought western governments closer to their people (A. D. Smith 1981). An analysis of civilian declines in infant mortality in England during World War I credits patriotic fervor for widespread support for institutional initiatives in health (Winter 1986).[10] In times of peace, the enemies of the nation were international (e.g., the Catholic church and international socialism) and regional (e.g., users of dialect and regional patriots) (Hobsbawm 1987; Grew 1984).

Important in nation building, I think, was education. Not only the higher levels of mass education were relevant for demographic behavior, but also students attended either state schools or schools subject to a considerable degree of regulation by the state. Schools taught national history and deliberately sought to inculcate civic loyalty (Katznelson and Weir 1985).[11] Ernest Gellner has argued that in the modern, industrial nation state this must be so.

> The *nation* is now supremely important, thanks both to the erosion of sub-groupings and the vastly increased importance of a shared, literary-dependent culture. The state, inevitably, is charged with the maintenance and supervision of an enormous social infrastructure (the cost of which characteristically comes close to one half of the total income of the society). The educational system becomes a very crucial part of it, and the maintenance of the cultural/linguistic medium now becomes the central role of education. The citizens can only breathe conceptually and operate within that

[10] Institutional initiatives in health were, Winter argues, seen as patriotic, a way in which those who were denied combat by age or sex could show their patriotic fervor. Agitation about infant welfare had a symbolic appeal; it "demonstrated that a nation which demanded the 'supreme sacrifice' at the front demonstrated its true humanity by preserving infant and maternal life at home" (Winter 1986, 191). As one medical officer put it, the establishment of centers for antenatal and postnatal care was "a form of war-work that called for the enlistment of many workers" (Winter 1986, 192).

[11] In France there was little difference in the curriculums of church schools and lay schools (Anderson 1970).

medium, which is co-extensive with the territory of the state and its educational and cultural apparatus, and which needs to be protected, sustained and cherished. (Gellner 1983, 63–64)

State control over education was not achieved smoothly, with opposition often (but not always) led by the church, but the essential victory went to the state.

National economic integration, state expansion, and nation building are obviously not entirely separable. The growth of capitalism was managed by the state, which viewed the encouragement of industrialization as its reponsibility (Grew 1984); political factors influenced the building of railways (as in Italy, where political unity led to the first railway boom [O'Brien 1983; Fenoaltea, 1983]); an autonomous market was one of the goals of nationalist leaders (A. D. Smith 1981). The adoption of national welfare policies and programs indicated an expansion of the morally relevant community from kin and neighbors to the nation state; this expansion of the morally relevant boundaries is a prerequisite for the functioning of a national market economy (Kohli 1986).

Nor should the list of processes that may reasonably be associated with the growth of a national community be confined to the economy, the state, or the nation. Sports tied people together. Goudsblom's (1967) description of the development of soccer in the Netherlands sounds much like the description of the diffusion of fertility control. He writes that soccer was introduced from England in the 1870s; that the game spread from one town to another; that initially the founding clubs had their homes in cities in two provinces, and their members were well-to-do young men. Subsequently, there was a rapid diffusion, first to cities in other parts of the country, then to urban working class districts, and finally to rural towns and villages. By 1940, the three national soccer federations (Roman Catholic, Orthodox Protestants, and a non-confessional type) had merged into one union, and by 1960 one-third of the male population above the age of twelve went to see a soccer game at least once a month. "Membership," he concludes, "is always in a local club, but through their club people are involved in a tightly organized national network" (Goudsblom 1967, 113–14). In the United Kingdom, "the topic of the day's matches would provide common ground for conversation between virtually any two male workers in England or Scotland, and a few score celebrated players provided a point of common reference for all" (Hobsbawm 1983, 288–89).

Increased literacy made provincial boundaries increasingly porous, as did newspapers. But the effective influence of newspapers stops at the frontiers of the language in which they are written (Tarde [1898] 1969, 306).

It is surprising to see that as nations intermingle and imitate one another, assimilate, and morally unite, the demarcation of nationalities becomes deeper, and their oppositions appear more irreconcilable. At first glance one cannot understand this contrast of the nationalistic 19th century with the cosmopolitanism of the previous century. But this result, however paradoxical, is actually very logical. While between neighboring or distant peoples the exchange of merchandise, ideas, all kinds of items multiplied, the exchange of ideas, in particular, between people speaking the same language progressed even more rapidly, thanks to newspapers. Therefore, even though the *absolute* difference between nations diminished, their relative and conscious differences grew. (Tarde [1898] 1969, 306)

A similar argument has been made by Benedict Anderson, who emphasizes the interactions of capitalism, printing, and the growth of standard vernacular languages in the formation of what he calls "imagined communities" (Anderson 1983). One of Anderson's central images is a newspaper; a newspaper is a one-day best seller, out-of-date tomorrow, read in privacy.

Yet each communicant is well aware that the ceremony he performs is being replicated simultaneously by thousands (or millions) of others of whose existence he is confident, yet of whose identity he has not the slightest notion. . . . What more vivid figure for the secular, historically-clocked, imagined community can be envisioned? (Anderson 1983, 39)

Imagined communities were not necessarily harmonious. But when there was conflict rather than consensus, these conflicts increasingly were fought out at the national rather than the local level. Expanded suffrage increasingly focused political discussions at the national rather than the local level. As politics nationalized, power centralized, and communications among dissident groups improved, the protest of local groups (such as guilds) was replaced by the protest of trade unions and political parties (Tilly 1981, 106).

EXCEPTIONS

There were several exceptions to the general pattern of internal demographic convergence. Demographic variation increased on at least one measure in the countries of the Mediterranean, and in Belgium, Ireland, and Norway. Trying to account for exceptions to a general pattern requires explicit consideration of historical, cultural, and political-economic particularities (Kohn 1987, 717). The attempt that follows, relying as it does on the secondary literature on various countries, can only sketch directions in which those more steeped in the history and sociology of the particular countries might proceed.

As noted earlier, the fertility transition occurred later in the Mediterranean countries; given the general pattern of an increase in variation during a time of demographic change, it is not surprising to find more variation there than elsewhere in 1960. But these countries also seem to have been relatively late in developing national institutions and a sense of a national community. The Italian railways were relatively expensive and, therefore, lightly used, permitting the large-scale survival of traditional local economies based on exchange between towns and nearby regions (Fenoaltea 1983). Italy's "poor sons learned that they were citizens only when they found themselves in military uniform and were sent to fight in the trenches. One may go so far as to say that a national Italian public opinion, in the widest sense of the term, emerged only with the First World War'' (Procacci 1968, 336). The south, which was demographically distinct throughout the period (Livi-Bacci 1977), was integrated into modern Italy "not through mass political alignments but through a multitude of clientalist arrangements which have prevented the development of a wider regional consciousness" (Orridge 1982, 64). Similarly, Spain's civil war may have retarded the formation of a national political community. In Spain, the national parties have not served to bridge linguistic, social, and economic cleavages between Catalonia and the rest of Spain (Linz 1967, 220–21).

Although it might be possible to account for the greater demographic diversity of the Mediterranean countries by pointing to country-specific economic and political factors, the differences in demographic integration may turn out to be largely those of the timing of demographic change. In both Italy and Portugal variation in fertility diminished substantially after 1960. In Portugal the midspread decreased from .223 in 1960 to .187 in 1970. It was not possible to calculate the indexes for 1970 or 1971 for either Italy or Spain (cross-tabulations of women by age and marital status for provinces were not published). A fertility survey taken in Italy in 1979–1980, however, shows that diversity in the median number of children by province had declined by 50 percent between 1961 and 1981 (data from the Istituto delle Ricerche, 1985; see also Caselli, Egidi, and Wilmoth 1987).

Let us now consider the more interesting cases of Norway, Ireland, and Belgium. We saw in chapter 5 that in Ireland, marital fertility was more diverse in 1960 than in 1870, but marriage was more uniform; in Belgium, it was the reverse. In Norway, demographic diversity increased on both measures. Ireland was divided by politics and religion, but not language; Belgium, by politics and language, but not religion; Norway, by debates about the writing of the language that appear to have political and religious significance. In what follows I will also consider Switzerland, where the cantons differed in religion and language but where these cultural divisions were not as politically salient as in Belgium or Ireland.

Although Norway was relatively homogeneous demographically both in 1870 and 1960, demographic diversity increased in both fertility and marriage. Norway was homogeneous linguistically, in the sense that most of the population (including the Lapps in the North) spoke Norwegian (Eidheim 1969). Debates continued, however, over how the language was to be written.

Norway was ruled by Denmark for centuries. Danish was the written language and a variety of dialects was the spoken language.[12] After independence

---

[12] There were also Finnish and Lappish speakers, but in 1926, less than 1 percent spoke Finnish or Lappish (Tesnière 1928, 413).

in 1814, the nationalist movement attempted reforms of the language. Two versions of a standard language dominated a debate that began in the middle of the nineteenth century and increased in intensity. Since 1900 the language issue has been highly divisive both politically and socially (Haugen 1959). It seems unlikely that disagreements about orthography would be reflected in demographic behavior, but it is relevant to note that the language debate has become associated with other political conflicts. The south and west not only are strongholds of the rural language movement, but also support Lutheran and pietistic fundamentalism (and distinctly Christian political parties) as well as temperance and prohibition movements (Rokkan 1967, 416–17). Currently, both versions of Norwegian have equal status in the government and in schools (Katzner 1986, 82–83). It also may be relevant that the Norwegian press is typically decentralized, with a large number of local papers with a relatively small readership (UNESCO 1975).

Compared to many other countries of western Europe, Ireland was demographically homogeneous in 1870. In 1920 partition divided Ireland into Eire, consisting of 26 counties, and Northern Ireland, consisting of the six northern counties that remained attached to England.[13] Migration after partition was considerable (Protestants moved north, and, to a lesser extent, Catholics moved south), which could be expected to make each part of the country more homogeneous and to magnify the differences between them.

To examine more closely what appears to be a demographic parallel to the political partition of Ireland, consider the results of an analysis of variance that compares variation between Eire and Northern Ireland to variation within each region of the country (table 6.2). In this analysis, Northern Ireland consists of five counties (Armagh, Londonderry, Tyrone, Fermanagh, and Antrim-Belfast-Down), while Eire includes the other twenty-six counties.[14]

In 1871 and 1911, before partition, for both marital fertility (I_g) and marriage (I_m) R^2s were low and the F-values were not statistically significant, which suggests that the distinction between Eire and Northern Ireland had little demographic meaning. In 1926 and 1961, however, the R^2 increased and F-values were statistically significant, which suggests a hardening of the demographic boundary between the two areas. Again, we can determine whether the increase in these statistics was due to increasing differences between regions (the between-region sum of squares) or increasing homogeneity within regions (the within-region sum of squares). It is clear that most of the increase was due to divergence between Northern Ireland and Eire. When we consider marital fertility (I_g), we see that the differences between regions increased more (from .00004 to .0279) than differences within regions (from .0308 to

---

[13] There is no single neutral term with which to refer to the twenty-six counties; apparently all have political connotations. I have chosen to use the term "Eire"; it was promoted by de Valera in the 1930s and remains in some use despite the establishment of the republic in 1949.

[14] Antrim Belfast, and Down were combined because of border changes.

TABLE 6.2

One-way Analysis of Variance of Marital Fertility (I_g) and Marriage (I_m) for Ireland by Region, Northern Ireland and Eire, in 1871, 1901, 1926, and 1961

Section 1	1871	1901	1926	1961
Marital Fertility (I_g)				
R²	.00	.05	.35	.35
F-value	.04	1.59	15.36***	15.37***
Sum of squares				
Between regions	.00004	.0026	.0282	.0279
Within regions	.0308	.0470	.0532	.0526
Marriage (I_m)				
R²	.09	.00	.37	.47
F-value	2.93	.09	17.33***	25.94***
Sum of squares				
Between regions	.0063	.00003	.0082	.0145
Within regions	.0617	.0104	.0137	.0161

Section 2	Eire		Northern Ireland	
	1871	1961	1871	1961
Marital Fertility (I_g)				
Standard deviation	.034	.033	.019	.080
Mean	.715	.625	.712	.543
Marriage (I_m)				
Standard deviation	.049	.022	.018	.034
Mean	.405	.486	.367	.544

Note: Probability values: *p<.05, **p<.01, ***p<.001

.0526). With marriage, only the difference between regions increased (from .0063 to .0145); the within-region sum of squares diminished (from .0617 to .0161).

Given the opposition of the Roman Catholic church to the control of fertility within marriage and the close relationship between church and state in Eire, it is not suprising to find that north-south differences in marital fertility increased after partition.[15] It is more surprising, however, to find that the north-south differentials increased in marriage as well.

It is unlikely that differences in divorce would account for this, because

[15] A clause in the constitution prohibited, until 1972, any laws that contravened the laws of the Catholic church (O'Reilly 1986).

both Catholics and Protestants in Ireland tend to disapprove of divorce. About a quarter of the Northern Ireland population is Catholic, and even among the Protestants of the north divorce rates were probably not high enough in either 1930 or in 1960 to affect I_m, which is more heavily influenced by the proportion married at younger ages.[16] Thus, if Eire and Northern Ireland were distinctive only with respect to marital fertility, the obvious interpretation would be that the political boundary is largely a proxy for a religious boundary; that the two regions differ with respect to marriage, however, suggests that there are more general consequences of the partition of Ireland. In any case, it is evident that the boundary mattered for the demographic behavior of Ireland where, it has been argued, the difference between Northern Ireland and Eire was as much a national, as a religious, issue (Connor 1977).

Section 2 of table 6.2 treats Eire and Northern Ireland separately, as if each were a country. Despite the relatively high fertility of Eire compared to the other countries of western Europe, demographic homogeneity increased there as well: the standard deviation diminishes for both marital fertility (barely) and marriage. Northern Ireland, in contrast, was more diverse on both measures in 1961 than it had been in 1871. Northern Ireland—perhaps because of its substantial Catholic minority—does not appear as a demographic nation, but Eire does. Indeed, postpartition Eire displays some of the same macrolevel processes that are associated with the decline in demographic diversity elsewhere. While the Free State (1922–1936) did not institute a policy of protectionism, it displayed an "obsession with enforcing public modes of 'Irishness,' " including the teaching of Irish history and the (unsuccessful) attempt to revive spoken Gaelic, as well as by a powerful and administratively centralized civil service (Foster 1988, 516–35).[17] The sense of belonging to a national community would have been heightened during World War II, when Northern Ireland was intensely engaged in the British war effort while Eire (although still in the Commonwealth) remained neutral. It is also probably relevant for demographic differences that after partition Eire was no longer in

[16] Whether the Catholic church in Ireland has historically been in favor of marriage or has tilted towards encouraging later marriage and more celibacy is debated (Connell 1968; Kennedy 1973; McKenna 1978). While the latest date in McKenna's analysis is 1911, it does suggest an influence of the church on marriage, one that we might expect to be stronger in the postpartition period.

[17] Economic relations between Eire and Great Britain were closer than those between Eire and Northern Ireland, as measured by the value of imports and exports. At every year between 1923 and 1968 Eire's trade with Great Britain was much greater than its trade with Northern Ireland (Mitchell 1976, 536). Trade statistics for external trade between Eire and her main trading partners (Germany, Great Britain, Northern Ireland, and the United States) published by Mitchell only go back to 1924, so it is not possible to use these to evaluate precisely the effect of partition on commercial relations. Imports and exports to Northern Ireland both dropped after 1924, but so did imports and exports to other countries (Mitchell 1976, 536). Figures for 1966–1970 show that the value of Eire's imports and exports was less for trade with Northern Ireland than for either Great Britain or "other countries," but they also show a small increase in the percentage of the total trade with Northern Ireland (Ireland Central Statistics Office 1974, 151).

the British welfare system, so that especially after the 1920s the benefits in the two regions were dramatically different.

Just as the political boundary appears to divide Ireland into two demographic communities, the linguistic boundary separates the demographic regimes of Flemish-speaking Flanders and French-speaking Wallonia in Belgium.[18] In the nineteenth and early twentieth centuries the Flemish nationalists fought for linguistic equality; since the 1930s, however, language legislation has tended to reduce areas of language contact, and the number of occasions of conversations between Walloons and Flemings has almost certainly diminished since the 1950s (Zolberg 1977; McRae 1986, 30, 62). The demographic differences between Flanders and Wallonia are much greater than the differences within either of the two regions. At every date and for both indexes, Flanders and Wallonia are quite different from one another (the F-values are large and statistically significant) (section 1, table 6.3).[19] However, the story is more complicated than that for Ireland. Because the trends in the two indexes are different, with marital fertility the two regions have come closer together (the R^2 diminished, largely due to the relatively large drop in the between-region sum of squares), whereas with marriage they have diverged (the R^2 increased slightly).

In Belgium as in Norway, other cleavages correspond to the linguistic cleavages. If we ask, however, whether the trend on these other dimensions has been towards greater polarization between Flanders and Wallonia, the story is mixed. The evolution of Flemish and Walloon political communities—what might be called regional nationalism—would predict greater demographic diversity over time, whereas the decline in regional economic inequality and the increase in national market integration would predict less demographic diversity. It is relevant to note that changes in religious practice probably cannot account for the observed trends. Flanders remains more devoutly Catholic, but levels of secularization have increased in both communities, with no significant increase in the difference between them (McRae 1986, 65–68).

The political salience of language in Belgium has increased over time (Zolberg 1977). The early stages of the Flemish movement were limited to intellectuals and the movement's goals were primarily cultural (Clough 1930; Rudolph 1982). In 1861 a Flemish organization emerged that had essentially

[18] Language also appears to connect Flanders and Wallonia with linguistically similar Netherlands and France, respectively; the Netherlands and the Flemish arrondissements hardly experienced a post-World War II baby boom, whereas many Walloon arrondissements and many departments in France did.

[19] Brussels has been omitted from this analysis. Brussels is officially bilingual, but it is largely French speaking. It is in Flanders, but shows distinctive demographic attitudes; a 1951 survey shows much higher approval of limiting the number of children than in the other arrondissements of Flanders (McRae 1986).

TABLE 6.3

One-way Analysis of Variance of Marital Fertility (I_g) and Marriage (I_m) for Belgium by Region, Flanders and Wallonia, in 1880, 1900, 1930, and 1961

Section 1	1871	1900	1930	1961
Marital Fertility (I_g)				
R^2	.73	.73	.32	.17
F-value	103.5***	103.3**	17.9***	7.7**
Sum of squares				
Between regions	.635	1.065	.189	.018
Within regions	.233	.392	.402	.088
Marriage (I_m)				
R^2	.22	.20	.19	.26
F-value	10.9**	9.4**	9.1**	13.2***
Sum of squares				
Between regions	.017	.025	.034	.021
Within regions	.058	.101	.141	.060

Section 2	Flanders		Wallonia	
	1880	1961	1880	1961
Marital Fertility (I_g)				
Standard deviation	.059	.050	.095	.045
Mean	.914	.332	.661	.290
Marriage (I_m)				
Standard deviation	.039	.029	.039	.049
Mean	.408	.676	.448	.722

Note: Probability values: *p<.05, **p<.01, ***p<.001

political goals (Rudolph 1982), but it was not until the 1919 elections that an explicitly ethnic party was modestly successful (Nielsen 1980). Political support for the Flemish nationalist movement has generally been higher in each successive election, with governments rising and falling principally over the language issue (Gordon 1978, 108; Nielsen 1980).[20]

While political differences between the linguistic groups have increased, economic differences have decreased. In the nineteenth century Flanders was poorer than Wallonia, but since the late nineteenth century Flanders' economic

[20] Clough credits the press with part of the success of the Flemish movement in carrying the message of the Flemish movement to the common people. In 1857 there were only 85 Flemish journals in Belgium; in 1900 there were 39 dailies and 334 weeklies (Clough 1930, 74).

position has improved and that of Wallonia has deteriorated (McRae 1986, 75–85). The country was increasingly united economically by railroads and canals, large firms that have holdings in both districts, banks that have investments in both regions, and the Belgian customs barrier, which tended to concentrate the trade of the country within itself (Clough 1930, 171). On most social statistics (e.g., cars per capita, private baths per household, telephones per household) not very much difference exists now between the two parts of the country, and, in general, they have been moving closer together rather than further apart (McRae 1986, 82–89). Another source of integration is the state. Although the strength of Belgian regionalism is expressed by titling the monarch "The King of the Belgians," the national government coordinates the activites of the networks of institutions that represent and serve the particularistic communities (Fox 1978).

Clearly, the story is not complete, because it is hard to account for the different trends over time in marital fertility and marriage. Regional differences in marital fertility diminished, while those in marriage increased. This suggests that economic integration may be more important for marital fertility, whereas the political community may have a larger influence on marriage, at least in Belgium. If we follow the story through to 1970 (analysis not shown), differences between Flanders and Wallonia are much less evident; the F-value for I_g is no longer statistically significant in 1970, whereas the F-value for I_m is smaller (down from 13.2 to 10.4) and is marginally less significant (at the .002 rather than the .001 level). The persistent regional demographic differences between 1870 and 1960 are consistent, however, with the continued political salience of the linguistic boundary. And the comparison with Ireland suggests that when cultural boundaries and national boundaries are congruent—as they are in Ireland but not in Belgium—they are particularly definite.

Switzerland suggests the importance of a national political culture in containing potentially divisive cultural differences. Some cantons are predominantly French speaking, others predominantly German speaking.[21] As in Belgium, migration within language areas is greater than across language boundaries (Mayer 1952, 282–83), and there is very little intermarriage across language groups (McRae 1983, 78).[22] The constitution of 1848 established a high degree of cantonal autonomy. Apart from officials of the post office, the Swiss railways, and a few other administrations, no federal officials were permitted in the cantons (Siegfried 1950, 161). There has been a great deal of decentralization: the educational system is cantonal, and the army is composed largely of linguistically homogeneous groups (McRae 1986, 211; Warburton 1976, 98). The Swiss press is characterized by small newspapers of low cir-

[21] Ticino and Grisons, predominantly Italian or Romansch speaking, respectively, in the nineteenth century, are now largely bilingual in either French or German.

[22] In 1930, 94 percent of the marriages were linguistically homogeneous, and in 1970, 91 percent of the marriages were linguistically homogeneous.

culation; their geographical and ideological fragmentation reflects and reinforces Swiss particularism (McRae 1986, 161).

On the other hand, there are a number of sources of national unity. Again, one is economic. The nineteenth century nationalist leaders created a national market, one in which products would be accessible to all parts of the country. They eliminated internal tariffs, unified the currency and weights and measures, and created a modern postal system (Warburton 1976, 89; Mayer 1952, 31). Even though Switzerland resisted the push towards much higher levels of centralization that characterize modern societies in general, the size of the federal bureaucracy has increased (Siegfried 1950, 162). Despite Switzerland's neutrality in both world wars, the wars were "fatal to the old-style federalism," because of the responsibility and power that were taken on by the central government to maintain order and the food supply (Siegfried 1950, 162).

Perhaps more importantly, the nineteenth century nationalist movement in Switzerland was not based on language, culture, or ethnicity, but on the concept of political community (Warburton 1976, 95). Public schools emphasize national history and national consensus (Warburton 1976, 95; McRae 1983). Somewhat paradoxically, cultural diversity—both religious and linguistic—has been enshrined in the political culture. The *Livre du soldat*, a manual of instruction formerly distributed to all male Swiss citizens, informs readers that among the core values of Swiss democracy is its linguistic and religious diversity (McRae 1983, 103). "One of the most striking features of contemporary Swiss political culture is its recognition and acceptance of diversity as a core value in itself" (McRae 1983, 105). A celebration of diversity appears to define what it is to be Swiss.[23]

CONCLUSIONS

There was less demographic diversity in 1960 than in 1870. This was the case for countries, which were more similar to each other in 1960 than they had been in 1870; for provinces of western Europe when national boundaries were

---

[23] This is supported by national referendums covering the period from 1918 to 1967 that show a relatively small degree of divergence from the majority view by language group (McRae 1983, 98). Although differences remain on specific issues such as female suffrage and entry into the Common Market, the majority of all language groups "see [the] Swiss political system as good or very good" (McRae 1983, 100). More interestingly, a 1972 voter survey asked respondents for their primary identities. In all cases, a higher percentage said that their primary identity was Swiss than answered that it was either the canton or the linguistic group (McRae 1983, 109). In the same survey, respondents were asked to compare their degrees of sympathy with the three main Swiss language groups with their sympathy to four outside nationalities. Those whose mother tongue was German (the majority of the population) expressed more sympathy for the French Swiss than for Germans; indeed, the score for sympathy with the Germans was only slightly higher than the degree of sympathy for Spaniards (McRae 1983, 96).

disregarded; and for provinces within countries. The decline in demographic variation within countries was greater than the decline in variation between them. This finding provides statistical support for the conclusion that between 1870 and 1960 in western Europe national boundaries became more important for demographic behavior.

Market integration, state formation, and nation building would have made the circumstances that influence demographic behavior more similar. If prices and incomes are important determinants of demographic behavior, then the greater homogeneity in prices and income that can be expected to follow the integration of national markets and the development of state welfare programs would result in greater demographic homogeneity. These processes of market integration, state expansion, and nation building presumably also knit local personal networks into larger national networks. If couples also take into account what other couples are doing—if, for example, they consider the demographic behavior of their friends and neighbors, and acquaintances—then the integration of diverse local communities into a national community would expand the geographical extent of these social networks. The increased importance of national demographic boundaries in 1960 and the decline in local linguistic diversity suggest that the relevant community for demographic behavior had become the national community.

CHAPTER 7

From Peasants into Frenchwomen

IN PREVIOUS chapters I showed that in most European countries demographic diversity was less in 1960 than in 1870. I speculated that the integration of national markets, state expansion, and nation building were all likely to be relevant. In this chapter, I will extend the previous argument by distinguishing more precisely between two, quite different, possible effects of these processes.

First, they may have made the circumstances in which local populations lived increasingly similar within each country. Market integration and state expansion would homogenize local circumstances. Market integration, for example, evened out wages and prices; state formation, and particularly the expansion of social welfare policies, increased this homogenization. If wages, prices, and welfare are relevant for demographic behavior, their greater homogeneity would lead to a reduction in demographic diversity.

Alternatively, market integration, state expansion, and nation building may have been important because they created a sense of participation in a national community. Production in a national market meant that people in the same country increasingly ate the same foods, bought the same toys, followed the same fashion. Until 1923 the beret was Basque; then "suddenly it was adopted as a French fashion, becoming almost a national uniform by 1932, when twenty-three million were manufactured, virtually one for every Frenchman" (Zeldin 1984, 36). States deliberately inculcated national identification by elaborating old traditions and inventing new ones, but a sense of belonging to a national community would have also been a by-product of the expansion of the state in other ways, such as universal compulsory education and military service. If demographic behavior is embedded in the community—perhaps because neighbors serve as models, perhaps because people do not like to be different from their neighbors, or perhaps because it is in the interaction with others that alternative family patterns are evaluated—then the reduction in demographic diversity would be the consequence of the creation of a national community, so that people in more distant areas came to be seen as neighbors.

The analysis in this chapter concerns only France and is, therefore, inadequate for distinguishing between these two alternative hypotheses. An ideal test would be multilevel; it would include comparable measures for all the provinces of western Europe as well as measures of national integration for each of the fifteen countries. One would like, for example, measures of income for all provinces, as well as measures such as the proportion of newspapers that were distributed nationally rather than locally. It would then be possible to compare the degree of association between demographic behavior and province-level characteristics, and demographic behavior and national-level characteristics. Although some reasonable and comparable measures at the level of the nation do exist (e.g., miles of railroads per capita, telephones per capita, etc.) for many western European countries from the late nineteenth century on, comparable measures of income and other influences at the level of the province are not available for all the provinces both in 1960 and at some earlier date.

Instead, the analysis in this chapter is confined to one country, France, and explores a more limited issue. In brief, I examine the association between demographic behavior and empirical measures that I interpret as crudely representing the importance of income, the integration of national markets, state expansion, and the development of a common national culture. I use income to represent departmental-level economic influences on childbearing, migration to represent the integration of national markets, the number of national bureaucrats to represent state expansion, and non-French languages to represent relative isolation from the national culture. I give most interpretive weight to income, because I think it is closest to the concepts expressed in the usual models that account for fertility in terms of changes in the costs and benefits of children, and to language, because I think that not speaking French in the nineteenth century was likely to be associated with distance from the national culture, as well as perhaps representing distinctive community values about demographic behavior. Thus, a finding that heterogeneity in income decreased and that income was importantly associated with demographic behavior both in the nineteenth and the twentieth centuries would support a view that it was the increasingly similar circumstances in which provincial populations lived that accounted for their increased demographic homogeneity. If, on the other hand, speaking a minority language was associated with demographic diversity, that would support a conclusion that it was the formation of a common culture between 1870 and 1960 that promoted demographic homogeneity.

I focus on two dates, with one analysis for variables measured around 1870, and the second for variables measured around 1960; the intervening period is not examined. Given the limited scope of this analysis that follows from the focus on one country and two dates, and given the gap between the measures and the concepts they are meant to capture, it is clear the analysis is to be taken as exploratory rather than confirmatory.

I do not argue that France is typical. In 1870, it was one of the more demographically diverse countries and the subsequent reduction in demographic diversity was particularly great. In addition, the French Revolution spurred the creation of a rhetoric of a distinctive national identity. The various governments in France over the near-century between 1871 and 1961 were probably more concerned to see political power concentrated in the center than were most other western European governments of the time.

Several further caveats are in order. First, it should be noted that the attempt to distinguish between common circumstances and the creation of a national community require sundering what are more properly seen as mutually reinforcing processes. Those who have similar incomes are more likely to feel part of the same community than those whose incomes are markedly different. Similarly, to the degree that there is a heightened sense of a national community, formerly tolerated differentials (e.g., of income) may no longer be acceptable, and the political process will be called upon to reduce intolerable inequalities (Gellner 1983). Despite the interactions of markets, states, and nations, however, their analytic separation is desirable, at least initially.

The second caveat concerns measurement and analysis. Even when we confine the analysis to France, it is difficult to find appropriate quantifiable indicators of the influences of markets, states, and nation-building. Those I have used will probably leave some readers dissatisfied: markets, states, and cultures are collapsed into crude indicators, somewhat like the stick-figures in children's drawings. Given the exploratory spirit of this chapter, I have deliberately chosen a rather parsimonious analysis, including only a few measures that I think are particularly appropriate rather than including several finer specifications of the same concept (e.g., I have used the total disposable income rather than classifying income by source). There is no doubt considerable measurement error: moreover, measurement error is likely to be greater in the nineteenth century than in the modern period.

Lastly, the analysis in this chapter is somewhat more statistical than in the preceding chapters, and I assume that the reader is familiar with standard regression techniques.

PRELIMINARY ANALYSES

Figures 7.1a–7.1c illustrate the diminution of demographic variation. (The actual values are given in appendix table A7.1.)

Consider first, marital fertility in figure 7.1a. (For a discussion of this graphic technique, see chapter 3.) Demographic variation slowly decreases to 1901, with a more rapid decrease subsequently. Until 1961 the distribution is concentrated at the low fertility end of the scale. The pattern for illegitimacy is quite similar: a slow decrease in the midspread (figure 7.1b). Again, the median is usually below the middle of the box, the distribution is skewed upwards, the most unusual departments are those with high rather than low fertility. The maximum is Paris, which is very distinctive in the early years, but increasingly becomes like the other departments. The distribution is more compressed for marriage (figure 7.1c) than for marital fertility and the most

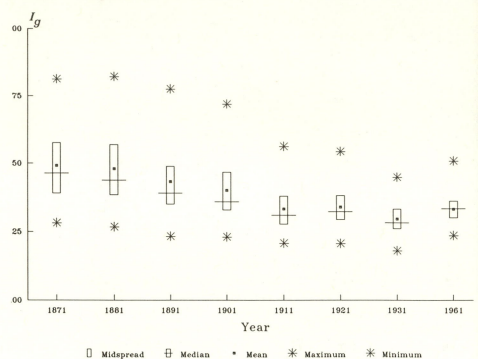

Figure 7.1a. Boxplots of Marital Fertility (I_g), France, 1871–1961

distinctive departments are those with low rather than high nuptiality. The most distinctive department in 1961 is Corsica, with very low nuptiality.

The boxplots describe departments, not individuals, and it is possible that variation among individuals within a department either remained the same or increased. We do not have comprehensive information on individuals for the nineteenth century, but a fertility survey taken in the mid-1970s (see table 5.8) shows little absolute variation among individuals in different socioeconomic categories. Although there is no baseline in the nineteenth century, these figures suggest that variation among individuals within departments may have decreased as well.

Which departments were most distant from the national pattern in 1961? Over the century, trends in demographic behavior were to lower marital fertility and higher proportions married during the reproductive ages, with little change in illegitimacy. Thus, low marital fertility and high nuptiality can be considered ''modern''; conversely, the twenty departments with the highest marital fertility and the lowest proportion married can be considered furthest from the national pattern. Figure 7.2a shows a map of France with the names of the departments; figure 7.2b shows those departments that were most distant from the national pattern in 1961, and table 7.1 is a list of those departments.

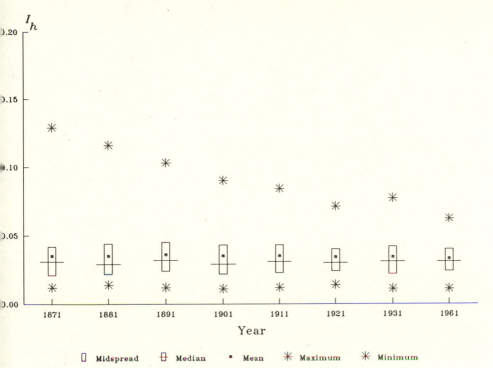

Figure 7.1b. Boxplots of Illegitimacy (I_h), France, 1871–1961

The list will surprise no one familiar with either the demographic history of France or its economic or social history. Most of these departments are in "backward" areas (e.g., LeRoy Ladurie and Dumont's [1971] analysis of other measures of backwardness—the famous maps of goiters and cripples). Most are south of the Saint-Malo–Geneva line (the conventional division between prosperous and poor France); most are near a border or relatively far from Paris, or—like the departments of the Massif Central—in mountainous areas; most of these areas were dominated by the politics of local autonomy and local resistance (LeBras 1986); many had significant proportions of the population who did not speak French in the nineteenth century. Corsica, an island department that only became part of France in the late eighteenth century, heads both lists, and both lists include several departments of Brittany (Morbihan, Finistère, and Ille-et-Vilaine), which despite its relatively early subjection to the crown retained a special status until the time of the revolution.

On the other hand, the sources of demographic backwardness are not as obvious as the preceding discussion suggests. Many departments in the south are demographically similar to the departments of northern and central France; several of the southern departments are of above-average wealth (e.g., Hé-

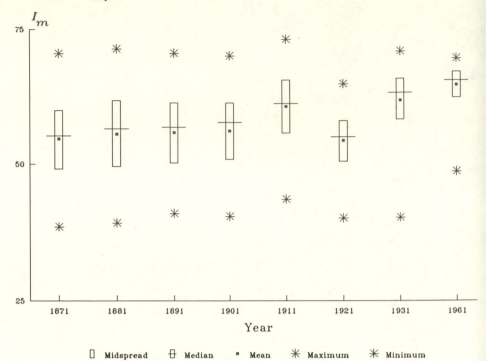

| □ Midspread | ⊞ Median | ▪ Mean | ✳ Maximum | ✳ Minimum |

Figure 7.1c. Boxplots of Marriage (I_m), France, 1871–1961

rault). While most of the low-nuptiality departments are somewhat backward on usual measures of development, the Seine (Paris) and Rhône (Lyons) are distinctive in 1961 because they are leaders in the new trend to later marriage that will characterize many more departments subsequently.

In what follows I will try to specify more precisely the characteristics associated with the general reduction in demographic variation over the long term and with greater or lesser integration into the national pattern in the modern period. The variables used were chosen because they are theoretically relevant and because they are comparable for dates close to 1871 and close to 1961. It was particularly important to use the same variables at both dates; thus, potentially relevant variables that were available at only one of these dates (or at intervening dates) were not used. It is likely that the quality of the data is better for the later than for the earlier date, but the variables should tap the same things.

The set of variables that will be used in the analysis that follows appears in table 7.2. Most variables are drawn from the work of Nicole Delefortrie and Janine Morice, who assembled comparable economic statistics for France for 1864 and 1954 (Delefortrie and Morice 1959). Most of the information for

Figure 7.2a. Map of the Departments of France, 1871–1914

1864 refers to the period 1861–1865; much of it comes from the agricultural census of 1862 and the industrial census of 1861–1865. For 1954, all of the information comes from 1954. The demographic measures are for 1871 and 1961. Because the demographic variables are measured at 1871 and 1961, for rhetorical ease in what follows I have labeled the analyses as 1871 or 1961. The issue of lags between socioeconomic and demographic change is relevant. I do not, however, know what an appropriate lag would be; thus, I have ignored that issue and used the nearest subsequent dates for which the demographic measures are available.

As is evident from table 7.2, relatively few variables are both theoretically relevant and roughly comparable at both dates. These are a measure of per capita disposable income, a measure of the intervention by the central government in local affairs, and migration.

Disposable income per person age sixteen to sixty was selected from among

Figure 7.2b. French Departments with Highest Marital Fertility (I_g) and Lowest Marriage (I_m) in 1961

those available as the income variable that should best capture the economic circumstances of the population of the departments. It also is usually correlated fairly closely with other macrolevel economic indicators (e.g., urbanization, the proportion in industry). It includes income from social welfare programs. I have calculated disposable income per person age sixteen to sixty (roughly the working age population) rather than disposable income per capita because the departments varied so greatly in fertility in the nineteenth century; thus, differences in per capita income would include the effect of fertility (a higher fertility would mean a lower per capita income) (*ceteris paribus*). Since our interest here is in the effects of income on fertility, using a measure of income that is affected by fertility would systematically bias the analysis.

To measure state penetration, I used an indirect measure of the number of *national bureaucrats*: the ratio of national civil and military salaries to the

TABLE 7.1

French Departments with the Highest Marital Fertility (I_g) and Lowest Marriage (I_m) in 1961

Marital Fertility (I_g) (Highest 20)	Marriage (I_m) (Lowest 20)
Corsica	Corsica
Maine-et-Loire	Lozère
Meuse	Haute-Loire
Vendée	Ardèche
Haute-Marne	Haute-Savoie
Morbihan	Seine
Doubs	Basses-Pyrénées
Ardennes	Ille-et-Vilaine
Haute-Saône	Finistère
Moselle	Morbihan
Loire-Inférieure	Aveyron
Manche	Rhône
Finistère	Jura
Vosges	Cantal
Calvados	Côtes-du-Nord
Mayenne	Hautes-Pyrénées
Lozère	Alpes-Maritimes
Aisne	Hérault
Deux-Sèvres	Savoie
Ille-et-Vilaine	Hautes-Alpes

Note: The departments are listed in rank order, from highest to lowest for I_g, and lowest to highest for I_m.

departmental population of working age sixteen to sixty. I assume a high degree of correspondence between salaries and the number of national officials stationed in the departments. Those departments with the least governmental presence (the smallest amount spent on salaries per person age sixteen to sixty) should be furthest from the national demographic patterns. Alternatively, if the government deliberately concentrates manpower in those departments perceived to be most distant from the center, the prediction would be reversed—those demographically most distant would be the departments with the highest proportion of national bureaucrats (the largest amount spent on salaries).

Migration is measured by the proportion of the population whose department of residence at the time of the relevant census differed from the department of birth, and thus is an estimate of in-migration. It is included for two reasons.

First, greater demographic homogeneity might be simply a consequence of the mixing of populations. To imagine how this might affect demographic

TABLE 7.2
Socioeconomic Variables for French Departments in 1871 and 1961

	Nineteenth Century
Disposable income per person age 16–60[a]	*Source*: The total private revenues minus direct taxes around 1866 (Delefortrie and Morice 1959, 49–50). The revenues are the sum of income from business, capital, salaries, wages, and social welfare payments. Direct taxes are those baesd on *richesse apparente*, rather than declarations. Disposable income is given in Delefortrie and Morice (1959, 196, col. 30). Disposable income is divided by the number of persons age 16–60. This figure is calculated from the total population in 1866 (ibid., 208, col. 51) times the proportion of the population aged 16–60 (ibid., 305, col. 209).
National bureaucracy[a]	*Source*: The combination of state salaries (ibid., 193, col. 9) and military salaries (ibid., 193, col. 10) per person age 16–60. The salaries are discussed in Delefortrie and Morice (1959, 33–38). State salaries include, for example, the personnel of the Ministry of Justice, the Ministry of the Interior (e. g., salaries of prefects, subprefects, etc.), and the Ministry of Finance (e. g., bureaucrats of the post office).
Migration, 1872[a]	*Source*: The number of residents born outside the department per 100 departmental residents in 1872. It is taken from LeBras and Todd (1981, 444, col. 3).
Language, 1863	*Source*: The proportion of the communes in a department that are non-French speaking (or French speaking). I have taken the information from a map published by Weber (1976, 68, map 3); his source is an 1863 survey by the Ministry of Public Education. Weber has distinguished seven categories: (1) all or nearly all communes non-French speaking; (2) 50% of communes non-French speaking; (3) significant proportion of communes non-French speaking; (4) cohesive groups of communes non-French speaking; (5) patois indicated; (6) questionable; and (7) French speaking. I have combined these into three categories: Group 1, which includes categories 1, 2, and 6; Group 2, which includes categories 3, 4, and 5; and French speaking (category 7). These two groups are compared to the French-speaking departments. Category 6 (questionable) was included in Group 1 because these departments are geographically contiguous to several predominantly non-French-speaking departments, and because qualitative evidence suggests widespread use of languages other than French.

TABLE 7.2 (cont.)

Language, 1863	*Language Group 1*[b]	*Language Group 2*[b]
	Alpes (Basses-)	Ain
	− Alpes (Maritimes-)	− Alpes (Hautes-)
	+ − Ardèche	Charente
	− Ariège	Côtes-du-Nord
	Aude	+ Doubs
	− Aveyron	Gard
	Bouches-du-Rhône	Gironde
	− Cantal	− Jura
	Corrèze	Lot-et-Garonne
	+ − Corsica	Meurthe-et-Moselle
	Dordogne	+ Meuse
	Drôme	− Morbihan
	+ − Finistère	Nièvre
	Garonne (Haute-)	Nord
	Gers	Rhin (Haut-)
	− Hérault	− Rhône
	+ − Ille-et-Vilaine	+ Saône (Haute-)
	Isère	− Savoie (Haute-)
	Landes	Tarn-et-Garonne
	− Loire (Haute-)	
	+ − Lozère	
	Lot	
	Puy-de-Dôme	
	− Pyrénées (Basses)	
	− Pyrénées (Hautes)	
	Tarn	
	Var	
	Vaucluse	
	Vienne (Haute)	

Disposable income per person age 16–60[a]	*Source*: Revenue minus direct taxes in 1954, discussed in Delefortrie and Morice (1959, 111–12; it is given on p. 246, col. 30). Total disposable income was divided by the population age 16–60 in 1954, which was calculated from the total population (ibid., 261, col. 51) times the proportion of the population age 16–60 (ibid., 305, col. 10).
National bureaucracy[a]	*Source*: The combination of state salaries (ibid., 237, col. 9) and military salaries (ibid., 237, col. 10) in 1954. The total state and military salaries was divided by the number of people age 16–60, as above, to give the amount spent on these salaries per person age 16–60.

TABLE 7.2 (*cont.*)

	Twentieth Century
Migration[a]	*Source*: The number of residents born outside the department per 100 departmental residents at the time of the census (1975). It is taken from LeBras and Todd (1981, 444, col. 6).
Agriculture	*Source*: The number of the departmental population in agriculture (ibid., 264, col. 56) divided by the number age 16–60, as above.
Telephones	*Source*: The number of telephones per 100 *residents principales*. This number includes not only households that have a telephone installed, but also those that can use a telephone installed in a part of the lodging that is for professional use exclusively. The data are taken from Croze (1976, 202–03, col. 5).

Sources: Croze (1976); Delefortrie and Morice (1959); LeBras and Todd (1981); Weber (1976).

[a] Measures comparable at both dates.

[b] The departments in Language Group 1 and Language Group 2 marked with a " + " or a " − " appear in Table 7.1 as high-fertility (+) or low nuptiality (−) departments.

behavior, consider an exaggerated case. Assume that individuals born in Morbihan in 1900 inherited one set of fertility preferences while individuals born at the same date in Hérault inherited another. Assume also that these preferences did not change between 1900 and 1930, but that half of the Morbihan birth cohort moved to Hérault, while half of the Hérault birth cohort moved to Morbihan. The result would be that for the populations of Morbihan and Hérault fertility would be the same in 1930. Children are not, of course, born with fertility preferences, and preferences do not remain stable. Nonetheless, to the degree that early childhood socialization in one department differed from that in another, and to the degree that some of this socialization persisted into adult reproductive behavior, internal migration would have had the effect of blending departmental differences in demographic behavior. Conversely, those departments with the least in-migration would be expected to remain most demographically distinct.

Second, although this conceptualization does not require that migration directly affect behavior, it is reasonable to believe that migrants change as a result of their move, and that they have effects on the community into which they move. In addition, and of particular relevance here, migration expands the networks of those that stay at home. These considerations would make the homogenizing effects of migration even greater than a simple arithmetic averaging would predict.

The measure of migration used here is the simple difference between department of birth and department of residence at the time of the census. It is thus a particularly inadequate measure of the way in which migration can knit together different parts of the country. Not only does this measure miss intervening moves, but it distinguishes neither the sex of the migrant nor the distance traveled, and it is silent on the contacts between those who left and those who remained.[1]

A few variables are not comparable over time, but were included because they were theoretically relevant or because specific departments that were outside the national pattern in 1961 suggested their importance. An example of the former is communications. Households with *telephones* would likely be more closely linked to the wider community than those without, and thus I have included the percentage of households with telephones. Another variable, the *proportion of the labor force in agriculture* was included because the departments with high fertility and/or low nuptiality in 1961 included many that were unusually agricultural (that is, they had a high ratio of persons in agriculture to all persons age sixteen to sixty). These might not only be poorer, but also might be particularly rural and socially isolated departments.

A common language is not a prerequisite for a sense of a national community, as the decrease in diversity in nuptiality in Switzerland between 1871 and 1961 discussed previously shows, but it is surely important. Distinctive languages inhibit the communication that is an important basis of community, and distinctive languages are also markers of distinctive cultures. A common language would facilitate interaction, and it is likely that its absence (ceteris paribus) would hinder the development of a sense of identification with fellow citizens. This was certainly thought to be the case in France. The National Convention legislatively abolished patois, and the use of languages other than French was thought by the Republicans to be associated with reaction. Successive governments legislated that education be in French, but with little success until the Third Republic (Gordon 1978; Weber 1976).

Using information from an 1863 survey of communes by the French Ministry of Public Education (Weber 1976), I have created three language categories: French speaking, mostly non-French speaking (*Language Group 1*), and largely non-French speaking (*Language Group 2*). Their locations are shown on the map in figure 7.3. A comparison of this map with figure 7.2 shows a high degree of overlap between demographically remote departments and non-French speaking departments.

---

[1] For migration, data for 1975 are used to represent 1961. Although place of birth was apparently asked in the 1961 census, I have not been able to find published tabulations of place of birth by place of residence. The pattern of migration in France between 1961 and 1975 was probably rather stable, however (the same departments sending, the same departments receiving); the correlation between the 1975 measure used here and the proportion of the departmental population moving between 1962 and 1968 (data from Desplanques 1975) is .90.

Figure 7.3. Map of Language Groups

The language variable deserves more extended comment, for there are reasons to be cautious about its quality. From the time of the revolution, French governments have been concerned because all French persons did not speak French; in the nineteenth and early twentieth centuries success at "Frenchifying" them was a marker of a government's success in nation building. Because the statistics tracing the decline of monolingual speakers in other than French languages were politically relevant, they should be approached cautiously.

In chapter 3 I noted that various estimates of the proportion of non-French speakers differed. The 1863 survey shows that about 11 percent of school children ages seven to thirteen spoke no French, and about 22 percent of the communes were non-French speaking (Weber 1976, 498–501). Estimates for an earlier period come from a report, based on a questionnaire sent to parish priests, given by Abbé Gregoire to the National Convention in 1794. He showed in the report that out of an estimated population of 25 million at least 6 million, especially in country districts in the south, knew no French at all, while another 6 million had only a smattering of the language and were unable to carry on a sustained conversation in it (Rickard 1974). In only about fifteen departments was the French language spoken exclusively (Lartichaux 1977). Levasseur's estimates of non-French speakers from the census of 1881 are higher than either Weber's or Abbé Gregoire's. He estimates that 22,790,000 out of a total population of 37,362,000 (60.5 percent) spoke French, so about 40 percent did not (Levasseur 1889, 394–95, fn. 2). Of those who did not, about half (12.7 million) spoke Provençal (Levasseur 1889, 393). Levasseur's estimates are probably overestimates because for Provençal he includes the entire population of the relevant departments, which surely included some French speakers.

French had been the language of officials and offical documents since the Ordinance of Villers-Cotterets (1539), while local populations spoke various different languages and dialects. Before the revolution, little attempt was made by the government to insist that French be spoken by the public. During the revolution, however, this changed; linguistic unity was seen as a prerequisite to political unity, and legislation was passed making schooling in French compulsory. These efforts were resisted in many French regions, the same areas where populations resisted government efforts in other spheres, such as conscription and tax collection. Great strides towards the spread of French are attributed to the reforms of Jules Ferry, the Minister of Public Instruction under the Third Republic; these affected the generations born after 1875 (Weber 1976).

The state's role in changing the linguistic world was not confined to schooling. In explaining the increasing dominance of French in France, Rickard lists as important the new governmental machine devised by Napoleon, which "brought even the most remote villager, willy-nilly, into contact with the world of administration, of documents, stamps, signatures and countersignatures" (Rickard 1974, 124). A mixed bag of state and private developments—improved communications, postal service, national and regional journals (invariably in French), male suffrage, and electoral campaigns—was also important. But the decline in other languages and dialects was especially rapid after the introduction of free, compulsory primary education.

In addition, contemporaries emphasized the rapid development of the network of railroads and roads. A school inspector in Tarn-et-Garonne wrote that the inhabitants of the countryside were avid for money and eager to sell their beets to the foreigners who came in by rail; to be understood, they had to give up their patois. The mobility of the population was also singled out. A schoolteacher in a village in the Vosges wrote, shortly before 1921, that patois was scarcely used among adults, in good part because there had been such an in-migration of foreign workers; the mixture of languages, he said, favored the adoption of a common language (Bloch 1921, 6).

There are apparently no surveys comparable to that by the Ministry of Public Instruction in 1863 that would make it possible to time precisely the successive abandonment of local languages. There is, however, a great deal of qualitative evidence concerning the timing and causes of their diminution. The major studies of specific local languages consistently agree that they were rapidly disappearing in the last quarter of the nineteenth century and the beginning of the twentieth century. In 1888, a speaker at the Congrès de Sociétés Savantes said that it was necessary to make haste to study regional languages because many had already disappeared and others were being ruined by French (Dauzat 1927, 8).

The nonmountainous departments of the Auvergne seem to have given up most easily; the last old women there who knew no French were reported to have died around 1880 (Dauzat 1927, 32). The generations born there between 1820 and 1830 understood but did not speak French; the generations born after 1875 were perfectly bilingual and were followed by the generations of those who preferred to speak French (Dauzat 1927, 32). Brun, writing of a small agricultural village in Provence, found only two or three people who could speak no French, although those over fifty—that is, those born before about 1875—still chose to speak Provençal. Of those under forty-five, the men spoke Provençal and the women French, while the children spoke no Provençal at all, a clear harbinger of the disappearance of the language; he argues that patois survived in Provence as long as it did because the area was isolated by its privileges and administered largely by locals (Brun 1927, 164–67).[2] In the Midi, by 1922 everyone not only understood French but used it daily; the last generation that understood French but did not use it daily had disappeared by around 1900 (Dauzat 1922, 211). Dauzat wrote in 1927 that to find those who spoke no French, it was necessary to go to "the most hidden corner" of the Alpes-Maritimes or Roussillon; both were among the last provinces to be politically united to the rest of France (Dauzat 1927).

Basque persisted into the twentieth century in the Basses-Pyrénées, which Bourdieu argues was due to the fact that the department stood apart from contemporary economic changes and more generally to its marginal situation (Bourdieu 1962, 114). Even there, however, by 1927 the great majority of Basques spoke and understood French (Dauzat 1927, 129–30). Brittany appears to have persisted longest in maintaining its own language. The change seems to have been even more abrupt in Brittany than in Provence; by 1925 only the aged were monolingual in Breton, whereas the children were monolingual in French (Dauzat 1945, 118; Loth 1926).

[2] The use of French in Provence varied by age and sex. A grandfather would speak Provençal to his wife and his son, but French to his grandson and, especially, to his granddaughter. Outside the home, Provençal tended to be used where men congregated—the barbershop, the *tabac*—whereas French predominated where the women shopped (Brun 1927, 165).

In 1961 French was not the mother tongue for some, but few except the children of recent migrants would have entered school not speaking French. From the point of view of language, almost all had access to the national culture. Nevertheless, it may be that language represents more than the ability to converse with others who speak French, to read national newspapers, and so on. Language may also capture cultural values that persist after the use, or even the knowledge, of the language has disappeared. If, as has been argued (Levy 1966), family values are among the last to change with modernization, past language may be a reasonable indicator of the persistence of distinctive family values. Thus, the analyses of 1961 that follow will include whether or not the department was French speaking a century earlier.

FINDINGS

Several measures of level and variation for the demographic and socioeconomic variables for all departments are shown in section 1 of table 7.3, while the means of the demographic and socioeconomic variables by language group are shown in section 2. Initial inspection of the distribution of the provinces on each variable showed that one of the extremes was usually either Paris or Corsica; these two provinces were outliers not only demographically but in almost every other way as well. They were thus omitted from the analyses that follow.

The mean level of all variables changed substantially, but the proportional change differed considerably across variables. Income is measured in current francs in both periods; because of inflation, it appears to increase enormously, as does the mean departmental amount spent on bureaucratic salaries. Delefortrie and Morice reevaluated 1871 (1864) income in 1954 francs and calculated a cost-of-living index that indicated that the cost of living increased about 250-fold (Delefortrie and Morice 1959, 323, col. 30B). Thus, the 500-fold increase in incomes corresponds to a doubling of real income. The increase in the amount spent on the salaries of national bureaucrats (about a 1000-fold) is in part due to inflation, in part due to increases in the real income of bureaucrats, and in part due to an increase in the number of bureaucrats. If their real incomes increased as did that of the entire population, the number of bureaucrats would have doubled.

Because of the substantial changes in the level of the variables, the coefficient of variation (the standard deviation divided by the mean) is the preferable measure of variation. For all variables, the coefficient of variation is less at the later date than at the earlier.[3] That there is a marked decrease in the diversity of income means that the decline in demographic diversity might simply

---

[3] This is a more general finding than the few variables listed here indicate. LeBras and Todd (1981) find a similar reduction of variation across a wide variety of measures, and I reached similar conclusions for other comparable economic statistics gathered by Delefortrie and Morice (1959).

TABLE 7.3
Descriptive Statistics for Socioeconomic and Demographic Variables
for French Departments in 1871 and 1961

Section 1[a]	Mean	Standard Deviation	Coefficient[b] of Variation
Income (francs per person age 16–60)[c]			
1871	774	274	35.41
1961	389,281	54,867	14.10
Bureaucracy (salaries in francs per person age 16–60)[c]			
1871	17	11	60.98
1961	19,093	8,018	42.00
Migration (migrants per 100 persons)			
1871	10	6	57.16
1961	27	7	26.98
Marital fertility (I_g)			
1871	.49	.12	25.28
1961	.33	.04	11.30
Illegitimacy (I_h)			
1871	.04	.02	47.21
1961	.03	.01	37.61
Marriage (I_m)			
1871	.54	.07	13.61
1961	.65	.03	4.62
Agriculture (per 100 persons age 16–60)			
1961	18	8	43.21
Telephones (per 100 households)			
1961	12	2.20	18.63

have been due to the fact that all departments were characterized by much more similar economic circumstances in 1961 than in 1871.

Note that the "backwardness" of the non-French-speaking departments (Language Group 1 and Language Group 2) is more evident in 1871 than in 1961 (section 2 of table 7.3). Compared to the French-speaking departments, the non-French-speaking departments were poorer; they showed more expen-

TABLE 7.3 (*cont.*)

		Means	
Section 2[a]	French	Language Group 1	Language Group 2
Income[c]			
1871	865	655	806
1961	400,574	357,199	415,956
Bureaucracy[c]			
1871	15	16	21
1961	18,108	20,056	19,799
Migration			
1871	11	8	12
1961	28	27	25
Marital fertility (I_g)			
1871	.42	.54	.51
1961	.34	.31	.33
Illegitimacy (I_h)			
1871	.04	.03	.04
1961	.66	.63	.64
Marriage (I_m)			
1871	.59	.52	.53
1961	.66	.63	.64
Agriculture			
1961	16	21	18
Telephones			
1961	13	12	12

[a]The variables are described in table 7.2.

[b]The coefficient of variation is the standard deviation divided by the mean.

[c]The increase in income and salaries of bureaucrats is due in part to inflation and in part to increases in real income. See text for discussion.

diture on national bureaucrats; and they had higher marital fertility and lower proportions married. In 1961 the picture is rather different, and in some respects, Language Group 1 and Language Group 2 have diverged. Marital fertility is now *slightly lower* in both these sets of departments than in those that were French-speaking in the nineteenth century, and the proportions married are also slightly lower. Language Group 1—the departments with the highest proportions of non-French-speakers in the nineteenth century—is still distinguished by relatively low incomes and high proportions in agriculture, but the departments of Language Group 2 (which include many departments on France's eastern border) have *higher* incomes than the departments that were French speaking in the nineteenth century.

Although low marital fertility was characterized earlier as "modern" because the long-term trend has been to fewer children, the postwar baby boom interrupted that trend. In France marital fertility continued to fall between 1931 and 1961 in about half the departments, but it rose in the other half. The baby boom was somewhat a fad, and the departments in Language Group 1 seem to have participated less than the other departments.[4] They were demographically "backward" in the nineteenth century when the trend was to low marital fertility and higher nuptiality and demographically backward after World War II when the trend was temporarily to higher marital fertility.

It is possible that the presence of a national bureaucracy, migration, the size of the agricultural labor force, and telephones are simply other ways of measuring per capita disposable income; in other words all we have is a list of more or less adequate measures of personal income. This does not appear to be consistently the case, as the correlations in table 7.4 between these variables and income show. The correlations between income and bureaucracy, and income and migration, are positive and significant in 1871; in 1961, however, the corresponding correlation coefficients are not statistically significant. There is an association in 1961 between income and the proportion in agriculture, but none with the proportion of households with a telephone. Although it is interesting that the number of telephones per 100 households is correlated with migration, as we shall see, this variable is not important in the multivariate analyses presented later.

Income is usually expected to be negatively related to fertility (the higher the income, the lower the fertility) and positively related to nuptiality (the higher the income, the higher the proportion married). This is the case for nuptiality, both in 1871 and 1961, but not for marital fertility (table 7.4). State penetration as measured by bureaucratic salaries is also unimportant, statistically significant only for I_h and I_m in 1871. Migration, like income, should be negatively related to fertility and positively related to nuptiality because we expect migrants to go to more "modern" areas, leaving the "backward" areas even more backward. In both 1871 and 1961 this is the case, and all coefficients are statistically significant.

The relation between the proportion of the population in agriculture in 1961 and marital fertility should be positive, and between agriculture and nuptiality it should be negative; only the latter meets expectations, but the correlation

---

[4] The departments missed by the baby boom are six contiguous departments in Brittany and Normandy (Finistère, Morbihan, Ille-et-Vilaine, Côtes-du-Nord, Manche, and Mayenne), five contiguous departments in the Massif Central (Aveyron, Cantal, Corrèze, Lozère, and Haute-Loire) and two contiguous Alpine departments on the far eastern border (Savoie and Hautes-Alpes). Most had relatively high fertility in 1931.

TABLE 7.4
Zero-order Correlation Matrix for Socioeconomic and Demographic Variables for French Departments in 1871 and 1961

	I_g	I_h	I_m	Income	Bureaucracy	Migration	Agriculture	Telephones
1871								
I_g	1.00	−.25**	.09	−.17	.006	−.41***		
I_h		1.00	.24**	.51***	.25**	.44***		
I_m			1.00	.21**	−.25***	.31***		
Income				1.00	.47***	.26**		
Bureaucracy					1.00	.28**		
Migration						1.00		
1961								
I_g	1.00	.09	−.20*	.14	−.15	−.35***	−.07	−.34***
I_h		1.00	.65***	.56***	.08	.31***	−.44***	.26**
I_m			1.00	.30***	.06	.24**	−.19*	.01
Income				1.00	.15	.13	−.52***	−.10
Bureaucracy					1.00	.26**	−.31***	−.04
Migration						1.00	−.25**	.57***
Agriculture							1.00	−.09
Telephones								1.00

Notes: Corsica and Paris (Seine) are excluded.

Probability values: *p<.10, **p<.05, ***p<.01.

coefficients are small. Lastly, the proportion of households with telephones should be negatively associated with marital fertility and positively associated with nuptiality. The association with marital fertility is as expected, but the association with nuptiality is not statistically significant.

In the analysis that follows the demographic indexes are the dependent variables and the socioeconomic variables are the independent variables (table 7.5). The regression procedure was ordinary least squares. Since the dependent variables (I_g, I_h, and I_m) can only vary between 0 and 1, the log of the indexes was the dependent variable.[5] The first two columns show the coefficients for models that include variables that are comparable at both dates: income, bureaucracy, migration, and language. The last column (Model 2) shows the estimates for 1961 when telephones and the proportion in agriculture are included.

The R^2s indicate the proportion of variation in demographic behavior accounted for by departmental levels of income, bureaucratic salaries, migration, and language. For I_g the R^2 is larger in 1871 than in 1961. Put another way, the proportion of variation *unexplained* was much larger in 1961 than in 1871. For I_m, the R^2 was about the same at both dates. Illegitimacy, which in 1961 varied more from department to department than did either marital fertility or nuptiality, is better accounted for in that year by departmental characteristics—the R^2 is almost twice as high for I_h as for I_g or I_m.[6] Surprisingly, the addition of telephones and the proportion in agriculture (Model 2) do not change the results: the R^2s remain virtually the same, and the coefficients are not significant for either marriage or marital fertility.

To test whether the differences in the coefficients in the two years were statistically significant, the regressions were run on a pooled data set that combined observations for both years and in which 1871 (1864) income was in constant francs (Delefortrie and Morice 1959, 323, col. 30A); the regression equation included interactions between year and all the other variables (i.e., year-income, year-bureaucracy, year-migration, and year-language). All the interactions between year and the other variables were statistically significant for I_g, but only the year-income interaction was significant for I_m. That the year-income interaction was statistically significant supports a conclusion that the relation between income and demographic behavior had changed over time. These results mean that the way in which income, bureaucracy, migration, and language influenced marital fertility changed over time, but the way

[5] In preliminary regressions squared terms for the predictor variables were not significant, which indicates that the relationship of the predictor variable to the logged index was approximately linear.

[6] Models were examined that included interactions among all the predictor variables. These had little effect on the R^2; thus, for simplicity, only the model with no interactions is presented here.

TABLE 7.5
Parameters for 1871 and 1961 Regressions, Income, Bureaucracy,
Migration, and Language, Logged I_g, I_h, and I_m

	Standardized Coefficients	Model 1 Standardized Coefficients	Model 2 Standardized Coefficients
	Log I$_g$ 1871	*Log I$_g$ 1961*	*Log I$_g$ 1961*
Income	−.29**	.03	−.001
Bureaucracy	.40***	−.06	−.12
Migration	−.35***	−.27**	−.17
Language 1	.28**	−.48***	−.47***
Language 2	.19*	−.16	−.17
Telephones			−.18
Agriculture			−.10
R²	.36	.22	.23
	Log I$_h$ 1871	*Log I$_h$ 1961*	*Log I$_h$ 1961*
Income	.34***	.42***	.41***
Bureaucracy	−.02	.05	.07
Migration	.37***	.21**	.11
Language 1	−.25***	−.43***	−.41***
Language 2	−.16	−.34***	−.32***
Telephones			.17*
Agriculture			−.001
R²	.40	.52	.53
	Log I$_m$ 1871	*Log I$_m$ 1961*	*Log I$_m$ 1961*
Income	.33**	.15	.24*
Bureaucracy	−.31**	.02	.08
Migration	.22**	.20*	.23*
Language 1	−.27**	−.43***	−.47***
Language 2	−.24**	−.29**	−.33***
Telephones			−.04
Agriculture			.20
R²	.27	.25	.25

Notes: Corsica and Paris (Seine) are excluded. The R² is the adjusted R².

Probability values: *p<.10, **p<.05, ***p<.01.

in which these variables influenced nuptiality remained rather similar—with the exception of income, the effect of which changed over the century.

The most relevant findings concern the effects of income and linguistic history. Income became less important for marital fertility and marriage, while language usually retained its influence. In 1871 the effect of income on marital fertility and nuptiality was statistically significant; in 1961 the effect of income on marital fertility and nuptiality (Model 1) cannot be distinguished from random variation.[7] Only for illegitimacy is income statistically significant in both years; departments with higher income have higher levels of illegitimacy.

Whether or not a department had large proportions who did not speak French in 1871 had an important effect in both 1871 and 1961, one that was independent of any association between language and the measures of income, state penetration, or migration. We saw earlier (table 7.3) that predominantly non-French-speaking departments (Language Group 1) in the nineteenth century had, in 1871, lower fertility and lower proportions married than predominantly French-speaking departments. In 1961 all or virtually all in these departments spoke French, but their history apparently continues to matter; demographic behavior is distinctive in these departments. While in the past that distinctiveness consisted of *higher* fertility and lower proportions married (that is, they were demographically "backward"), in 1961 the distinctiveness consisted of *lower* fertility as well as lower proportions married.[8] While it was expected that telephones would be part of the explanation for the relevance of language, in Model 2 we see that the addition of telephones had little effect on the R^2, and is statistically significant only for illegitimacy.

An examination of the largest and smallest residuals from the 1961 regression (excluding telephones and agriculture) shows that there is some tendency for the departments with the largest residuals to fall into clusters of geographically contiguous departments. However, in marital fertility, there are clusters of large positive residuals and clusters of large negative residuals, and these two occur in departments that are generally not geographically contiguous. Although departments with a distinctive language include those with higher than expected marital fertility as well as lower than expected marital fertility, in the event the negative residuals more than counterbalance the positive ones, so that the overall effect of a distinctive language is negative in 1961 (as seen earlier in table 7.5). But the more important conclusion is that a distinctive

---

[7] There may, however, have been a threshold effect. This cannot be tested with the available data.

[8] When language was excluded, the R^2 was much lower (about .07 for both I_g and I_m). In an exploratory stepwise regression (in which variables are considered one by one and entered into the analysis in the order of their statistical importance) for I_g Language Group 1 entered the analysis first, and Language Group 2 entered third; in this analysis, income never attained the threshold level of statistical significance to enter the equation.

language is associated with distinctive fertility, whether it is unusually high or unusually low.

This result can be explored further by an examination of regional differences in demographic behavior in France, where regions are larger groupings of departments. There are several ways of combining departments into regions (see, for example, Wrigley [1985]). Here I follow a regionalization based on the prerevolutionary provinces of France, which groups departments into clusters of contiguous departments that had a common political history (often as separate entities before coming under control of the crown) and often a common culture, expressed in similar language or dialects. They were probably knit together in other ways as well, ways that would only be visible with more detailed information: for example, in the period of the Vendée rebellion after the revolution, personal contacts, markets, and marriages created a community of interest between the villagers of Chanzeaux and towns in the Mauges, a part of the larger region of Anjou (Wylie 1966, 20). The regions are shown in appendix table 7.2.

In France location in a particular region accounts for a good deal of a department's demographic behavior; analysis of variance shows that the differences within regions are much smaller than the differences among regions (table 7.6). Moreover, regions are important in accounting for demographic variation in 1961 as well as in 1871; for marital fertility and illegitimacy, they account for more variation at the latter date than at the former (the R^2s are higher). Controlling for income does not change these results.

We might expect that where regions were distinctive demographically at the start of the transition and remained distinctive in 1961, the regional order

TABLE 7.6

Analysis of Variance of Marital Fertility (I_g), Illegitimacy (I_h), and Marriage (I_m) by Regions of France for 1871 and 1961

	Marital Fertility (I_g)		Illegitimacy (I_h)		Marriage (I_m)	
	1871	1961	1871	1961	1871	1961
R^2	.55	.70	.48	.64	.52	.46
F-value[a]	5.83	10.96	4.52	10.44	5.17	3.99
Sum of squares						
Between regions	.551	.061	.009	.007	.183	.024
Within regions	.456	.027	.009	.004	.171	.028
Total	1.007	.088	.018	.011	.354	.052

Note: The twelve regions are shown in appendix table A7.2.

[a] All F-values are significant at the .001 level or better. There are a total of 64 degrees of freedom, 11 for the model and 53 for the error.

would remain the same or be similar; that is, regions with relatively high marital fertility in 1871 would also be regions with relatively high marital fertility in 1961. We speak to this question by showing the rank order of the regions in table 7.7. In general, most regions retain their relative positions, but the amount of switching can be substantial, as for Picardy, which changed from one of the regions with the lowest marital fertility in 1871 to the middle of the distribution, or Languedoc, which had relatively high fertility in 1871 but relatively low fertility in 1961. Scatter plots and rank order correlation coefficients (not shown) show that the rank order of regional means is more stable for both illegitimacy and nuptiality than for marital fertility. The switching of regions, especially for marital fertility, suggests it is not so much that regions are distinguished by a stable preference for relatively high marital fertility or relatively low nuptiality, rather, they are characterized by a persistent demographic integrity; departments in the same region change in a similar fashion over time.

CONCLUSIONS

Demographic diversity declined in France between 1871 and 1961. This may have been the result of increased homogeneity in the circumstances in which departmental populations lived; alternatively, it is what would be expected if national-level influences increasingly drew the departments into the same na-

TABLE 7.7
Rank Order of Regional Means, Marital Fertility (I_g),
Illegitimacy (I_h), and Marriage (I_m) in 1871 and 1961

Region	Name	Marital Fertility (I_g)		Illegitimacy (I_h)		Marriage (I_m)	
		1871	1961	1871	1961	1871	1961
1	Picardy	12	6	1	1	1	1
2	Champagne	11	4	3	2	2	3
3	Berry	9	8	4	4	3	2
4	Burgundy	10	7	6	5	4	4
5	Guyenne	7	11	8	6	5	8
6	Loire	6	3	10	10	6	7
7	Languedoc	2	10	11	11	8	11
8	Auvergne	5	12	7	9	7	5
9	Normandy	8	5	2	3	9	6
10	Provence	3	9	9	8	10	9
11	Brittany	1	2	12	12	12	12
12	Franche-Comté	4	1	5	7	11	10

Note: 1 = highest I_g, I_h, and I_m; 12 = lowest.

tional community. The period between 1871 and 1961 was characterized by accelerated market integration, state formation, and nation building; these either would have evened out the economic and social landscapes in which departmental populations lived, or promoted the sense of belonging to a national community, or both.

The analysis in this chapter evaluated the relative importance of each of these three factors by examining their association with departmental variation in demographic behavior in 1871 and in 1961. Market integration was represented by disposable income, which would be expected to become more similar across departments, and by migration; state expansion was represented by an increase in the number of national bureaucrats in the department; nation building was represented by language—that is, by distinguishing between those departments whose populations in the nineteenth century were largely non-French-speaking and those whose inhabitants predominantly spoke French. None of the variables considered can be neatly packaged with one hypothesis or the other; the separation made here was purely analytic and exploratory. Perhaps the least untidy separation is between income and language. If the reduction in demographic diversity was largely due to the increased similarity in the circumstances in which departmental populations lived, we would expect income to be closely associated with demographic behavior both in 1871 and in 1961. If, however, the reduction in demographic diversity was largely due to the creation of a national community, we would expect those departments that were non-French-speaking in the nineteenth century to be unusual still in 1961, even though their populations by then spoke French. Those departments that had large proportions speaking languages such as Breton and Basque would have been somewhat isolated, I think, from the main currents of national life; in addition, language can be taken as a marker of other cultural differences that might continue to influence marriage and childbearing even if the populations of these departments were fully bilingual, or when there were few who spoke the local language.

In 1871 when the fertility transition was in full flood, there was considerable diversity in the measures of market integration and state formation. A multivariate analysis showed that disposable income, the proportion of the population born outside the department, the number of state bureaucrats, and whether or not the department was largely French speaking together "explained" a considerable degree of the variation in marital fertility, illegitimacy, and marriage. Moreover, each of these measures was important; that is, the coefficients were statistically significant (with the exception of the relation between state bureaucrats and illegitimacy).

In 1961 income, the number of state bureaucrats and the proportion of migrants varied less across departments, showing that in these respects circumstances had indeed become more similar since 1871. The association between these measures and demographic behavior, however, had changed in important ways. Taken together, the association between these variables and marital fertility had weakened (the amount of variation that they "explained" diminished), but the association with marriage remained about the same strength, while the association with illegitimacy increased. Although it is possible that a longer list of explanatory variables might have improved our understanding of modern variations in demographic behavior, that there is so little variation to account for suggests that more full-scale attacks on the sources of modern differences in fertility may not repay our attempts.

The most interesting results concerned the relative effects of income and language. Income, which had a statistically highly significant association with marital fertility, illegitimacy, and marriage in 1871, no longer mattered in 1961 (Model 1) for either marital fertility or for marriage (though it remained quite important for illegitimacy). In contrast, whether or not the population of a department was largely French speaking was associated with all three of these demographic behaviors in the nineteenth century; by 1961, when the populations of all departments were largely French speaking, linguistic history mattered. In chapter 6, the decline in linguistic diversity was interpreted as a sign of the growth of a sense of participation in a national community. The analyses in this chapter showed that their linguistic history—perhaps indicating the persistence of distinctive family values—continued to matter.

Although national-level influences on departmental demographic behavior could not be addressed directly in an analysis confined to one country, the effect of communities larger than the department was explored by "recreating" prerevolutionary regions (e.g., Burgundy, Brittany). These regions had a common political history and, often, a common language, but had been divided into departments at the time of the revolution. For each measure of demographic behavior, and at both dates (1871 and 1961) the differences between regions were greater than the differences within them. The persistent importance of regions was not simply a consequence of their relatively high or relatively low level in 1871; the order of the regions—which regions had high fertility, which had low—changed over the century. Rather, the regional groups seem to have had demographic integrity; the departments within them changed together.

France, wrote Le Bras and Todd, contains not one people but a hundred, who differ in their conceptions of life and death (Le Bras and Todd 1981, 76). This statement more aptly characterizes the demography of France in the nineteenth century than in 1961. Yet, although the demographic map of France was far more uniform in 1961 than it was a century earlier, the outlines of an earlier culture—seen in the influence of past language and of prerevolutionary regions on demographic behavior—remained evident.

Conclusions

FROM PROVINCES INTO NATIONS

ERNEST GELLNER has written that there are two ethnographic maps, one drawn up before the age of nationalism, and the other after.

> The first map resembles a painting by Kokoschka. The riot of diverse points of colour is such that no clear pattern can be discerned in any detail, though the picture as a whole does have one. A great diversity and plurality and complexity characterizes all distinct parts of the whole: the minute social groups, which are the atoms of which the picture is composed, have complex and ambiguous and multiple relations to many cultures; some through speech, others through their dominant faith, another still through a variant faith or set of practices, a fourth through administrative loyalty, and so forth. When it comes to painting the political system, the complexity is not less great than in the sphere of culture. . . .
>
> Look now instead at the ethnographic and political map of an area of the modern world. It resembles not Kokoschka, but, say, Modigliani. There is very little shading; neat flat surfaces are clearly separated from each other, it is generally plain where one begins and another ends, and there is little if any ambiguity or overlap. (Gellner 1983, 139–40)

The demographic measures used here for the approximately 500 provinces (cantons, counties, departments) in the fifteen countries of western Europe permit us to imagine two corresponding maps of western Europe, one before the major declines in marital fertility and illegitimacy and the increases in marriage, and one after. These maps would look much the same as the ethnographic maps. Around 1870 there was a great deal of diversity among the provinces within each country; by 1960 provincial demographic diversity had diminished. Even though countries had become more similar to one another, national demographic boundaries had hardened.

Placing the description of provincial diversity in the nineteenth century in the context of what is known about the determinants of pretransition demographic behavior suggests the importance of local communities. The most important source of local diversity in marital fertility in historical populations is the duration and intensity of breastfeeding. While we have little direct knowledge of breastfeeding practices in the past, studies in contemporary developing countries permit us to infer that in those provinces with high levels of marital fertility most women weaned their children earlier than in those provinces where marital fertility was low. And it seems likely that breastfeeding practices were not left entirely to the individual, but were shaped by the community—what kin and neighbors were doing and what they advised the new mother to do.

Differences in the proportion of women who were married are best interpreted in the context of a widespread consensus across western Europe that couples should not marry until they had enough resources to set up housekeeping apart from their parents. Diversity in marriage would be due to local variations in economic conditions, but also to local definitions of what constituted enough resources. Just as the poor married with less than the rich, it seems likely that some local communities considered a higher standard of living appropriate, while others were satisfied with less. Whether to have sex before marriage, and what to do if the woman became pregnant, were the areas of demographic behavior with the most local option. In some provinces, there were virtually no recorded births before marriage, while in others the distinction between legitimate and illegitimate births seems to have been slight.

Local demographic diversity was substantial, but not unconstrained. Demographic diversity was limited by the location of the province in western Europe; some patterns found elsewhere in the world were not found in western Europe. Marriage patterns were most distinctive, with considerably later female marriage and higher proportions of spinsters than most other parts of the world, but there is some evidence that both marital fertility and illegitimacy may have been higher than elsewhere as well. Even in the nineteenth century demographic diversity was also limited by location in a particular country; provinces were more similar to other provinces in the same country than to provinces across a national border. Were it possible to examine demographic diversity at a lower level of aggregation, villages within a province probably were more similar to one another than to villages in other provinces; there is some evidence from the few countries where data for smaller units than the province are available that this was the case.

Other limits to demographic diversity became evident by a comparison across countries. Around 1870 the most diverse countries were multilingual (Belgium, France, Germany, and Switzerland), which suggests that language boundaries were also demographic boundaries. A comparison of England and France pointed to other limits to demographic diversity. There was relatively little demographic diversity in England, where there was a more developed national market, long unification under the same crown, and more extensive circulation of newspapers and mail that brought news of *Pamela's* marriage to outlying areas. In contrast, demographically diverse France had a less-developed national market, was more recently unified, and had less circulation of newspapers and mail, as well as a variety of languages and dialects.

By 1960 the limits to provincial diversity in marital fertility, illegitimacy, and marriage were greater, not less, than they had been earlier. Demographic diversity diminished across all western European provinces; countries were more similar to each other; and provinces within a country were—with some exceptions—more similar to each other. That country boundaries increased in salience was evident in analyses that considered all countries, in analyses that focused on border provinces, and analyses that examined each country separately. In Northwestern Europe and in Scandinavia, variation in marital fertility and nuptiality decreased by 25 to 50 percent, with even greater declines in France. There were exceptions. In the countries of the Mediterranean, where the fertility decline had begun later than elsewhere and steep declines occurred after 1960, demographic diversity was, not surprisingly, often greater than it had been in 1870. The increases in demographic diversity in the Mediterranean countries simply may have been the result of their later decline; in Italy and Portugal, diversity diminished subsequently. The other exceptions were Belgium (where diversity in marriage increased), Ireland (where diversity in marital fertility increased), and Norway (where diversity on both measures increased).

Because the fertility decline among urban populations and the upper classes had already begun by the first date that it is possible to calculate the measures used here, an analysis of demographic diversity by socioeconomic group would show it to be great around 1870 and would thus inappropriately exaggerate the decline in diversity by 1960. But sketchy evidence suggests that the patterns for socioeconomic groups may be similar to the increasing national demographic integration shown for spatial groups. Class fertility differentials typically increased up to World War I and then typically converged. Fertility surveys in the mid-1970s show that the differences in fertility among groups categorized by religion, education, occupation, income, rural and urban residence, and wife's work status were large in percentage terms, but in absolute terms they were small.

The power of the forces that resulted in diminished demographic diversity within countries was also highlighted by comparing variation in mortality with variation in marriage. Although we can assume that people were more likely to share a concern about child survival, as well as a considerably enhanced ability to achieve lower mortality, than they were to share views about the proper age or circumstances for marriage, in most countries in 1960 there was little more diversity in marriage than in infant mortality rates.

The patterns described above are quite robust; a variety of approaches give similar results. It is important to stress, however, that interpreting the story told by the numbers requires inference, and the conclusions are necessarily more tentative. Neither the local communities nor the networks that connected them with each other are directly visible in the demographic data that describe provincial aggregates. But just as the aggregate demographic data are the precipitates of courtship and sex among ordinary people in the past, so also do these data trace the tracks between communities in the past. By examining these tracks, we can partially re-create the networks that connected them.

The local community comes closer if we visualize women gossiping as they washed their clothes or walking to the market together to sell their thread. From their stories of shotgun weddings unmarried women would have learned to be very careful before marriage, or, in other communities, that it was all right to take a risk. They would have chatted about a neighbor who nursed her child too long, or, in other communities, too little, and what happened as a result. In doing so, they created shared intepretations of marriage and childbearing.

It seems likely that in the past as well as in the present the "others" that had the most influence on demographic behavior were kin and friends. These are the people one observes most frequently, with whom one converses. They are also likely to be seen as "like us." Therefore, their examples are more likely to be followed than those who are distinctly different—their opinions taken most seriously, their praise or censure felt most comforting or painful. In the past, these kin and friends were likely to be neighbors, either living in the local community or nearby. It was with kin and neighbors that women gossiped, telling stories of a young couple who married too soon, or a spinster left on the shelf because she was too picky. Not only the storytellers but also the characters in the stories were likely to be members of the local community; it was those "like us" whose stories were relevant for one's own behavior, not stories about exotic people from faraway.

Although these conversations took place largely in the context of the local community and in the course of day-to-day interaction, local communities of the midnineteenth century were not isolated from communities elsewhere. Migration and marriage created paths for visits, letters, and, later, telephone calls. These connected villages in the same provinces; to a lesser extent they connected provinces in the same country; and to an even lesser extent they connected provinces in different countries.

At a less personal level, regional, national, and international institutions also connected villages, provinces, and nations. The Roman Catholic church provided all of western Europe with elements of a shared culture, the persistence of which after the Reformation can be seen in the high proportion of spinsters in Protestant as well as in Catholic countries. International trade also provided some links that stretched across western Europe. The influence of other institutions, such as states and the press, largely stopped at the territorial borders.

These connections among communities come into high relief during the fertility transition. The control of fertility within marriage by the cessation of childbearing after a desired (and ever smaller) number of children had been reached was an innovation, first evident on a national scale in France in the late eighteenth century, and then in the other countries of western Europe at the end of the nineteenth century. Typically this innovation was adopted first by the more educated, the wealthier, and those who lived in cities, and then later by the less educated, the poorer, the rural dwellers. Its spread was rapid compared to the previous centuries of stability in marital fertility. In 1870 few provinces showed signs of the onset of the fertility transition; by 1930 few did not.

The geographical spread of fertility control within marriage is consistent with the existence of networks that stretched across western Europe; the fertility transition was a pan-European phenomenon, affecting all countries. The patterns of fertility decline are also consistent with the assumption that these networks decayed with distance, that they were denser and stronger within countries than between them.

It seems likely that new information about fertility control and new images of ideal family size came into the local communities through personal networks as well as through national institutions such as the press and, eventually, state health and welfare bureaucracies. But the new information and the new images would have been discussed and interpreted by women gossiping with each other in the course of their daily routines, or by men at cafés or in workshops. These conversations would have provided opportunities to assess reactions to complaints about too many children, to hear about a friend of a friend who used birth control, to evaluate its pros and cons. Again, the more the stories were about kin, friends, and friends of friends, the more relevant they were as examples of permissible or desirable behavior.

How can we account for the decrease in demographic diversity between 1870 and 1960? I have argued that market integration, state expansion, and nation building were all important in diminishing the demographic differences between provinces in the same country. These processes went on at a level that seems quite distant from day-to-day conversations and even more distant from bedrooms and courting parlors. What they did that was relevant, I think, was to expand the density and range of personal networks and to make it more likely that at the other end of the network would be someone ''like us.''

The expansion of networks across provincial boundaries was in part due to improvements in transportation that made it easier to get around and improvements in methods of communication that made it easier to keep in touch. There is some evidence that over the century migrants went further and that the proportion of marriages with those outside the province increased. The expansion of higher education, the proliferation of national organizations such as labor unions, political parties, and soccer leagues, also would have broadened the geographical range of personal networks.

More important is that market integration, state expansion, and nation building would have made those that one encountered in the progress along these networks more similar to those in the local community. In part, these macrolevel processes made the circumstances—and thus, presumably, behavior—in one province more similar to those in another. Thus, for example, market integration evened wages and prices and made it likely that periods of prosperity or distress would be the same in all parts of the country. Similarly, state bureaucrats applied the same rules and regulations to those in Morbihan as they did to those in Allier, at least in principle.

In addition, market integration, state expansion, and nation building would have created a sense of membership in a national community. Department stores made the same fashions available in all parts of the country, thus making it more likely that those coming into the local community, or those met outside, would be dressed more similarly. The sense of membership in a national community would have been enhanced by the development of national welfare programs, a sort of "nationalization of compassion." These programs not only reduced incentives to have children for insurance in times of illness or old age, but also forged links between the citizen and the state. Although the provision of expanded welfare benefits was justified by rhetoric that emphasized the rights of individuals, and although welfare programs in different countries had much in common, entitlements depended on citizenship.

War would have further enhanced the sense that those living in the same country shared a common fate, one different from the fate of those across the border, who indeed may have been enemies. Probably the most important aspect of nation building was schooling, and particularly the insistence on schooling in the national language (or, languages, in the few countries where more than one language was politically protected).

The conclusion that there was a greater sense of participation in a national community in 1960 than in 1870 and that this was relevant for fertility and marriage is supported by consideration of Belgium and Ireland, where demographic diversity increased between 1870 and 1960 (in marriage in Belgium, in marital fertility in Ireland). In both of these countries the sense of membership in a national community appeared to be weaker than elsewhere. Partition divided Ireland into two political units, and in Belgium the political salience of linguistic differences increased over time.

The relevance of political integration for demographic behavior is suggested by the areas that have generated movements for separatism or greater regional political autonomy. These movements have used linguistic and ethnic differences symbolically in their political manuevering, but have not insisted that use of the movement's language be compulsory in everyday life. Whatever the bases of these movements, they indicate that the integration of these areas into the national community is relatively weak. It is noteworthy that they have often occurred in just those areas that were furthest from the national demographic pattern in 1960—North Wales, Corsica and Brittany in France, the Basque provinces and Catalonia in Spain—indicating that the political community and the demographic community can be seen as roughly congruent.

The story of demographic nationalism is also supported by a consideration of the parallel decline in linguistic diversity. Demographic diversity and linguistic diversity appear to go together. This statement needs to be qualified by calling attention to the imprecision of the measurements of language and to the level of aggregation. Both the demographic data and the linguistic data are highly aggregated, so that the correspondence could evaporate for smaller units or for individuals. Nevertheless, the association is impressive. In 1870 the most diverse countries demographically were those with more than one significant language. A common language facilitated the diffusion of new fertility practices and/or norms and values about appropriate family size, and linguistic boundaries acted as temporary brakes to fertility decline. But a common language is more than a vehicle for the diffusion of innovation. It is a necessity for intimate interaction: for courtship and for gossip. In contrast, a distinctive language or dialect—much like a distinctive dress—is an outward and visible sign of otherness, of unspecified, and often unspecifiable, differences. In Italy, deep dialectical differences at the time of unification do not show up in demographic diversity in 1870, but may be partly responsible for the huge increase in variation in marriage and fertility between 1870 and 1960.

A common language is both a cause and a consequence of the increased interaction across provinces that accompanied market integration, the expansion of state activities, and nation building, all processes that increased in intensity in the nineteenth century and that have been associated with the increasing dominance of a standard language over local dialects and patois. Pierre-Jakez Hélias wrote in his autobiography that his mother tongue was Breton, but he learned French because the French state insisted that education be in French and because elders told him that the world had changed; in the new world if he spoke only Breton he would be "like a cow on a short tether" (Hélias 1978). Once he could speak French, however, he could go further. Migration increased over this period; more significant is evidence that this was related to an expansion in the geographical scope of the marriage market.

An important tradition of sociologists from Marx to Parsons predicted that the "primordial" bases of community such as language and ethnicity would diminish in salience. This is only partly supported by the analyses presented here. The reduction in linguistic diversity does parallel the reduction in demographic diversity. On the other hand, the analysis of France showed that although both linguistic and demographic diversity diminished, cultural residues may be seen in demographic behavior. An analysis that took departmental differences in per capita income into account showed that whether or not the department had been largely non-French speaking in the nineteenth century was statistically important in understanding departmental variations both in marriage and in marital fertility in 1960. Although local languages were replaced by national ones, the demographic differences with which they were associated persisted in the new context of reduced demographic diversity. When artists paint a new work over an earlier work, it is sometimes possible to see the old outlines under the new paint; so also the old demographic patterns associated with language remained to form a pentimento visible under the surface.

The idea of national communities can be made more concrete by considering the empirical work of geographers on "mental maps" (Gould and White 1986). One test of knowledge of geography is to ask people to write in a limited time all the place names they can think of. Young children typically know nearby places, the capital, and perhaps a favorite resort area or a place recently in the headlines. Older children are able to add more places, until as school graduates they are able to fill in the map fairly completely. Language and religious boundaries often appear on these maps as "fault" lines—test takers are less likely to know about a place across a linguistic or religious border.

Such an experiment was conducted around 1970 in two villages on each side of the Norway-Sweden border. The villages were separated by no more than a few miles, and the dialects spoken in each were similar. As expected, the older children knew more places than the younger, but interestingly, the Norwegian children's maps showed a marked preferential bias toward places in Norway, whereas the Swedish children's maps showed a bias toward locations in Sweden. The territorial boundary acted much like religious and linguistic boundaries. Gould and White write that "the border with Norway is analagous to a geological fault line, for on the Norwegian side the surface has slipped down to much lower levels" (Gould and White 1986, 143).

Roger Thabault's account of the commune of Mazières from the midnineteenth to the early twentieth century provides a historical analogy to the filling out of mental maps (Thabault 1971). In 1872 few inhabitants of the commune had been born outside the commune or neighboring communes (Thabault 1971, 47). Most showed little interest in events beyond the local—even the wars of the Second Empire and the revolution of 1848 seem hardly to have penetrated (Thabault 1971, 48, 106). In subsequent decades horizons widened.

Part of the explanation lies in migration. Places became known not because people found them on maps, but because they had been there, or knew someone who had. The villagers of Mazières knew Rivarenne not because it was near Tours, but because "Rivarenne is where M's son went to work" (Thabault, 1971, 165). Letter writing became more general, as did visiting.

Nearly everyone who had relatives living at a distance (and they were many) allowed themselves to be tempted by the demon of adventure and would arrange to go and visit them—*en famille*—at least once in their life if they were old, more often if they were young. . . . Neighbours, too, became interested in these distant places where, after all, people lived just as they did at Mazières. . . . One knew—dimly as yet—

that wherever French was spoken, a peasant born and bred in Mazières-en-Gâtine could fit in and live his life. (Thabault 1971, 164–65)

We might expect that as more of the commune's inhabitants traveled, had friends or relatives who traveled, and read about distant places in the newspapers, their mental maps would have filled in. But as in the villages in Norway and Sweden, it is likely that the maps were filled in largely with places in France.

The filling in of mental maps, as a historical process, nicely parallels Benedict Anderson's concept of "imagined communities" (Anderson 1983). Anderson's central image is of a newspaper; it is read in privacy, but on the same day by people all over the country who are presumed to be interested in some of the same events. Readers

gradually became aware of the hundreds of thousands, even millions, of people in their particular language-field, and at the same time that *only those* hundreds of thousands, or millions, so belonged. These fellow-readers, to whom they were connected through print, formed, in their secular, particular, visible invisibility, the embryo of the nationally-imagined community. (Anderson 1983, 47)

SIGNIFICANCE

The description and interpretation presented is by no means complete. Many questions remain. Closer examination of pretransition demographic regimes using smaller populations and finer measures might show either more demographic diversity or more demographic homogeneity. The former would probably be the case in Italy, which was quite demographically homogeneous in 1861, when dialect differences divided the small populations only recently unified. Both in 1870 and 1960 some countries were diverse in marital fertility but not in marriage, or vice versa. It is not surprising that demographic diversity would have increased in Belgium by 1960, but why is this evident only in nuptiality and not in marital fertility? Are the debates about language in Norway—debates about orthography, though linked to other political issues—really enough to account for its increased demographic diversity in both marriage and marital fertility?

Nonetheless, the description of greater national demographic homogeneity in 1960 than in 1870 and the interpretation of the sources of demographic diversity as well as the account of its decrease suggest further lines of speculation.

First, these findings raise questions about the dominant paradigm within which we have tried to account for demographic behavior, a paradigm that stresses individual calculations according to a sort of cost-benefit calculus in which economic costs and benefits are usually given most weight. The demographic data used here do not permit distinguishing the behavior of individuals.

It may be that data on individuals would, in fact, support a model that abstracts individuals from their communities. But the local diversity in demographic behavior in the nineteenth century and the increased importance of national boundaries in the twentieth suggest the importance of membership in communities and by implication the importance of the networks that link individuals with each other.

Differences in income or occupation do help account for the leaders of the fertility decline and thus for the substantial differentials among groups during the fertility transition. But income differentials are less important in accounting for demographic diversity either before or after the fertility transition. In France, the one country examined here in detail, differences in per capita income among departments were not statistically significant in accounting either for variations in marital fertility or in the proportions married in 1960. It may be that income will turn out to be more important in other countries than in France, or that other measures of economic circumstances are more sensitive predictors of fertility and marriage. Given the findings summarized above, it would seem to be more fruitful to proceed in the future by giving more attention to communities, to cultural characteristics, particularly language, and to the effect of political institutions on demographic behavior.

Second, the correspondence of language and demographic behavior provides the strongest support for paying more attention to cultural influences on marriage and fertility. Language plays a direct role in the diffusion of innovations. Once new information or new attitudes about fertility control within marriage entered the community, its adoption was likely to proceed from the innovators to those closest to them in geographical and social space, and these were likely to be those who spoke the same language. In addition, language is often a marker of more diffuse cultural differences, a boundary between those who share the same view of the world and those who do not. It is likely that these shared views would also extend to matters of birth and marriage. The greater demographic diversity of certain multilingual countries suggests that this is the case.

Third, there is an association between the political community and the demographic community. The links between the state and demographic change have not been well specified; my speculations have been based more on logical extrapolations from consistent findings than on the direct analysis of links between state activities and demographic change. The role of the state seems to be of two major sorts. One, it evens out local circumstances so that the economic and social environments in which citizens live become more similar within the nation's territory. Two, the state influences the creation of a community. Important in this was the elaboration of the concepts of citizenship; by the 1960s it included a vastly more extended set of rights than in the nineteenth century.

The findings here that support an emphasis on language are consistent with some previous findings of others, particularly in the examination of the fertility transition in western Europe and in the Third World. The focus on political boundaries and political processes, including both the expansion of state activities and nationalist movements, for demographic behavior is less common (in this respect Geoffrey McNicoll is an exception [McNicoll 1980, 1983]). It is significant that national political processes are evident not only in public behavior but in behavior that we normally think of as quintissentially private. We can speculate that other sorts of private preferences would show the same influence of the expansion of a sense of community from local to national.

Lastly, it is not difficult to accept a considerable role for communities in regulating demographic behavior in the past. It is harder to see how the larger "imagined" communities of the present could influence demographic behavior. Yet the evidence suggests that they do.

The evidence of increased demographic homogeneity within countries is best seen from the perspective of what might have happened, the expansion of the "horizons of the possible," in Braudel's phrase. We would expect to find more, not less, diversity in 1960 than in 1870. Some constraints on demographic behavior were much less in 1960 than they were in 1870. In 1960 the contraceptive pill was not yet in widespread use, but substantial proportions of married couples used other, obviously effective, forms of contraception. In addition to the relaxation of these technological and economic constraints, the advance and elaboration of individualistic and secular philosophies would lead us to expect more diversity in demographic behavior. There is no reason to doubt an increasing rhetorical stress on the primacy of individual choice in marriage and childbearing over the last century. On modern surveys that interrogate individuals about their demographic behavior, they are usually likely to answer as if the decision were up to them, made for their own reasons.

It is necessary to repeat that individuals are not well described by the data used in this analysis and that the measures of demographic behavior are limited. The connection between these large-scale social processes and demographic patterns is largely based on parallel changes. The patterns and the exceptions to the patterns are consistent with links between these processes and the private behavior of provincial populations. Only rarely are there glimpses of individuals: Hélias learning French so that he will not be a cow on a short tether in the world that has changed; the village women of France traveling further than their mothers did in search of spouses; the woman in Lancashire who says, "My own opinion is that people wish to have a small family on account of public opinion which has now hardened into custom."

But the increasing homogeneity of national communities with respect to demographic behavior ought to make us question descriptions of fertility or marriage as moving from social control to individual control. Despite better contraception and more individualistic rhetoric, we see less, not more, demographic diversity within nations. It may be that circumstances are so similar for everyone that each individual's cost-benefit calculations reach the same sum. This is a more intuitively appealing account for the homogeneity in marital fertility than it is for marriage, however, and it remains troubling why the wealthier and better educated are so similar to other parts of the population in terms of their demographic behavior. The results presented here are more consistent with a shift from social control by a smaller group to social control by a larger group than they are with a shift from social control to individual control. We cannot visualize the process of social control as well for national communities as we can for small face-to-face communities. In the nineteenth century, it is likely that social control was exercised at the level of the local community, not only by example and precept of others in the village but also by punishing deviance and rewarding conformity. In the modern world such direct sanctions for improper demographic behavior are rare; nonetheless, the community—now national—would still seem to provide potent models for behavior.

The search for the bonds that hold modern society together has been a feature of sociological analysis since its early days. Durkheim's distinction between mechanical and organic society, Toennie's shift from Gemeinschaft to Gesellschaft are in this tradition. Most analysts who focus on demographic behavior are searching for its determinants. For example, Why is fertility higher in some groups or lower in others? But how populations give birth and marry are signs of social integration, or of its absence. Demographic boundaries may help us define communities and subcommunities.

After 1960

Will national boundaries be less significant for demographic behavior in the future? There are two reasons to expect that this might be the case. The first derives its implications from the ethnic resurgence movements of the 1970s and 1980s, which usually focus on communities smaller than the nation, and the second from economic and political integration over a larger area than the nation, specifically the European Economic Community, as well as from the crossing of national boundaries by the media.

William McNeill has argued that the century between the French Revolution and World War I was unusual in the degree of national ethnic homogeneity that it aimed for and achieved (McNeill 1986). Earlier empires were likely to be multiethnic, and modern societies, he says, may be multiethnic as well. The prosperity of the 1950s and 1960s drew migrants to western Europe from further and further away, and the idea that they can be assimilated has faded. Others have proposed that ethnic identification becomes increasingly attractive in a sterile modern world (Bell 1975), or that ethnic identification becomes important because it is a basis of claims on the resources of the state (e.g., Hannan 1979; Nagel and Olzak 1982; Beer 1980).

It seems highly unlikely, however, that vigorous movements of ethnic re-surgence would attempt a pronatalist policy, which would appear to be even more difficult than a language policy (which most of them have eschewed), or that such movements would have the unintended consequences of raising fer-tility levels. Since the late nineteenth century the trends in fertility have been almost without exception to lower fertility; even deliberate and expensive pro-natalist policies have not had an unambiguous effect. Low fertility appears to be irresistible in modern societies, and I see little reason to expect that the Basques or Bretons or Scots would attempt to reverse this, or that they would be successful.

What about convergence within western Europe, which would also reduce the salience of national boundaries? Marx and Engels predicted that some na-tional differences would diminish with the advance of capitalism. "National differences and antagonisms between people are daily more and more vanish-ing, owing to the development of the bourgeoise, to freedom of commerce, to the world market, to uniformity in the mode of production and in condition of life corresponding thereto" (Marx and Engels [1848] 1967, 102). Differences between countries were smaller in 1960 than they had been in 1870, but only slightly.

In the future, economic boundaries are less likely to coincide with national boundaries. Levels of economic integration are higher now than they were when the European Coal and Steel Community was formed in 1950 and will be higher after 1992. While political integration has lagged behind, an analysis of a series of surveys in the EEC countries has found increasing support for supranational organizations over national ones (Inglehart 1977). And, signifi-cantly, Ron Lesthaeghe and Dominique Meekers have found some evidence for a connection between support for internationalization and demographic behavior (Lesthaeghe and Meekers 1986). Using the limited demographic in-formation available in these surveys, they show that those who are more likely to support supranational organizations and who are less committed to their own nation are also more likely to cohabit.

International organizations now penetrate even the most geographically iso-lated areas of western Europe. An article by Jane Kramer on a French peasant family illustrates this nicely (Kramer 1985). The family lives in a village in the Périgord, a region in France that corresponds approximately to the depart-ment of Dordogne in southwest France. The farm has been in the family for centuries. The current owners, the Pelletiers, went away for a holiday only once (their honeymoon). In 1964 they went to Paris to take their son to a doctor. They left in the morning, saw the doctor, and headed home without another stop.

It was not that Paris intimidated the Pelletiers, or put them off. The Pelletiers had a book of photographs of Paris. They knew Paris from their book and from the evening news and from the pictures in *Le Pèlerin*, the Catholic weekly that Fernande's mother gets in the mail on Friday. (Kramer 1985, 74)

Although the Pelletiers think of themselves as traditional *paysans*, their farming is highly influenced by the Common Market. Fernande Pelletier's lamb chops sell for less than lamb chops from England (or Australia, or New Zealand); the local representative of the Crédit Agricole tells her to concentrate on crops that have not yet made the EEC agenda, and to "spread her risk." One year an agricultural advisor from the city told them to raise beef, on his next visit to forget beef and grow tobacco, and on yet another visit to grow walnuts.

What about linguistic differences among European countries in the future? Will national languages be abandoned, much as local languages were replaced by national languages between 1870 and 1960? It is hard to imagine a monolingual western Europe: it seems likely that Frenchwomen will continue to speak French. It is easier to imagine, however, that national languages may matter somewhat less in the future. One of the European languages may come to be a de facto lingua franca; more Europeans may become fluent in other national languages; at the least, we can expect more neologisms such as "Euro-dollar," "Euro-TV," and "Euro-babble."

Based on the analyses in this book, I predict that in the future national boundaries will become less deeply etched on the demographic map of western Europe. Further economic and political integration are likely; some increase in identification with the western European community and some decline in the salience of national languages are possible. But just as those French departments in which many spoke languages other than French were demographically distinct in 1960, I expect that national differences will persist as shadings of tone if not of color on the demographic map of western Europe.

Appendix

APPENDIX TABLE A3.1
Midspread and Median of Provincial Marital Fertility (I_g), Illegitimacy (I_h),
and Marriage (I_m), Each Country, First Date

	Marital Fertility (I_g)		Illegitimacy (I_h)		Marriage (I_m)	
	Midspread	Median	Midspread	Median	Midspread	Median
Northwestern Europe						
Belgium	.233	.846	.027	.032	.054	.420
England and Wales	.031	.679	.014	.050	.045	.482
France	.161	.556	.021	.032	.104	.521
Germany	.141	.759	.042	.066	.070	.466
Ireland	.031	.718	.007	.011	.069	.386
Netherlands	.125	.822	.013	.024	.049	.419
Scotland	.035	.755	.032	.056	.063	.393
Switzerland	.141	.729	.016	.023	.073	.412
Scandinavia						
Denmark	.073	.669	.036	.059	.063	.443
Finland	.153	.692	.013	.057	.063	.504
Norway	.047	.767	.040	.052	.024	.409
Sweden	.107	.706	.025	.050	.086	.419
Mediterranean						
Italy	.059	.690	.021	.043	.037	.547
Portugal	.081	.711	.040	.059	.089	.471
Spain	.073	.666	.029	.036	.099	.622
All provinces	.113	.698	.033	.042	.105	.462

APPENDIX TABLE A3.2
Rank Order of the Midspread of Marital Fertility (I_g), Illegitimacy (I_h), and Marriage (I_m), Each Country, First Date

	Marital Fertility (I_g)	Illegitimacy (I_h)	Marriage (I_m)
Northwestern Europe			
Belgium	15	9	5
England and Wales	1.5	4	3
France	14	6.5	15
Germany	12.5	15	10
Ireland	1.5	1	9
Netherlands	10	2.5	4
Scotland	3	11	7
Switzerland	12.5	5	11
Scandinavia			
Denmark	6.5	12	7
Finland	11	2.5	7
Norway	4	13.5	1
Sweden	9	8	12
Mediterranean			
Italy	5	6.5	2
Portugal	8	13.5	13
Spain	6.5	10	14

Note: 1 = smallest midspread, 15 = largest midspread. If two countries have the same midspread, both are given the average of the two positions they would occupy (e.g., 2.5). If three countries have the same midspread, they are given the same ranking.

APPENDIX TABLE A3.3
Variation in Marital Fertility (I_g) and Marriage (I_m) for Selected Countries,
According to Number of Sub-units into Which Country Is Divided

Country	Number of Units	Range	Midspread
Marital fertility (I_g)			
Denmark	07	.130	.065[a]
Denmark	19	.175	.056
Italy	14	.116	.058[a]
Italy	75	.211	.053
Spain	14	.365[a]	.073[a]
Spain	48	.316	.071
Marriage (I_m)			
Denmark	07	.120	.060[a]
Denmark	19	.122	.051
Italy	14	.075	.035
Italy	75	.199	.057
Spain	14	.250	.097
Spain	48	.281	.098

[a] The grouping with the *smaller* number of provinces in each pair has the greater variation. See text.

APPENDIX TABLE A3.4

Number of Provinces within Each Country with a 10-percent Decline in Marital Fertility (I_g) or I_g below .600 at First Date

	Number of Provinces with 10% Decline in I_g by First Date	Number of Provinces with I_g below .600 at First Date
Northwestern Europe		
Belgium	5	5
England and Wales	0	0
France	52	28
Germany	1	1
Ireland	0	1
Netherlands	0	0
Scotland	0	0
Switzerland	0	1
Scandinavia		
Denmark	0	1
Finland	0	1
Norway	1	0
Sweden	0	1
Mediterranean		
Italy	0	0
Portugal	1	1
Spain	6	6
Total	66	46

Note: By convention, a 10-percent decline in I_g from a previous plateau indicates the onset of an irreversible decline in marital fertility; an I_g level of .600 or less usually indicates deliberate fertility control (Coale and Treadway 1986). A province can be in both columns. The methods used to estimate the date of the 10-percent decline in I_g are described in Coale and Treadway (1986).

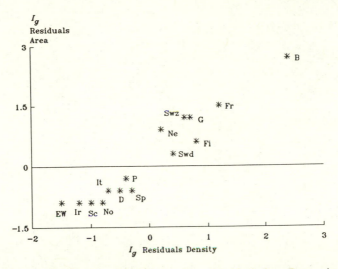

Figure A3.1a. Marital Fertility (I_g), Relationship of Residuals from Regression Analyses

Residuals area = residual from model: Midspread of $I_g = \alpha + \beta$ (area)

Residuals density = residual from model: Midspread of $I_g = \alpha + \beta$ (population density)

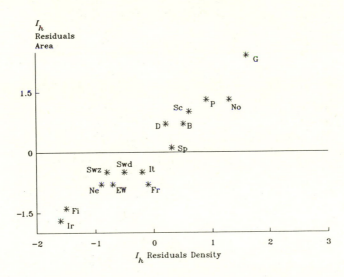

Figure A3.1b. Illegitimacy (I_h), Relationship of Residuals from Regression Analyses

Residuals area = residual from model: Midspread of $I_h = \alpha + \beta$ (area)

Residuals density = residual from model: Midspread of $I_h = \alpha + \beta$ (population density)

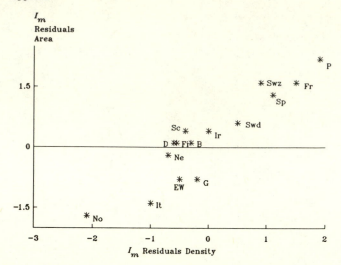

Figure A3.1c. Marriage (I_m), Relationship of Residuals from Regression Analyses

Residuals area = residual from model: Midspread of $I_m = \alpha + \beta$ (area)

Residuals density = residual from model: Midspread of $I_m = \alpha + \beta$ (population density)

APPENDIX TABLE A4.1
Countries, Dates, and Number of Provinces Used
in the Analyses in Chapter 4 and Chapter 5

	1870[a]	1900	1930	1960	Provinces Omitted	Provinces Used[b]
Northwestern Europe						
Belgium	1880	1900	1930	1961	0	41
England and Wales	1871	1901	1931	1961	0	45
France	1871	1901	1931	1961	3	87
Germany	1871	1900	1933	—	5	66
Ireland	1871	1901	1936	1961	0	31
Netherlands	1869	1899	1930	1960	0	11
Scotland	1871	1901	1931	1961	0	33
Switzerland	1870	1900	1930	1960	0	25
Scandinavia						
Denmark	1870	1901	1930	1960	3	19
Finland	1880	1900	1930	1960	1	8
Norway	1875	1900	1930	1960	0	20
Sweden	1880	1900	1930	1960	0	25
Mediterranean						
Italy	1871	1901	1931	1961	2	16
Portugal	1890	1900	1930	1960	1	21
Spain	1887	1900	1930	1960	2	48

[a] Dates: In some countries, the first date at which data are available is after 1871. Generally, this first date is used to represent 1870. If, however, it is important that roughly equal periods of time be compared (e.g., 1870–1900, 1900–1930, etc.) then if the first date is after 1880, the analysis for 1870–1900 is omitted. Because of boundary changes, Germany is omitted from most analyses of 1960.

[b] Provinces: The number of provinces used in the analyses in chapters 4 and 5 differs slightly from the number or provinces used in the first-date analyses in chapters 2 and 3 (see text).

APPENDIX TABLE A5.1

Number of Provinces in Which Marital Fertility (I_g), Illegitimacy (I_h), and Marriage (I_m) Fell or Rose between 1870 and 1960, by Country and by Period

	1870–1960		1870–1900		1900–1930		1930–1960	
	Fell	Rose	Fell	Rose	Fell	Rose	Fell	Rose
Northwestern Europe								
Belgium								
I_g	41	0	39	2	41	0	26	15
I_h	41	0	26	14	40	1	28	12
I_m	0	41	4	37	0	41	0	41
England and Wales								
I_g	45	0	45	0	45	0	23	22
I_h	32	13	45	0	45	0	0	45
I_m	0	45	43	2	2	43	0	45
France								
I_g	78	7	82	3	83	2	13	72
I_h	44	36	41	38	46	37	43	36
I_m	0	85	18	65	1	84	13	71
Germany								
I_g	66	0	60	6	66	0	—	—
I_h	64	2	34	28	66	0	—	—
I_m	6	59	2	63	18	48	—	—
Ireland								
I_g	31	0	17	14	31	0	17	14
I_h	14	17	30	1	3	27	25	6
I_m	4	27	31	0	29	2	2	29
Netherlands								
I_g	11	0	8	3	11	0	10	1
I_h	11	0	11	0	11	0	4	6
I_m	1	10	1	10	0	11	0	11
Scotland								
I_g	33	0	33	0	33	0	30	3
I_h	28	5	32	1	24	7	11	20
I_m	0	33	23	10	6	27	0	33
Switzerland								
I_g	25	0	22	3	25	0	15	10
I_h	19	5	21	3	22	1	0	24
I_m	1	24	19	6	18	7	0	25

APPENDIX TABLE A5.1 (*cont.*)

	1870–1960		1870–1900		1900–1930		1930–1960	
	Fell	Rose	Fell	Rose	Fell	Rose	Fell	Rose
Scandinavia								
Denmark								
I_g	19	0	12	7	19	0	17	2
I_h	15	4	17	2	18	1	2	17
I_m	0	19	2	17	1	18	0	19
Finland								
I_g	8	0	5	3	8	0	7	1
I_h	8	0	7	1	8	0	7	1
I_m	0	8	2	6	8	0	0	8
Norway								
I_g	20	0	18	2	20	0	19	1
I_h	18	2	20	0	20	0	3	17
I_m	0	20	13	6	4	16	0	20
Sweden								
I_g	25	0	23	2	25	0	23	2
I_h	18	7	9	13	23	2	20	4
I_m	0	25	10	14	10	15	0	25
Mediterranean								
Italy								
I_g	16	0	8	8	2	14	16	0
I_h	16	0	9	6	16	0	16	0
I_m	7	9	13	3	12	4	2	13
Portugal								
I_g	20	1	—	—	4	17	20	1
I_h	17	4	—	—	9	12	17	3
I_m	1	20	4	17	6	15	2	19
Spain								
I_g	48	0	—	—	48	0	48	0
I_h	48	0	—	—	36	12	45	3
I_m	32	16	—	—	45	3	10	38
Totals								
Northwestern Europe								
I_g	264	7[a]	306	31	335	2	134	137[a]
I_h	189	76[a]	240	85	257	73	111	149[a]
I_m	6	265[a]	141	193	74	263	15	255[a]

APPENDIX TABLE A5.1 (*cont.*)

	1870–1960		1870–1900		1900–1930		1930–1960	
	Fell	Rose	Fell	Rose	Fell	Rose	Fell	Rose
Scandinavia								
I_g	72	0	58	14	72	0	66	6
I_h	59	13	52	16	69	3	32	39
I_m	0	72	27	43	23	49	0	72
Mediterranean								
I_g	84	1	(8)	(8)	54	31	84	1
I_h	81	4	(9)	(6)	61	24	78	6
I_m	40	45	(17)	(20)	63	22	14	70
Grand Total								
I_g	420	8[a]	372	53	461	33	284	144[a]
I_h	329	95[a]	302	107	387	100	221	194[a]
I_m	46	441[a]	185	254	160	334	29	397[a]

Note: Parentheses around figures for Mediterranean countries in 1870–1900 indicate that only Italy is included for I_g and I_h, and only Portugal and Italy for I_m. Occasionally there was no change in an index over a period, so the country total may be less than the number of provinces.

[a] Since Germany is omitted in 1960, the maximum in these columns is 271 provinces for Northwestern Europe and 428 for the Grand Total.

APPENDIX TABLE A5.2a
Midspread of Marital Fertility (I_g), All Dates, by Country

Country	1870	1880	1890	1900	1910	1920	1930	1940	1950	1960
Northwestern Europe										
Belgium	—	.233	.301	.356	.314	.210	.148	—	.115	.060
England and Wales	.036	.043	.039	.048	.062	.041	.041	—	—	.024
France	.185	.184	.139	.139	.102	.088	.072	—	—	.061
Germany	.158	.133	.144	.165	.179	.137	.122	—	—	—
Ireland	.031	.049	.040	.072	.094	—	.054	.038	—	.038
Netherlands	.111	.139	.122	.105	.101	.141	.132	—	—	.072
Scotland	.047	.075	.100	.079	.077	.064	.067	—	—	.035
Switzerland	.143	.099	.150	.200	.264	.285	.301	.204	.160	.148
Scandinavia										
Denmark	.064	.082	.095	.093	.101	.114	.089	—	—	.045
Finland	—	.153	.096	.080	.082	.121	.131	.130	.141	.094
Norway	—	.047	.050	.064	—	.099	.117	—	—	.079
Sweden	—	.107	—	.134	—	—	.090	—	.037	.023
Mediterranean										
Italy	.049	.043	.046	.075	.142	.223	.255	—	.250	.243
Portugal	—	—	.065	.071	.067	.118	.143	.169	.217	.223
Spain	—	—	.076	.084	.101	.094	.135	.159	—	.105

APPENDIX TABLE A5.2b
Midspread of Illegitimacy (I_h), All Dates, by Country

Country	1870	1880	1890	1900	1910	1920	1930	1940	1950	1960
Northwestern Europe										
Belgium	—	.027	.027	.021	.017	.014	.011	—	.010	.011
England and Wales	.016	.014	.011	.008	.010	.009	.006	—	—	.011
France	.022	.022	.022	.022	.021	.017	.021	—	—	.016
Germany	.045	.043	.042	.040	.035	.025	.022	—	—	—
Ireland	.007	.006	.005	.006	.006	—	.008	.009	—	.006
Netherlands	.014	.014	.015	.009	.005	.002	.003	—	—	.005
Scotland	.032	.030	.027	.022	.018	.015	.018	—	—	.013
Switzerland	.016	.014	.012	.015	.009	.005	.004	.003	.004	.005
Scandinavia										
Denmark	.031	.023	.018	.020	.026	.021	.021	—	—	.013
Finland	—	.013	.020	.024	.022	.015	.012	.008	.006	.005
Norway	—	.040	.039	.034	—	.022	.019	—	—	.015
Sweden	—	.025	—	.026	—	—	.019	—	.021	.022
Mediterranean										
Italy	.032	.033	.027	.023	.023	.019	.015	.009	.008	.004
Portugal	—	—	.040	.045	.057	.059	.065	.067	.043	.049
Spain	—	—	.030	.027	.032	.032	.030	.015	—	.006

APPENDIX TABLE A5.2c
Midspread of Marriage (I_m), All Dates, by Country

Country	1870	1880	1890	1900	1910	1920	1930	1940	1950	1960
Northwestern Europe										
Belgium	—	.054	.063	.067	.061	.083	.088	—	.063	.071
England and Wales	.052	.057	.056	.055	.056	.043	.038	—	—	.038
France	.110	.122	.114	.105	.099	.076	.077	—	—	.049
Germany	.070	.051	.072	.064	.054	.060	.085	—	—	—
Ireland	.069	.046	.026	.027	.010	—	.030	.030	—	.033
Netherlands	.051	.046	.043	.049	.059	.051	.049	—	—	.034
Scotland	.063	.065	.063	.090	.097	.071	.059	—	—	.033
Switzerland	.075	.049	.055	.038	.032	.042	.051	.066	.043	.053
Scandinavia										
Denmark	.043	.025	.030	.029	.032	.033	.027	—	—	.022
Finland	—	.063	.053	.073	.078	.069	.042	.027	.020	.014
Norway	—	.024	.031	.047	—	.047	.053	—	—	.043
Sweden	—	.086	—	.070	—	—	.041	—	.027	.020
Mediterranean										
Italy	.029	.055	.035	.030	.046	.059	.046	.053	.072	.091
Portugal	—	—	.089	.093	.085	.084	.066	.063	.085	.060
Spain	—	—	.100	.096	.097	.091	.077	.048	—	.060

APPENDIX TABLE A5.3

One-way Analysis of Variance between Countries in Marital Fertility (I_g), Illegitimacy (I_h), and Marriage (I_m) for Countries of Northwestern Europe and Scandinavia in 1870, 1900, 1930, and 1960

	1870	1900	1930	1960
Marital Fertility (I_g)				
R^2	.59	.58	.59	.81
F-value[a]	47.12	45.70	47.56	143.14
Sum of squares				
Between country	4.23	4.91	3.02	2.81
Within country	2.99	3.59	2.12	.66
Total	7.22	8.51	5.14	3.47
Illegitimacy (I_h)				
R^2	.41	.46	.51	.57
F-value	22.75	27.06	34.55	44.95
Sum of squares				
Within country	.07	.06	.04	.05
Between country	.10	.07	.04	.04
Total	.17	.13	.08	.09
Marriage (I_m)				
R^2	.54	.68	.81	.75
F-value	38.53	70.98	139.53	101.15
Sum of squares				
Between country	1.14	1.80	2.75	1.21
Within country	.99	.85	.66	.40
Total	2.13	2.65	3.40	1.61
Degrees of freedom				
Between country	10	10	10	10
Within country	334	334	334	334
Total	344	344	344	344

Note: Germany, Italy, Portugal, and Spain are omitted.

[a]All F-values are significant at the .0001 level.

APPENDIX TABLE A5.4a
Descriptive Statistics for Marital Fertility (I_g), by Country
in 1870, 1900, 1930, and 1960

Country	1870	1900	1930	1960
Northwestern Europe				
Belgium				
Median	.846	.651	.351	.306
Mean	.791	.666	.355	.310
Range	.564	.603	.608	.257
Standard				
deviation	.149	.193	.124	.053
Midspread	.233	.356	.148	.060
Midspread				
of logit	1.509	1.727	.675	.283
England and Wales				
Median	.693	.555	.288	.290
Mean	.695	.562	.285	.290
Range	.142	.166	.217	.056
Standard				
deviation	.032	.039	.044	.014
Midspread	.036	.048	.041	.024
Midspread				
of logit	.173	.195	.202	.117
France				
Median	.463	.358	.282	.334
Mean	.491	.399	.294	.331
Range	.531	.488	.268	.273
Standard				
deviation	.125	.108	.055	.042
Midspread	.185	.139	.072	.061
Midspread				
of logit	.752	.584	.346	.274
Germany				
Median	.748	.662	.276	—
Mean	.757	.671	.294	—
Range	.369	.518	.321	—
Standard				
deviation	.090	.115	.079	—
Midspread	.158	.165	.122	—
Midspread				
of logit	.891	.752	.593	—

APPENDIX TABLE A5.4a (*cont.*)

Country	1870	1900	1930	1960
Ireland				
Median	.718	.702	.615	.617
Mean	.714	.710	.614	.612
Range	.185	.156	.314	.293
Standard				
deviation	.032	.041	.052	.052
Midspread	.031	.072	.054	.038
Midspread				
of logit	.153	.352	.161	.162
Netherlands				
Median	.830	.755	.449	.408
Mean	.841	.773	.471	.401
Range	.181	.335	.316	.112
Standard				
deviation	.066	.108	.094	.040
Midspread	.111	.105	.132	.072
Midspread				
of logit	.863	.569	.536	.303
Scotland				
Median	.754	.634	.395	.325
Mean	.755	.631	.396	.328
Range	.189	.199	.219	.114
Standard				
deviation	.043	.054	.050	.024
Midspread	.047	.079	.067	.035
Midspread				
of logit	.253	.341	.282	.158
Switzerland				
Median	.747	.680	.386	.394
Mean	.729	.651	.417	.394
Range	.570	.555	.474	.288
Standard				
deviation	.119	.133	.150	.090
Midspread	.143	.200	.301	.148
Midspread				
of logit	.753	.913	1.254	.622
Scandinavia				
Denmark				
Median	.653	.617	.346	.283
Mean	.663	.640	.357	.289
Range	.183	.357	.265	.112

APPENDIX TABLE A5.4a (*cont.*)

Country	1870	1900	1930	1960
Denmark				
Standard deviation	.051	.078	.064	.029
Midspread	.064	.093	.089	.045
Midspread of logit	.288	.411	.383	.219
Finland				
Median	.692	.699	.468	.328
Mean	.694	.687	.468	.350
Range	.193	.156	.339	.167
Standard deviation	.073	.051	.103	.059
Midspread	.153	.080	.131	.094
Midspread of logit	.734	.366	.530	.417
Norway				
Median	.767	.720	.425	.332
Mean	.756	.707	.402	.332
Range	.220	.190	.341	.155
Standard deviation	.052	.046	.082	.044
Midspread	.047	.064	.117	.079
Midspread of logit	.258	.308	.491	.360
Sweden				
Median	.706	.667	.325	.244
Mean	.691	.657	.321	.247
Range	.330	.388	.361	.068
Standard deviation	.073	.096	.075	.017
Midspread	.107	.134	.090	.023
Midspread of logit	.502	.596	.417	.127
Mediterranean				
Italy				
Median	.661	.670	.516	.347
Mean	.662	.650	.512	.358
Range	.115	.220	.377	.329
Standard deviation	.031	.055	.135	.118

APPENDIX TABLE A5.4a (*cont.*)

Country	1870	1900	1930	1960
Italy				
Midspread	.049	.075	.255	.243
Midspread				
of logit	.219	.329	1.046	1.084
Portugal				
Median	.711	.686	.569	.460
Mean	.702	.696	.583	.439
Range	.248	.294	.426	.464
Standard				
deviation	.060	.066	.112	.142
Midspread	.065	.071	.143	.223
Midspread				
of logit	.390	.336	.590	.937
Spain				
Median	.667	.668	.591	.412
Mean	.662	.662	.566	.402
Range	.316	.343	.403	.227
Standard				
deviation	.060	.072	.104	.064
Midspread	.076	.084	.135	.105
Midspread				
of logit	.337	.379	.556	.439
All provinces				
Median	.696	.638	.351	.325
Mean	.682	.613	.391	.358
Range	.772	.738	.643	.494
Standard				
deviation	.131	.145	.141	.103
Midspread	.121	.167	.195	.103
Midspread				
of logit	.574	.721	.846	.462

APPENDIX TABLE A5.4b

Descriptive Statistics for Illegitimacy (I_h), by Country in 1870, 1900, 1930, and 1960

Country	1870	1900	1930	1960
Northwestern Europe				
Belgium				
Median	.032	.033	.014	.009
Mean	.037	.034	.014	.012
Range	.082	.054	.024	.029
Standard				
deviation	.019	.015	.006	.008
Midspread	.027	.021	.011	.011
Midspread				
of logit	.793	.670	.867	1.082
England and Wales				
Median	.045	.022	.014	.037
Mean	.046	.023	.015	.038
Range	.049	.020	.015	.037
Standard				
deviation	.012	.005	.004	.008
Midspread	.016	.008	.006	.011
Midspread				
of logit	.364	.340	.441	.319
France				
Median	.032	.030	.032	.031
Mean	.036	.035	.034	.033
Range	.117	.079	.066	.051
Standard				
deviation	.019	.018	.015	.012
Midspread	.022	.022	.021	.016
Midspread				
of logit	.739	.716	.680	.533
Germany				
Median	.070	.060	.030	—
Mean	.068	.063	.033	—
Range	.128	.111	.070	—
Standard				
deviation	.031	.027	.016	—
Midspread	.045	.040	.022	—
Midspread				
of logit	.764	.719	.712	—
Ireland				
Median	.011	.007	.014	.011
Mean	.012	.008	.014	.012

APPENDIX TABLE A5.4b (*cont.*)

Country	1870	1900	1930	1960
Ireland				
Range	.023	.013	.016	.140
Standard deviation	.006	.004	.005	.004
Midspread	.007	.006	.009	.006
Midspread of logit	.636	.795	.702	.517
Netherlands				
Median	.023	.017	.008	.008
Mean	.023	.017	.008	.008
Range	.023	.011	.007	.009
Standard deviation	.008	.004	.002	.003
Midspread	.014	.009	.003	.005
Midspread of logit	.615	.607	.409	.611
Scotland				
Median	.053	.028	.024	.029
Mean	.057	.033	.028	.030
Range	.084	.057	.050	.055
Standard deviation	.023	.014	.013	.011
Midspread	.032	.022	.018	.013
Midspread of logit	.593	.739	.684	.432
Switzerland				
Median	.024	.019	.010	.019
Mean	.025	.019	.011	.018
Range	.031	.031	.010	.014
Standard deviation	.010	.008	.003	.003
Midspread	.016	.015	.004	.005
Midspread of logit	.710	.876	.372	.293
Scandinavia				
Denmark				
Median	.059	.046	.039	.046
Mean	.063	.049	.036	.045
Range	.076	.061	.041	.031

APPENDIX TABLE A5.4b (*cont.*)

Country	1870	1900	1930	1960
Denmark				
Standard deviation	.020	.018	.012	.009
Midspread	.031	.020	.021	.013
Midspread of logit	.540	.463	.670	.301
Finland				
Median	.057	.045	.030	.020
Mean	.055	.046	.029	.020
Range	.055	.037	.016	.007
Standard deviation	.016	.014	.006	.003
Midspread	.013	.024	.012	.005
Midspread of logit	.259	.606	.439	.250
Norway				
Median	.052	.034	.016	.019
Mean	.050	.039	.022	.026
Range	.069	.070	.065	.079
Standard deviation	.021	.018	.017	.021
Midspread	.040	.034	.019	.015
Midspread of logit	.936	.984	1.023	.790
Sweden				
Median	.050	.061	.044	.053
Mean	.057	.058	.045	.053
Range	.082	.063	.053	.065
Standard deviation	.020	.018	.015	.017
Midspread	.025	.026	.019	.022
Midspread of logit	.488	.533	.496	.457
Mediterranean				
Italy				
Median	.039	.047	.023	.010
Mean	.046	.048	.026	.010
Range	.078	.105	.033	.012
Standard deviation	.021	.028	.009	.003

APPENDIX TABLE A5.4b (*cont.*)

Country	1870	1900	1930	1960
Italy				
Midspread	.032	.023	.015	.004
Midspread of logit	.765	.620	.597	.516
Portugal				
Median	.059	.058	.065	.040
Mean	.068	.062	.068	.048
Range	.114	.125	.123	.104
Standard deviation	.030	.033	.037	.031
Midspread	.040	.045	.065	.049
Midspread of logit	.680	.829	1.164	1.215
Spain				
Median	.036	.031	.027	.007
Mean	.038	.035	.032	.010
Range	.092	.077	.084	.034
Standard deviation	.021	.019	.021	.008
Midspread	.030	.027	.030	.006
Midspread of logit	.909	.874	1.138	.813
All provinces				
Median	.041	.032	.023	.024
Mean	.045	.038	.028	.027
Range	.136	.133	.130	.112
Standard deviation	.026	.024	.020	.018
Midspread	.035	.032	.024	.026
Midspread of logit	.912	.989	1.023	1.179

APPENDIX TABLE A5.4c
Descriptive Statistics for Marriage (I_m), by Country in 1870, 1900, 1930, and 1960

Country	1870	1900	1930	1960
Northwestern Europe				
Belgium				
Median	.420	.452	.566	.695
Mean	.427	.464	.577	.697
Range	.186	.228	.275	.178
Standard				
deviation	.043	.056	.066	.045
Midspread	.054	.067	.088	.071
Midspread				
of logit	.222	.273	.359	.339
England and Wales				
Median	.501	.469	.511	.711
Mean	.504	.468	.507	.709
Range	.173	.170	.147	.161
Standard				
deviation	.037	.040	.029	.031
Midspread	.052	.055	.038	.038
Midspread				
of logit	.206	.221	.154	.183
France				
Median	.551	.573	.630	.655
Mean	.545	.561	.617	.646
Range	.320	.296	.307	.210
Standard				
deviation	.072	.067	.055	.035
Midspread	.110	.105	.077	.049
Midspread				
of logit	.445	.427	.326	.215
Germany				
Median	.467	.517	.533	—
Mean	.467	.508	.527	—
Range	.161	.177	.256	—
Standard				
deviation	.041	.046	.061	—
Midspread	.070	.064	.085	—
Midspread				
of logit	.282	.254	.344	—
Ireland				
Median	.386	.311	.359	.492
Mean	.399	.315	.360	.495

APPENDIX TABLE A5.4c (*cont.*)

Country	1870	1900	1930	1960
Ireland				
Range	.189	.073	.110	.160
Standard deviation	.048	.019	.027	.032
Midspread	.069	.027	.030	.033
Midspread of logit	.288	.125	.131	.132
Netherlands				
Median	.448	.463	.500	.632
Mean	.440	.454	.506	.636
Range	.115	.142	.112	.093
Standard deviation	.035	.042	.031	.028
Midspread	.051	.049	.049	.034
Midspread of logit	.203	.198	.196	.147
Scotland				
Median	.391	.363	.428	.659
Mean	.398	.383	.419	.658
Range	.274	.268	.194	.122
Standard deviation	.058	.061	.044	.030
Midspread	.063	.090	.059	.033
Midspread of logit	.265	.384	.243	.145
Switzerland				
Median	.413	.434	.438	.570
Mean	.414	.442	.433	.568
Range	.240	.089	.124	.150
Standard deviation	.060	.024	.032	.036
Midspread	.075	.038	.051	.053
Midspread of logit	.312	.154	.208	.216
Scandinavia				
Denmark				
Median	.464	.484	.518	.681
Mean	.456	.481	.517	.677
Range	.135	.086	.092	.161

APPENDIX TABLE A5.4c (*cont.*)

Country	1870	1900	1930	1960
Denmark				
Standard				
deviation	.034	.021	.023	.033
Midspread	.043	.029	.027	.022
Midspread				
of logit	.173	.116	.108	.102
Finland				
Median	.504	.469	.413	.599
Mean	.495	.483	.407	.602
Range	.124	.151	.060	.045
Standard				
deviation	.041	.051	.023	.014
Midspread	.063	.073	.042	.014
Midspread				
of logit	.253	.294	.176	.061
Norway				
Median	.410	.423	.418	.672
Mean	.410	.425	.411	.664
Range	.170	.119	.137	.176
Standard				
deviation	.034	.032	.037	.043
Midspread	.024	.047	.053	.043
Midspread				
of logit	.100	.192	.218	.197
Sweden				
Median	.419	.420	.434	.629
Mean	.420	.423	.429	.629
Range	.201	.197	.126	.124
Standard				
deviation	.049	.048	.030	.015
Midspread	.086	.070	.041	.020
Midspread				
of logit	.353	.288	.170	.084
Mediterranean				
Italy				
Median	.563	.519	.504	.573
Mean	.558	.527	.507	.568
Range	.113	.110	.138	.151
Standard				
deviation	.027	.029	.036	.045

APPENDIX TABLE A5.4c (*cont.*)

Country	1870	1900	1930	1960
Italy				
Midspread	.029	.030	.046	.091
Midspread				
of logit	.119	.120	.185	.372
Portugal				
Median	.471	.461	.484	.562
Mean	.462	.466	.485	.561
Range	.212	.203	.187	.183
Standard				
deviation	.062	.057	.048	.049
Midspread	.089	.093	.066	.060
Midspread				
of logit	.356	.375	.265	.243
Spain				
Median	.618	.582	.524	.543
Mean	.587	.567	.513	.552
Range	.281	.259	.260	.175
Standard				
deviation	.080	.071	.059	.042
Midspread	.100	.096	.077	.060
Midspread				
of logit	.420	.397	.308	.242
All provinces				
Median	.469	.477	.510	.638
Mean	.478	.481	.506	.626
Range	.420	.411	.402	.339
Standard				
deviation	.083	.087	.089	.072
Midspread	.114	.109	.130	.100
Midspread				
of logit	.460	.438	.525	.430

APPENDIX TABLE A7.1

Measures of Variation, France, Marital Fertility (I_g),
Illegitimacy (I_h), and Marriage (I_m), All Dates

	1831	1841	1851	1861	1871	1881	1891	1901	1911	1921	1931	1961
					Marital Fertility (I_g)							
Mean	.559	.525	.490	.486	.489	.478	.431	.399	.332	.339	.296	.332
Median	.556	.518	.480	.474	.460	.436	.388	.358	.310	.322	.284	.335
Midspread	.159	.153	.147	.172	.186	.184	.139	.139	.102	.088	.072	.061
Standard deviation	.111	.108	.104	.112	.125	.132	.120	.108	.079	.066	.055	.042
Coefficient of variation	.198	.206	.211	.230	.256	.275	.279	.270	.238	.196	.185	.127
					Illegitimacy (I_h)							
Mean	.035	.035	.034	.036	.035	.035	.036	.035	.035	.034	.034	.033
Median	.033	.034	.033	.032	.031	.029	.032	.029	.031	.030	.031	.031
Midspread	.021	.018	.017	.022	.022	.022	.022	.022	.021	.017	.021	.016
Standard deviation	.016	.014	.013	.019	.019	.018	.018	.018	.017	.014	.015	.012
Coefficient of variation	.463	.407	.373	.537	.539	.524	.498	.507	.475	.410	.438	.379
					Marriage (I_m)							
Mean	.519	.526	.539	.545	.546	.555	.558	.561	.606	.543	.617	.646
Median	.521	.535	.549	.550	.552	.565	.568	.577	.612	.555	.632	.655
Midspread	.103	.110	.111	.116	.110	.122	.114	.105	.099	.076	.077	.049
Standard deviation	.068	.066	.068	.072	.072	.073	.070	.067	.059	.051	.056	.035
Coefficient of variation	.130	.126	.126	.132	.132	.132	.125	.120	.098	.094	.090	.054

Source: The indexes were calculated by Etienne van de Walle and are published in van de Walle (1974) as well as in Coale and Treadway (1986, app. A). Because of obvious errors in some of the nineteenth century censuses, van de Walle corrected the distributions of women by marital status upon which the indexes are based. Some departments were omitted from his reconstruction: those in which there were major border changes (Alpes-Maritimes, Belfort, Meurthe-et-Moselle, Savoie and Haute-Savoie) and the most urbanized departments (Seine and Seine-et-Oise [Paris], Rhône [Lyons], and Bouches-du-Rhône [Marseilles]). Since the purpose of this table is comparison over time, only those departments with data available at all dates are included in the measures presented here. This accounts for slight discrepancies with table 7.3 and tables A5.4a–c.

APPENDIX TABLE A7.2
Regions of France

Region	Departments
1. Picardy	Somme Oise Aisne
2. Champagne	Aube Ardennes Marne Marne (Haute-)
3. Berry and Orléanais	Eure-et-Loir Loiret Loir-et-Cher Cher Indre-et-Loire
4. Burgundy	Ain Côte-d'Or Nièvre Saône-et-Loire Yonne
5. Guyenne	Aveyron Dordogne Gers Gironde Landes Lot Tarn-et-Garonne Lot-et-Garonne Pyrénées (Hautes-)
6. Pays de la Loire	Sèvres (Deux-) Vendée Vienne Maine-et-Loire Mayenne Sarthe
7. Languedoc	Ardèche Ariège Aude Gard Garonne (Haute-) Hérault Loire (Haute-)

APPENDIX TABLE A7.2 (*cont.*)

Region	Departments
7. Languedoc	Lozère
	Tarn
8. Auvergne-Limousin-Marche	Corrèze
	Creuse
	Vienne (Haute-)
	Cantal
	Puy-de-Dôme
9. Normandy	Calvados
	Eure
	Manche
	Orne
	Seine-Inférieure
10. Provence	Alpes (Basses-)
	Bouches-du-Rhône
	Alpes (Hautes-)
	Drôme
	Isère
	Var
11. Brittany	Côtes-du-Nord
	Finistère
	Ille-et-Vilaine
	Loire-Inférieure
	Morbihan
12. Franche-Comté	Doubs
	Jura
	Saône (Haute-)

Note: Regions that consisted of one of two provinces were omitted from the analysis.

References

Adams, Paul Vauthier. 1982. "Changes in Fertility, Nuptiality, and Family Structure: Five Villages in Mediterranean France." Paper presented at the seventh annual meeting of the Social Science History Association, Indiana University, November 1982.

Agulhon, Maurice. 1981. *Marianne into Battle*. Cambridge: Cambridge University Press.

Alter, George. 1988. *Family and the Female Life Course: The Women of Verviers, Belgium, 1849–1880*. Madison: University of Wisconsin Press.

Anderson, Barbara. 1986. "Regional and Cultural Factors in the Decline of Marital Fertility in Western Europe." In Ansley J. Coale and Susan C. Watkins, eds., *The Decline of Fertility in Europe*, pp. 293–313. Princeton, N.J.: Princeton University Press.

Anderson, Benedict. 1983. *Imagined Communities*. London: Verso Editions.

Anderson, Eugene, and Pauline R. Anderson. 1967. *Political Institutions and Social Change in Continental Europe in the Nineteenth Century*. Berkeley: University of California Press.

Anderson, Robert. 1970. "The Conflict in Education." In Theodore Zeldin, ed., *Conflicts in French Society*, pp. 51–93. London: George Allen and Unwin.

Annuaire Statistique de la Belgique et du Congo Belge. 1964. Brussels: Lesigne.

Ascoli, G. 1910. *Encyclopaedia Brittanica*, 11th ed. s.v. "Italian language."

Bade, Klaus J. 1980. "German Emigration to the United States and Continental Immigration to Germany in the Late Nineteenth and Early Twentieth Centuries." *Central European History* 13(4):348–77.

Baines, E. D. 1981. "The Labour Supply and the Labour Market 1860–1914." In Roderick Floud and Donald McCloskey, eds., *The Economic History of Britain since 1700*, 2:144–74. Cambridge: Cambridge University Press.

Banks, Joseph A. 1954. *Prosperity and Parenthood: A Study of Family Planning among the Victorian Middle Classes*. London: Routledge and Kegan Paul.

Barclay, G. W., A. J. Coale, M. Stoto, and T. J. Trussell. 1976. "A Reassessment of the Demography of Traditional Rural China." *Population Index* 42(4):606–35.

Barth, Fredrik. 1969. "Introduction." In F. Barth, ed., *Ethnic Groups and Boundaries*, pp. 9–38. Boston: Little Brown.

Beales, Derek. 1971. *The Risorgimento and the Unification of Italy*. London: George Allen and Unwin.

Beer, William R. 1980. *The Unexpected Rebellion: Ethnic Activism in Contemporary France*. New York: New York University Press.

Bell, Daniel. 1975. "Ethnicity and Social Change." In Nathan Glazer and Daniel P. Moynihan, eds., *Ethnicity: Theory and Experience*, pp. 141–74. Cambridge: Harvard University Press.

Bellah, Robert N., Richard Madsen, William M. Sullivan, Ann Swidler, and Steven M. Tipton. 1985. *Habits of the Heart*. Berkeley: University of California Press.

Belmont, Nicole. 1979. *Arnold van Gennep: The Creator of French Ethnography*, translated by Derek Coltman. Chicago: University of Chicago Press.

Berent, Jerzy. 1982. "Family Planning in Europe and USA in the 1970s." In *Comparative Studies: ECE Analysis of WFS Surveys in Europe and USA*. Geneva: Population Activities Unit, UN Economic Commission for Europe.

Blake, J. 1985. "The Fertility Transition: Continuity or Discontinuity with the Past?" *International Population Conference* 3:393–405.

Blau, Peter M. 1977. *Inequality and Heterogeneity*. New York: Free Press.

Bloch, Marc. 1966. *French Rural History*. Berkeley: University of California Press.

Bloch, Oscar. 1921. *La pénétration du français dans les parlers des Vosges meridionales*. Paris: E. Champion.

Blome, Richard. 1673. *Britannia: . . . . A Geographical Description of the Kingdom of England, Scotland, and Ireland, with the Isles and Territories Thereto Belonging. . . .* London: Printed by R. Roycroft for R. Blome.

Bongaarts, John. 1978. "A Framework for Analyzing the Proximate Determinants of Fertility." *Population and Development Review* 4(1):105–32.

Bongaarts, John, and Jane Menken. 1983. "The Supply of Children: A Critical Essay." In R. Bulatao and R. Lee, eds., *Determinants of Fertility in Developing Countries*, 1:27–60. New York: Academic Press.

Botein, Stephen, Jack R. Censer, and Harriet Ritvo. 1981. "The Periodical Press in Eighteenth-Century English and French Society: A Cross-cultural Approach." *Comparative Studies in Society and History* 23(3):464–90.

Bourdieu, Pierre. 1962. "Célibat et condition paysanne." *Études Rurales* 5/6:32–135.

———. 1977a. "The Economics of Linguistic Exchange." *Social Science Information* 16(6):645–68.

———. 1977b. *Outline of a Theory of Practice*. Cambridge: Cambridge University Press.

Bourgeois-Pichat, Jean. 1981. "Recent Demographic Change in Western Europe: An Assessment." *Population and Development Review* 7(1):19–42.

Braudel, Fernand. 1982. *The Wheels of Commerce*. New York: Harper and Row.

———. 1984. *The Perspective of the World*. New York: Harper and Row.

———. 1988. *The Identity of France*. New York: Harper and Row.

Brown, Peter. 1988. *The Body and Society: Men, Women, and Sexual Renunciation in Early Christianity*. New York: Columbia University Press.

Brun, Auguste. 1923a. *L'introduction de la langue française en Béarn et en Roussillon*. Paris: Champion.

———. 1923b. *Recherches historiques sur l'introduction du français dans les provinces du Midi*. Paris: Champion.

———. 1927. *La langue française en Provence*. Marseille: Institut Historique de Provence.

Brustein, William. 1988. *The Social Origins of Political Regionalism: France, 1849–1981*. Berkeley: University of California Press.

Buchanan, William, and Hadley Cantril. 1972. *How Nations See Each Other: A Study in Public Opinion*. Westport, Conn.: Greenwood Press.

Burke, Peter. 1978. *Popular Culture in Early Modern Europe*. London: Temple Smith.

Cachinero-Sánchez, Benito. 1982. "La evolución de la nupcialidad en España (1887–1975)." *Revista Española de Investigaciones Sociológias* 20:81–99.

Caldwell, John C. 1976. "Toward a Restatement of Demographic Transition Theory." *Population and Development Review* 2(3,4):321–66.

Caldwell, J.C., and Pat Caldwell. 1977. "The Role of Marital Sexual Abstinence in Determining Fertility: A Study of the Yoruba in Nigeria." *Population Studies* 31(2):193–217.

Caselli, Graziella, Viviana Egidi, and John Wilmoth. 1987. "Fertility, Development, and Female Activity: The Evolution of Territorial Differences in Italy." Paper presented at the European Population Conference, Jyväskylä, Finland, June 1987.

Casterline, John, Susheela B. Singh, John Cleland, and Hazel Ashurst. 1984. "The Proximate Determinants of Fertility." *WFS Comparative Studes*, no. 39. Voorburg, Netherlands: International Statistical Institute.

Chamie, Joseph. 1981. *Religion and Fertility: Arab Christian-Muslim Differentials.* Cambridge: Cambridge University Press.

Chatelain, Abel. 1976. *Les migrants temporaires en France de 1800 à 1914.* Paris: Publications de l'Université de Lille.

Chaunu, Pierre. 1973. "Réflexions sur la démographie Normande." In *Sur la population française au XVIIIe et XIXe siècles*, pp. 97–117. Paris: Société de Démographie Historique.

Christian, William A., Jr. 1972. *Person and God in a Spanish Valley.* New York: Academic Press.

Cleland, John. 1985. "Marital Fertility Decline in Developing Countries: Theories and the Evidence." In John Cleland and John Hobcraft, eds., *Reproductive Change in Developing Countries*, pp. 223–49. London: Oxford University Press.

Cleland, John, and Chris Wilson. 1987. "Demand Theories of the Fertility Transition: An Iconoclastic View." *Population Studies* 41:5–30.

Clough, Shepard. 1930. *A History of the Flemish Movement in Belgium.* New York: Richard R. Smith.

Clyne, Michael. 1984. *Language and Society in the German-Speaking Countries.* Cambridge: Cambridge University Press.

Coale, Ansley J. 1973. "The Demographic Transition Reconsidered." In *International Population Conference, Liège, 1973*, 1:53–72. Liège: International Union for the Scientific Study of Populations.

———. 1986. "The Decline of Fertility in Europe since the Eighteenth Century as a Chapter in Human Demographic History." In Ansley J. Coale and Susan C. Watkins, eds., *The Decline of Fertility in Europe*, pp. 1–30. Princeton, N.J.: Princeton University Press.

Coale, Ansley J., Paul Demeny and Barbara Vaughan. 1983. *Regional Model Life Tables and Stable Populations*, 2d ed. New York: Academic Press.

Coale, Ansley J., and Roy Treadway. 1986. "A Summary of the Changing Distribution of Overall Fertility, Marital Fertility, and the Proportion Married in the Provinces of Europe." In Ansley J. Coale and Susan C. Watkins, eds., *The Decline of Fertility in Europe*, pp. 31–181. Princeton, N.J.: Princeton University Press.

Coale, Ansley J., and Susan C. Watkins, eds., 1986. *The Decline of Fertility in Europe.* Princeton, N.J.: Princeton University Press.

Collins, Irene. 1959. *The Government and the Newspaper Press in France, 1814–1881*. London: Oxford University Press.

Connell, K. H. 1968. *Irish Peasant Society: Four Historical Essays*. Oxford: Clarendon Press.

Connor, Walker. 1977. "Ethnonationalism in the First World." In M. Esman, ed., *Ethnic Conflict in the Western World*, pp. 19–45. Ithaca, N.Y.: Cornell University Press.

Cooper, Robert L. 1982. "A Framework for the Study of Language Spread." In Robert L. Cooper, ed., *Language Spread: Studies in Diffusion and Social Change*, pp. 5–36. Bloomington: Indiana University Press.

Cornell, Laurel. 1984. "Why Are There No Spinsters in Japan?" *Journal of Family History* 9(4):326–39.

Corrigan, Philip, and Derek Sayer. 1985. *The Great Arch: English State Formation as Cultural Revolution*. Oxford: Basil Blackwell.

Courgeau, Daniel. 1970. *Les champs migratoires en France*. Paris: Presses Universitaires de France.

Cranfield, G. A. 1962. *The Development of the Provincial Newspaper*. Oxford: Clarendon Press.

Croze, Marcel. 1976. *Tableaux démographiques et sociaux*. Paris: Institut National de Études Démographiques.

Dauton, M. J. 1985. *Royal Mail: The Post Office since 1840*. London: Athlone Press.

Dauzat, Albert. 1922. *La géographie linguistique*. Paris: Flammarion.

———. 1927. *Les patois*. Paris: Delagrave.

———. 1945. *Études de linguistique française*. Paris: D'Artrey.

Davis, Natalie. 1983. *The Return of Martin Guerre*. Cambridge: Harvard University Press.

Delefortrie, N., and J. Morice. 1959. *Les revenus départementaux en 1864 et en 1954*. Paris: Armand Colin.

Desplanques, Guy. 1975. *Les migrations intercensitaires de 1962 à 1968*, Les Collections de l'INSEE, no. 157, series D, no. 39, Paris.

Deutsch, Karl W. 1966. *Nationalism and Social Communications*, 2d ed. Cambridge: MIT Press.

Devoto, Giacomo. 1978. *The Languages of Italy*. Chicago: University of Chicago Press.

Dixon, Ruth. 1970. "Hallelujah the Pill?" *Trans-action* 8(1/2):44–49, 92.

Dorian, N. C. 1980. "Linguistic Lag as an Ethnic Marker." *Language in Society* 9:33–41.

Duby, Georges. 1974. *The Early Growth of the European Economy: Warriors and Peasants from the Seventh to the Twelfth Century*. Ithaca, N.Y.: Cornell University Press.

Dupâquier, J. 1972. "De l'animal à l'homme: Le mécanisme autorégulateur des populations traditionnelles." *Revue de l'Institut de Sociologie, Université Libre de Bruxelles* 2:177–211.

Durand, Yves. 1984. *Vivre au pays au XVIIIe siécle*. Paris: Presses Universitaires de France.

Durkheim, Emile. [1893] 1964. *The Division of Labor in Society*. New York: Free Press.

Eidheim, Harald. 1969. "When Ethnic Identity Is a Social Stigma." In F. Barth, ed., *Ethnic Groups and Boundaries*, pp. 39–54. Boston: Little, Brown, and Company.

Elias, Norbert. 1982. *Power and Civility*. New York: Pantheon.

Eversley, D.E.C. 1966. "Population History and Local History." In E. A. Wrigley, ed., *An Introduction to English Historical Demography*, pp. 14–43. New York: Basic Books.

Fabre, Claudine. 1981. "Glossaire." In Jacques Le Goff and Jean-Claude Schmitt, eds., *Le Charivari*, pp. 429–34. Paris: Mouton.

Feldman, A. S., and W. E. Moore. 1960. "The Society." In *Labor Commitment and Social Change in Developing Areas*. New York: Social Science Research Council.

Fenoaltea, Stefano. 1983. "Italy" In Patrick O'Brien, ed., *Railways and the Economic Development of Western Europe, 1830–1914*, pp. 49–120. London: Macmillan.

Fildes, Valerie A. 1986. *Breasts, Bottles and Babies*. Edinburgh: Edinburgh University Press.

Fishman, J. A. 1968. "Some Contrasts between Linguistically Homogenous and Linguistically Heterogenous Polities." In J. Fishman, C. A. Ferguson, and J. das Gupta, eds., *Language Problems of Developing Nations*. New York: John Wiley and Sons.

————. 1977. "Language and Ethnicity." In Howard Giles, ed., *Language, Ethnicity and Intergroup Relations*, pp. 15–57. New York: Academic Press.

————. 1985. "Macrosociolinguistics and the Sociology of Language in the Early Eighties." *Annual Review of Sociology* 11:113–27.

Flinn, Michael. 1981. *The European Demographic System, 1500–1820*. Baltimore, Mary.: Johns Hopkins University Press.

Foster, R. F. 1988. *Modern Ireland 1600–1972*. London: Penguin Press.

Fox, Renée C. 1978. "Why Belgium?" *European Journal of Sociology* 19:205–28.

Freedman, Ronald. 1987. "The Contribution of Social Science Research to Population Policy and Family Planning Program Effectivness." *Studies in Family Planning* 18(2):57–82.

Garden, Maurice. 1970. *Lyon et les Lyonnais au XVIIIe siècle*. Paris: Les Belles-Lettres.

Gaskell, E. C. 1857. *The Life of Charlotte Bronte*. New York: D. Appleton.

Gaskin, Katherine. 1978. "Age at First Marriage in Europe before 1850: A Summary of Family Reconstitution Data." *Journal of Family History* 3(1):23–36.

Geertz, Clifford. 1971. "The Integrative Revolution: Primordial Sentiments and Civil Politics in the New States." In Jason L. Finkle and Richard W. Gable, eds., *Political Development and Social Change*, 2d ed., pp. 655–69. New York: John Wiley and Sons.

Gellner, Ernest A. 1983. *Nations and Nationalism*. Ithaca, N.Y.: Cornell University Press.

Giddens, Anthony. 1971. *Capitalism and Modern Social Theory*. Cambridge: Cambridge University Press.

Gillis, John R. 1974. *Youth and History*. New York: Academic Press.

Glass, D. V. 1938. "Changes in Fertility in England and Wales, 1851 to 1931." In L. Hogben, ed., *Political Arithmetic*, pp. 1–52. London: G. Allen and Unwin.

Goode, William. 1970. *World Revolution and Family Patterns*. New York: Free Press.

Gordon, David C. 1978. *The French Language and National Identity (1930–1975)*. The Hague: Mouton.

Goudsblom, Johan. 1967. *Dutch Society*. New York: Random House.

Gould, Peter, and Rodney White. 1986. *Mental Maps*, 2d ed. Boston: George Allen and Unwin.

Granger, C.W.J., and C. M. Elliott. 1967. "A Fresh Look at Wheat Prices and Markets in the Eighteenth Century." *Economic History Review* 20, no. 2:257–65.

Granovetter, Mark S. 1973. "The Strength of Weak Ties." *American Journal of Sociology* 78(6):1360–80.

Grew, Raymond. 1984. "The Nineteenth-century European State." In Charles Bright and Susan Harding, eds., *State-Making and Social Movements*, pp. 83–120. Ann Arbor: University of Michigan Press.

Gullickson, Gay L. 1986. *Spinners and Weavers of Auffay: Rural Industry and the Sexual Division of Labor in a French Village, 1750–1850*. Cambridge: Cambridge University Press.

Hajnal, John. 1965. "European Marriage Patterns in Perspective." In D. V. Glass and D.E.C. Eversley, eds., *Population in History*, pp. 101–43. London: Edward Arnold.

———. 1982. "Two Kinds of Pre-Industrial Household Formation System." *Population and Development Review* 8(3):449–94.

Hall, Arthur, and W. B. Ransom. 1906. "Plumbism from the Ingestion of Diachylon as an Abortifacient." *Lancet* (February 24): 510–12.

Hannan, Michael T. 1979. "The Dynamics of Ethnic Boundaries in Modern States." In John W. Meyer and Michael T. Hannan, eds., *National Development and the World System*, pp. 253–75. Chicago: University of Chicago Press.

Haugen, Einar. 1959. "Planning for a Standard Language in Modern Norway." *Anthropological Linguistics* 1(3):8–21.

———. 1976. *The Scandinavian Languages: An Introduction to Their History*. London: Faber and Faber.

Hechter, Michael. 1975. *Internal Colonialism. The Celtic Fringe in British National Development: 1536–1966*. Berkeley: University of California Press.

Heckscher, Eli F. 1954. *An Economic History of Sweden*. Cambridge: Harvard University Press.

Heffer, Jean, Jacques Mairesse, and Jean-Marie Chanut. August 1986. "La culture du blé en France au milieu du XIXe siècle: rendement, prix, salaires et autres coûts." Typescript.

Hélias, Pierre-Jakez. 1978. *The Horse of Pride*. New Haven, Conn.: Yale University Press.

Henry, Louis. 1961. "Some Data on Natural Fertility." *Eugenics Quarterly* 8(2):81–91.

Hill, Christopher. 1964. *Puritanism and Revolution*. New York: Schocken Books.

Himes, Norman E. [1936] 1970. *Medical History of Contraception*. New York: Schocken Books.

Hobsbawm, Eric. 1983. "Mass-producing Traditions: Europe, 1870–1914." In Eric Hobsbawm and Terence Ranger, eds., *The Invention of Tradition*. Cambridge: Cambridge University Press.

———. 1987. *The Age of Empire, 1875–1914*. New York: Pantheon.

Hochstadt, Steve. 1981. "Migration and Industrialization in Germany, 1815–1977." *Social Science History* 5(4):445–68.

Hoffman, George W., ed. 1969. *A Geography of Europe*, 3d ed. New York: Ronald Press.

Hunt, E. H. 1973. *Regional Wage Variations in Britain 1850–1914*. Oxford: Clarendon Press.

Inglehart, Ronald. 1977. *The Silent Revolution*. Princeton, N.J.: Princeton University Press.

Inkeles, Alex. 1981. "Modernization and Family Patterns: A Test of Convergence Theory." In Dwight W. Hoover and John T. A. Koulmoulides, eds., *Conspectus of History*, 1:31–63. Muncie, Ind.: Department of History, Ball State University.

Ireland Central Statistics Office. 1974. *Statistical Abstract of Ireland 1970–71*. Dublin: Stationary Office.

Istituto di Ricerche Sulla Popolazione. 1985. "The Italian Population: An Overview." Paper presented at the Twentieth Congress of the International Union for the Scientific Study of Population, Florence, Italy: Consiglio Nacionale delle Ricerche.

Jalland, Pat. 1986. *Women, Marriage and Politics, 1860–1914*. Oxford: Clarendon Press.

Johnston, R. J. and J. C. Doornkamp. 1982. *The Changing Geography of the United Kingdom*. London: Methuen.

Jones, E. L. 1988. *Growth Recurring*. Oxford: Clarendon Press.

Jones, Elise F. 1982. "Socio-Economic Differentials in Achieved Fertility." In *Comparative Studies: ECE Analyses of WFS Surveys in Europe and USA*. Geneva: Population Activities Unit, UN Economic Commission for Europe.

Joyce, Herbert. 1893. *The History of the Post Office from Its Establishment down to 1836*. London: Richard Bentley and Son.

Judt, Tony. 1979. *Socialism in Provence 1871–1914*. Cambridge: Cambridge University Press.

Katznelson, Ira, and Margaret Weir. 1985. *Schooling for All: Class, Race, and the Decline of the Democratic Ideal*. New York: Basic Books.

Katzner, Kenneth. 1986. *The Languages of the World*. New York: Funk and Wagnalls.

Kennedy, Robert E., Jr. 1973. *The Irish: Emigration, Marriage and Fertility*. Berkeley: University of California Press.

Kenwood, A. G., and A. L. Lougheed. 1983. *The Growth of the International Economy*. London: George Allen and Unwin.

Kertzer, David I. and Dennis P. Hogan. 1989. *Family, Political Economy, and Demographic Change: The Transformation of Life in Casalecchio, Italy, 1861–1921*. Madison: University of Wisconsin Press.

Kintner, Hallie. 1985. "Trends and Regional Differences in Breastfeeding in Germany from 1871 to 1937." *Journal of Family History* 10(2):163–82.

Kirk, Dudley. 1946. *Europe's Population in the Interwar Years*. New York: League of Nations.

Kloss, Heinz. 1968. "Notes Concerning a Language-Nation Typology." In J. A. Fishman, C. A. Ferguson, and J. das Gupta, eds., *Language Problems of Developing Nations*. New York: John Wiley and Sons.

Knodel, John. 1967. "Law, Marriage and Illegitimacy in 19th Century Germany." *Population Studies* 20(3):279–94.

————. 1974. *The Decline of Fertility in Germany, 1871–1939*. Princeton, N.J.: Princeton University Press.

————. 1983. "Natural Fertility: Age Patterns, Levels and Trends." In R. Bulatao and R. D. Lee, eds., *Determinants of Fertility in Developing Countries: A Summary of Knowledge* 1:61–102. New York: National Academy Press.

————. 1986. "Demographic Transitions in German Villages." In Ansley J. Coale and Susan C. Watkins, eds., *The Decline of Fertility in Europe*, pp. 337–89. Princeton, N.J.: Princeton University Press.

————. 1988. *Demographic Behavior in the Past: A Study of Fourteen German Village Populations in the Eighteenth and Nineteenth Centuries*. New York: Cambridge University Press.

Knodel, John, Havanon Napaporn, and Anthony Pramuelratana. 1984. "Fertility Transition in Thailand: A Qualitative Analysis." *Population and Development Review* 10 (2):297–328.

Knodel, John, and Etienne van de Walle. 1967. "Breast Feeding, Fertility and Infant Morality: An Analysis of Some Early German Data." *Population Studies* 21(2):109–31.

————. 1986. "Lessons from the Past: Policy Implications of Historical Fertility Studies." In Ansley J. Coale and Susan C. Watkins, eds., *The Decline of Fertility in Europe*, pp. 390–419. Princeton, N.J.: Princeton University Press.

Kohli, Martin. 1986. "Retirement and the Moral Economy: An Historical Interpretation of the German Case." Working Paper no. 3, Institut für Soziologie der Freien Universität: Berlin, West Germany.

Kohn, Melvin L. 1987. "Cross-National Research as an Analytic Strategy." *American Sociological Review* 52(6):713–31.

Kramer, Jane. 1985. "Letter from Europe." *The New Yorker* (January 21): 74–91.

Kussmaul, Ann. 1981. *Servants in Husbandry in Early Modern England*. Cambridge: Cambridge University Press.

————. 1985. "Agrarian Change in Seventeenth-century England: The Economic Historian as Paleontologist." *Journal of Economic History* 45(1):1–30.

Laponce, J. A. 1987. *Languages and Their Territories*. Toronto: University of Toronto Press.

Lartichaux, J-Y. 1977. "Linguistic Politics during the French Revolution." *Diogenes* (97):65–84.

Laslett, Peter. 1972. "Introduction: The History of the Family." In Peter Laslett and Richard Wall, eds., *Household and Family in Past Time*, pp. 1–89. Cambridge: Cambridge University Press.

————. 1980. "Introduction: Comparing Illegitimacy over Time and between Cultures." In Peter Laslett, Karla Oosterveen, and Richard M. Smith, eds., *Bastardy and Its Comparative History*, pp. 1–70. Cambridge: Harvard University Press.

Leasure, J. William. 1963. "Factors Involved in the Decline of Fertility in Spain 1900–1950." *Population Studies* 16(3):271–85.

Le Bras, Hérve. 1986. *Les trois France*. Paris: Odile Jacob.

Le Bras, Hérve, and Emmanuel Todd. 1981. *L'invention de la France*. Paris: Librairie Générale Française.

Lee, Robert. 1981. "Family and 'Modernisation': The Peasant Family and Social Change in Nineteenth Century Bavaria." In Richard J. Evans and W. R. Lee, eds., *The German Family*, pp. 84–119. London: Croom Helm.

Lehning, James. 1984. "The Decline of Marital Fertility: Evidence from a French Department, La Loire (1851–1891)." *Annales de Demographie Historique*, pp. 201–17.

LeRoy Ladurie, Emmanuel, and Paul Dumont. 1971. "Quantitative and Cartographical Exploitation of French Mililtary Archives, 1819–1826." *Daedalus* 100(2): 397–44.

Lesthaeghe, Ron. 1977. *The Decline of Belgian Fertility, 1800–1970*. Princeton, N.J.: Princeton University Press.

———. 1983. "A Century of Demographic and Cultural Change in Western Europe." *Population and Development Review* 9(3):411–35.

Lesthaeghe, Ron, and Dominique Meekers. 1986. "Value Changes and the Dimensions of Familism in the European Community." *European Journal of Population* 2(3/4):225–68.

Lesthaeghe, Ron, and Chris Wilson. 1986. "Modes of Production, Secularization and the Pace of the Fertility Decline in Western Europe, 1870–1930." In Ansley J. Coale and Susan C. Watkins, eds., *The Decline of Fertility in Europe*, pp. 261–92. Princeton, N.J.: Princeton University Press.

Levasseur, E. 1889. *La population française*, Vol. 1. Paris: Arthur Rousseau.

Levine, David. 1977. *Family Formation in an Age of Nascent Capitalism*. New York: Academic Press.

———. 1985. "Industrialization and the Proletarian Family in England." *Past and Present*, no. 107:168–203.

———. 1987. *Reproducing Families: The Political Economy of English Population History*. Cambridge: Cambridge University Press.

Levy, Marion J., Jr. 1966. *Modernization and the Structure of Societies: A Setting for International Affairs*. Princeton, N.J.: Princeton University Press.

Lieberson, Stanley. 1982. "Forces Affecting Language Spread: Some Basic Propositions." In Robert L. Cooper, ed., *Language Spread: Studies in Diffusion and Social Change*, pp. 37–62. Bloomington: University of Indiana Press.

Lieberson, Stanley, Guy Dalto, and Mary Ellen Marsden. 1981. "The Course of Mother-Tongue Diversity in Nations." In Stanley Lieberson, ed., *Language Diversity and Language Contact*, pp. 48–82. Stanford, Cal.: Stanford University Press.

Lieberson, Stanley, and Lynn K. Hansen. 1974. "National Development, Mother-Tongue Diversity, and the Comparative Study of Nations." *American Sociological Review* 39:523–41.

Linz, Juan J. 1967. "The Party System of Spain: Past and Future." In Seymour M. Lipset and Stein Rokkan, eds., *Party Systems and Voter Alignments: Cross-National Perspectives*, pp. 197–282. New York: Free Press.

Lithell, Ulla-Britt. 1981. "Breast-Feeding Habits and Their Relation to Infant Mortality and Marital Fertility." *Journal of Family History* 6(2):182–94.

Livi-Bacci, Massimo. 1971. *A Century of Portuguese Fertility*. Princeton, N.J.: Princeton University Press.

———. 1977. *A History of Italian Fertility during the Last Two Centuries*. Princeton, N.J.: Princeton University Press.

———. 1986. "Social Group Forerunners of Fertility Control in Europe." In Ansley J. Coale and Susan C. Watkins, eds., *The Decline of Fertility in Europe*, pp. 182–200. Princeton, N.J.: Princeton University Press.

Le livre de poste, ou départ de Paris des couriers de la poste aux lettres. 1816. Administration des Postes, Paris: Valade, Imprimeur du Roi.

Lockridge, K. A. 1983. "The Fertility Transition in Sweden." The Demographic Data Base, Report no. 3, University of Umeå.

Loth, J. 1926. "Les langues bretonne et le français." *Revue Critique* 43:419–27.

Lutz, Wolfgang. 1987. "Factors Associated with the Finnish Fertility Decline since 1776." *Population Studies* 41(3): 463–82.

McBride, Theresa M. 1976. *The Domestic Revolution: The Modernisation of Household Service in England and France, 1820–1920*. London: Croom Helm.

McEvedy, Colin, and Richard Jones. 1978. *Atlas of World Population History*. New York: Penguin Books.

Macfarlane, Alan. 1977. *Reconstructing Historical Communities*. New York: Cambridge University Press.

McKenna, Edward E. 1978. "Age, Region and Marriage in Post-Famine Ireland: An Empirical Examination." *Economic History Review*, 31, 2d series: 236–56.

McLaren, A[ngus]. 1983. *Sexuality and Social Order: The Debate over the Fertility of Women and Workers in France, 1770–1920*. New York: Holmes and Meier.

———. 1984. *Reproductive Rituals*. New York: Methuen.

———. Forthcoming. "The Sexual Politics of Reproduction." In J. Gillis, D. Levine, and L. Tilly, eds., *The European Experience of Declining Fertility*. Cambridge, Mass.: Basil Blackwell.

McNeill, William H. 1986. *Polyethnicity and National Unity in World History*. Toronto: University of Toronto Press.

McNicoll, Geoffrey. 1980. "Institutional Determinants of Fertility Change." *Population and Development Review* 6(4):441–62.

———. 1983. "Notes on the Local Context of Demographic Change." Population Council, New York: Center for Policy Studies, working paper no. 98.

McQuillan, Kevin. 1978. "Modernization and Internal Migration: The Cases of Nineteenth Century England and France." Ph.D. diss., Princeton University, Princeton, N.J.

McRae, Kenneth D. 1983. *Conflict and Compromise in Multilingual Societies: Switzerland*. Waterloo: Wilfred Laurier University Press.

———. 1986. *Conflict and Compromise in Multilingual Societies: Belgium*. Waterloo: Wilfred Laurier University Press.

Markham, James M. 1987. "Sowing a Language's Seed in Brittany." *New York Times*, 31 October, p. 4.

Marshall, T. H. 1975. *Social Policy in the Twentieth Century.* London: Hutchinson University Library.

Marx, Karl, and Frederich Engels. [1848]. 1967. *The Communist Manifesto.* Harmondsworth, England: Penguin Books.

Mathiessen, P. C. 1985. *The Limitation of Family Size in Denmark.* Copenhagen: Munksgaard.

Mayer, Kurt B. 1952. *The Population of Switzerland.* New York: Columbia University Press.

Mead, W. R. 1981. *A Historical Geography of Scandinavia.* London: Academic Press.

Medick, Hans. 1984. "Village Spinning Bees: Sexual Culture and Free Time among Rural Youth in Early Modern Germany." In Hans Medick and David Warren Sabean, eds., *Interest and Emotion: Essays on the Study of Family and Kinship*, pp. 317–39. Cambridge: Cambridge University Press.

Meillet, A. 1928. *Les langues dans L'Europe nouvelle.* Paris: Payot.

Meyer, John W., and Michael T. Hannan, eds. 1979. *National Development and the World System.* Chicago: University of Chicago Press.

Mill, John Stuart. [1859] 1956. *On Liberty.* Indianapolis: Bobbs-Merrill.

Miller, Michael B. 1981. *The Bon Marché: Bourgeois Culture and the Department Store, 1869–1920.* Princeton, N.J.: Princeton University Press.

Mitchell, B. R. 1976. *European Historical Statistics 1750–1970.* New York: Columbia University Press.

Mitterauer, Michael, and Reinhard Sieder. 1982. *The European Family.* Oxford: Basil Blackwell.

Moch, Leslie. 1983. *Paths to the City.* Beverly Hills, Cal.: Sage Publications.

―――. Forthcoming. "The History of Migration and Fertility Decline: The View from the Road." In J. Gillis, D. Levine, and L. Tilly, eds., *The European Experience of Declining Fertility.* Cambridge, Mass.: Basil Blackwell.

Moore, Wilbert E. 1965. *The Impact of Industry.* Englewood Cliffs, N.J.: Prentice-Hall.

―――. 1979. *World Modernization: The Limits of Convergence.* New York: Elsevier.

Morgan, Kenneth O. 1981. *Rebirth of a Nation: Wales, 1880–1980.* New York: Oxford University Press.

Muchembled, Robert. 1985. *Popular Culture and Elite Culture in France 1400–1750.* Baton Rouge: Louisiana State University Press.

Nagel, Joane, and Susan Olzak. 1982. "Ethnic Mobilization in New and Old States: An Extension of the Competition Model." *Social Problems* 30(2):139–43.

Nielsen, François. 1980. "The Flemish Movement in Belgium after World War II: A Dynamic Analysis." *American Sociological Review* 45:76–94.

O'Brien, Patrick K., ed. 1983. *Railways and the Economic Development of Western Europe, 1830–1914,* London: Macmillan.

O'Brien, Patrick K., and S. L. Engerman. 1981. "Changes in Income and Its Distribution during the Industrial Revolution." In Roderick Floud and Donald McCloskey, eds., *The Economic History of Britain since 1700*, 1:164–81. Cambridge: Cambridge University Press.

Ó'Gráda, Cormac. 1981. "Agricultural Decline 1860–1914." In Roderick Floud and

Donald McCloskey, eds., *The Economic History of Britain* 2:175–97. Cambridge: Cambridge University Press.

———. 1988. *Ireland before and after the Famine*. New York: St. Martin's Press.

O'Neill, Brian Juan. 1987. *Social Inequality in a Portuguese Hamlet*. Cambridge: Cambridge University Press.

O'Reilly, Kevin R. 1986. "Contraception, Ideology and Policy Formation: Cohort Change in Dublin, Ireland." In W. Penn Handwerker, ed., *An Anthropological Critique of Demographic Transition Theory*, pp. 221–36. Boulder: Westview Press.

Orridge, A. W. 1982. "Separatist and Autonomist Nationalisms: The Structure of Regional Loyalties in the Modern State." In Colin H. Williams, ed., *National Separatism*, pp. 43–74. Cardiff: University of Wales Press.

Page, Hilary, and Ron Lesthaeghe, eds. 1981. *Child-spacing in Tropical Africa: Traditions and Change*. London: Academic Press.

Parsons, Talcott. 1975. "Some Theoretical Considerations on the Nature and Trends of Change in Ethnicity." In Nathan Glazer and Daniel Moynihan, *Ethnicity: Theory and Experience*, pp. 53–83. Cambridge: Harvard University Press.

Phythian-Adams, Charles. 1985. "Little Images of the Great Country: English Rural Communities and English Rural Contexts." Paper presented at a conference, The Social World of Britain and America 1600–1820: A Comparison from the Perspective of Social History, Williamsburg, Virginia.

Pinchemel, Philippe. 1969. *France: A Geographical Survey*. New York: Praeger.

Pollard, Sidney. 1981. *The Integration of the European Economy since 1845*. London: George Allen and Unwin.

Poussou, Jean-Pierre. 1983. *Bordeaux et le sud-ouest au XVIIIe siècle: Croissance économique et attraction urbaine*. Paris: Editions de L'École des Hautes Études en Sciences Sociales.

Preston, Samuel H. 1985. "Resources, Knowledge and Child Mortality: A Comparison of the U.S. in the Late Nineteenth Century and Developing Countries Today." *International Population Conference* 4:373–88.

Price, Roger. 1975. *The Economic Modernization of France, 1730–1880*. New York: John Wiley and Sons.

Procacci, Guiliano. 1970. *History of the Italian People*. London: Weidenfeld and Nicolson.

Quetelet, Lambert Adolphe Jacques. 1848. *Du système social et des lois qui le régissent*. Paris: Guillaumin et Cie.

Rickard, Peter. 1974. *A History of the French Language*. London: Hutchinson University Library.

Robinson, Geoffrey. 1977. *Hedingham Harvest*. London: Constable.

Robinson, Howard. 1953. *Britain's Post Office*. London: Oxford University Press.

Rogers, Everett. 1983. *Diffusion of Innovations*, 3d ed. New York: Free Press.

Rokkan, Stein. 1967. "Geography, Religion, and Social Class: Cross-cutting Cleavages in Norwegian Politics." In Seymour M. Lipset and Stein Rokkan, eds., *Party Systems and Voter Alignment: Cross-National Perspectives*, pp. 367–444. New York: Free Press.

———. 1975. "Dimensions of State Formation and Nation-Building." In Charles

Tilly, ed., *The Formation of National States in Western Europe*, pp. 562–600. Princeton, N.J.: Princeton University Press.

Rudolph, Joseph R., Jr. 1982. "Belgium: Controlling Separatist Tendencies in a Multinational State." In Colin H. Williams, ed., *National Separatism*, pp. 263–98. Cardiff: University of Wales Press.

Rumpf, Erhard, and A. C. Hepburn. 1977. *Nationalism and Socialism in Twentieth Century Ireland*. Liverpool: Liverpool University Press.

Ryder, Norman B. 1974. "Comment." In T. W. Schultz, ed., *Economics of the Family*, pp. 76–80. Chicago: University of Chicago Press.

Sapir, Edward. 1931. "Dialect." In *Encyclopedia of the Social Sciences* 5:123–26. New York: Macmillan.

Schneider, Jane, and Peter Schneider. 1984. "Demographic Transitions in a Sicilian Rural Town." *Journal of Family History* 9(3):245–72.

Schulte, Regina. 1984. "Infanticide in Rural Bavaria in the Nineteenth Century." In Hans Medick and David Warren Sabean, eds., *Interest and Emotion: Essays on the Study of Family and Kinship*, pp. 77–102. Cambridge: Cambridge University Press.

Scott, J. C. 1976. *The Moral Economy of the Peasant*. New Haven, Conn.: Yale University Press.

Seccombe, Wally. 1983. "Marxism and Demography." *New Left Review* 137:22–47.

Segalen, Martine. 1983. *Love and Power in the Peasant Family*. Oxford: Basil Blackwell.

Sharlin, Allen. 1986. "Urban-Rural Differences in Fertility in Europe during the Demographic Transition." In Ansley J. Coale and Susan C. Watkins, eds., *The Decline of Fertility in Europe*, pp. 234–60. Princeton, N.J.: Princeton University Press.

Sheehan, M. M. 1978. "Choice of Marriage Partner in the Middle Ages: Development and Mode of Application of a Theory of Marriage." *Studies in Mediaeval and Rennaisance History*, 1:3–33.

Shils, Edward. 1963. "On the Comparative Study of the New States." In Clifford Geertz, ed., *Old Societies and New States: The Quest for Modernity in Asia and Africa*, pp. 1–26. New York: Free Press.

Shorter, Edward. 1975. *The Making of the Modern Family*. New York: Basic Books.

Siegfried, André. 1950. *Switzerland: A Democratic Way of Life*. New York: Duell, Sloan, and Pearce.

Simmel, Georg. 1955. *Conflict* and *The Web of Group-Affiliations*. New York: Free Press.

Skinner, G. William. 1964. "Marketing and Social Structure in Rural China." *Journal of Asian Studies* 24(1):3–43.

———. 1985. "Rural Marketing in China: Revival and Reappraisal." In Stewart Plattner, ed., *Markets and Marketing*, pp. 7–47. Lanham, Md.: University Press of America.

Smith, Anthony D. 1981. "War and Ethnicity: The Role of Warfare in the Formation of Self-Images and Cohesion of Ethnic Communities." *Ethnic and Racial Studies* 4:375–97.

———. 1986. *The Ethnic Origins of Nations*. Oxford: Basil Blackwell.

Smith, Daniel Scott. 1978. "A Homeostatic Demographic Regime: Patterns in West

European Family Reconstitution Studies." In R. D. Lee, ed., *Population Patterns in the Past*, pp. 19–51. New York: Academic Press.

Smith, Richard [M.] 1981. "The People of Tuscany and Their Families." *Journal of Family History*, 6(1):107–28.

———. 1984. "Pre-Industrial European Demograhic Regimes." In Serge Feld and Ron Lesthaeghe, eds., *Population and Societal Outlook*. Brussels: Fondation Roi Baudouin.

———. 1986. "Marriage Processes in the English Past: Some Continuities." In Lloyd Bonfield, Richard Smith, and Keith Wrightson, eds., *The World We Have Gained*, pp. 43–99. London: Basil Blackwell.

Soloway, R. A. 1982. *Birth Control and the Population Question in England, 1877–1930*. Chapel Hill: University of North Carolina Press.

Souboul, A. 1956. "The French Rural Community in the Eighteenth and Nineteenth Centuries." *Past and Present* 10:78–95.

Spacks, Patricia Meyer. 1986. *Gossip*. Chicago: University of Chicago Press.

Spagnoli, Paul G. 1977. "Population History from Parish Monographs: The Problem of Local Demographic Variation." *Journal of Interdisciplinary History* 7(3):427–52.

Stephens, Meic. 1976. *Linguistic Minorities in Western Europe*. Llandysul, Dyfed, Wales: Gomer Press.

Stone, Lawrence. 1977. *The Family, Sex and Marriage in England, 1500–1800*. New York: Harper and Row.

Stone, Lawrence, and Jeanne Stone. 1984. *An Open Elite? England, 1540–1880*. Oxford: Clarendon Press.

Sutherland, James, ed. 1977. *The Oxford Book of Literary Anecdotes*. New York: Simon and Schuster.

Sutter, Jean. 1958. "Évolution de la distance séparant le domicile des futurs époux (Loir-et-Cher 1870–1954; Finistère 1911–1953)." *Population* 13(2):227–58.

Sutter, Jean, and Léon Tabah. 1955. "L'évolution des isolats de deux départements français: Loir-et-Cher, Finistère." *Population* 10(4):645–74.

Swaan, Abram de. 1988. *In Care of the State: Health Care, Education and Welfare in Europe and the USA in the Modern Era*. Cambridge, England: Polity Press.

Szreter, Simon R. 1983. "The Decline of Marital Fertility in England and Wales c. 1870–1914: A Critique of the Theory of Social Class Differentials through an Investigation of its Historical Origins and an Examination of Data for the Constituent Male Occupations." Ph.D. diss., University of Cambridge, England.

Tabouret-Keller, A. 1968. "Sociological Factors of Language Maintenance and Language Shift: A Methodological Approach Based on European and African Examples." In J. A. Fishman, C. Ferguson, and J. das Gupta, eds., *Language Problems of Developing Nations*. New York: John Wiley and Sons.

Tarde, Gabriel. [1898] 1969. *On Communication and Social Influence*. Chicago: University of Chicago Press.

Teitelbaum, Michael S. 1984. *The British Fertility Decline*. Princeton, N.J.: Princeton University Press.

Tesnière, L. 1928. "Statistique des langues de L'Europe." In A. Meillet, *Les langues dans L'Europe Nouvelle*, app. Paris: Payot.

Thabault, Roger. 1971. *Education and Change in a Village Community: Mazières-en-Gâtine 1848–1914*. New York: Schocken Books.

Tilly, Charles. 1975. "Reflections on the History of European State-Making." In Charles Tilly, ed., *The Formation of National States in Western Europe*, pp. 3–83. Princeton, N.J.: Princeton University Press.

————. 1981. *As Sociology Meets History*. New York: Academic Press.

Tipton, Frank B., Jr. 1976. *Regional Variations in the Economic Development of Germany During the 19th Century*. Middletown, Conn.: Wesleyan University Press.

Tortella Casares, D. Gabriel. 1984. "La historia económica comparada de los países del sur de Europa: Los casos de España, Italia y Portugal." Inaugural lecture 17 October 1984 at the Universidad de Alcalá de Henares, Spain.

Trudgill, Peter. 1983. *Sociolinguistics: An Introduction to Language and Society*. Harmondsworth, England: Penguin.

Tugault, Yves. 1973. *La mesure de la mobilité*. Institut National d'Études Démographiques Cahier no. 67. Paris: Presses Universitaires de France.

UNESCO. 1975. *World Communications*. Paris: UNESCO Press.

United Nations. 1955. *Demographic Yearbook 1955*. New York: Statistical Office, Department of Economic and Social Affairs, United Nations.

van de Walle, Etienne. 1968. "Marriage and Marital Fertility." *Daedalus* 97(2):486–501.

————. 1974. *The Female Population of France in the Nineteenth Century: A Reconstruction of 82 Departments*. Princeton, N.J.: Princeton University Press.

————. 1980. "Motivations and Technology in the Decline of French Fertility." In R. Wheaton and T. Hareven, eds., *Family and Sexuality in French History*, pp. 135–78. Philadelphia: University of Pennsylvania Press.

van de Walle, Etienne, and Francine van de Walle. 1985. "On the Paradigm of the Fertility Transition." Paper presented at a conference, Historical Studies of Fertility Change, Michigan State University.

van de Walle, Francine. 1977. "One Hundred Years of Decline: The History of Swiss Fertility from 1869 to 1960." Office of Population Research, Princeton, N.J. Typescript.

————. 1986. "Infant Mortality and the European Demographic Transition." In Ansley J. Coale and Susan C. Watkins, eds., *The Decline of Fertility in Europe*, pp. 201–33. Princeton, N.J.: Princeton University Press.

van Poppel, Frans W. A. 1981. "Regional Mortality Differences in Western Europe: A Review of the Situation in the Seventies." *Social Science and Medicine* 15D:341–52.

————. 1983. "Differential Fertility in the Netherlands: An Overview of Long-term Trends with Special Reference to the Post-World War I Marriage Cohorts." Working paper no. 39. Netherlands: Interuniversity Demographic Institute.

————. 1985. "Late Fertility Decline in the Netherlands: The Influence of Religious Denomination, Socioeconomic Group and Region." *European Journal of Population* 1(4):347–73.

Verdery, Katherine. 1985. "The Unmaking of an Ethnic Collectivity: Transylvania's Germans." *American Ethnologist* 12(1):62–83.

Wallerstein, Immanuel. 1974. *The Modern World System: Capitalist Agriculture and the Origins of the European World-Economy in the Sixteenth Century.* New York: Academic Press.

Warburton, T. Rennie. 1976. "Nationalism and Language in Switzerland and Canada." In Anthony D. Smith, ed., *Nationalist Movements*, pp. 88–109. New York: St. Martin's Press.

Watkins, Susan C. 1980. "Variation and Persistence in Nuptiality: Age-Patterns of Marriage in Europe, 1870–1960." Ph.D. diss., Princeton University, Princeton, N.J.

———. 1981. "Regional Patterns of Nuptiality in Europe, 1870–1960." *Population Studies* 35(2):199–215.

———. 1984. "Spinsters." *Journal of Family History* (winter):310–25.

———. 1986. "Conclusions." In Ansley J. Coale and Susan C. Watkins, eds., *The Decline of Fertility in Europe*, pp. 420–50. Princeton, N.J.: Princeton University Press.

———. 1987. "The Fertility Transition: Europe and the Third World Compared." *Sociological Forum* 2(4):645–73.

Watkins, Susan C., John Casterline, and Maria Pereira. 1987. "Geography as Destiny: Regional Differences in Demographic Behavior in Europe and the Third World." Paper presented at the European Population Conference, Jyväskylä, Finland, June 1987.

Watkins, Susan C., and James McCarthy. 1980. "The Female Life Cycle in a Belgian Commune: La Hulpe 1847–1866." *Journal of Family History* 5(2):167–79.

Weber, Eugen. 1976. *Peasants into Frenchmen: The Modernization of Rural France, 1870–1914.* Stanford, Cal.: Stanford University Press.

Weinberg, Ian. 1976. "The Problem of Convergence of Industrial Societies: A Critical Look at the State of a Theory." In Cyril E. Black, ed., *Comparative Modernization*, pp. 353–67. New York: Free Press.

Weir, David. 1983. "Fertility Transition in Rural France, 1740–1829." Ph.D. diss., Stanford University, Stanford, Cal.

———. 1984a. "Life under Pressure: France and England, 1670–1870." *Journal of Economic History* 44(1):27–47.

———. 1984b. "Rather Never than Late: Celibacy and Age at Marriage in English Cohort Fertility." *Journal of Family History* 9(4):340–54.

———. 1989. "Markets and Mortality in France, 1600–1789." In Roger Schofield and John Walter, eds., *Famine, Disease, and the Social Order in Early Modern Society*, pp. 201–34. Cambridge: Cambridge University Press.

Weiss, John. 1983. "Origins of the French Welfare State: Poor Relief in the Third Republic, 1871–1914." *French Historical Studies* 13(1):47–78.

Wiles, R. M. 1965. *Freshest Advices: Early Provincial Newspapers in England.* Columbus: Ohio State University Press.

Wilke, Gerhard, and Kurt Wagner. 1981. "Family and Household: Social Structure in a German Village between the Two World Wars." In Richard G. Evans and W. R. Lee, eds., *The German Family*, pp. 120–47. London: Croom Helm.

Williams, Colin H. 1982. "Introduction" and "Separatism and the Mobilization of Welsh National Identity." In Colin H. Williams, ed., *National Separatism*, pp. 1–10 and 145–201. Cardiff: University of Wales Press.

Williams, Colin H., and A. D. Smith. 1983. "The National Construction of Social Space." *Progress in Human Geography* 7:502–18.

Williamson, Jeffrey G. 1965. "Regional Inequality and the Process of National Development: A Description of the Patterns." *Economic Development and Cultural Change* 13(4, pt. 2):3–84.

Wilson, C[hris]. 1984. "Natural Fertility in Pre-industrial England." *Population Studies* 38:225–40.

———. 1986. "The Proximate Determinants of Marital Fertility in England, 1600–1799." In Lloyd Bonfield, Richard Smith, and Keith Wrightson, eds., *The World We Have Gained*, pp. 203–30. New York: Basil Blackwell.

Winter, Jay. 1986. *The Great War and the British People*. Cambridge: Harvard University Press.

Wonnacott, Thomas H., and Ronald J. Wonnacott. 1984. *Introductory Statistics for Business and Economics*. New York: John Wiley and Sons.

Woods, R. I. 1987. "Approaches to the Fertility Transition in Victorian England." *Population Studies* 41:283–311.

Woods, R. I., and P.R.A. Hinde. 1985. "Nuptiality and Age at Marriage in Nineteenth Century England." *Journal of Family History* 10(2):119–44.

Wrightson, Keith, and David Levine. 1979. *Poverty and Piety in an English Village: Terling, 1525–1700*. New York: Academic Press.

Wrigley, E. A. 1967. "A Simple Model of London's Importance in Changing English Society and Economy 1650–1750." *Past and Present* 37:44–70.

———. 1978. "Fertility Strategy for the Individual and the Group." In Charles Tilly, *Historical Studies of Changing Fertility*, pp. 135–54. Princeton, N.J.: Princeton University Press.

———. 1985. "The Fall of Marital Fertility in Nineteenth Century France: Exemplar or Exception?" (Pt. 1, pt. 2). *European Journal of Population* 1:31–60, 141–77.

Wrigley, E. A., and R. S. Schofield. 1981. *The Population History of England, 1541–1871*. Cambridge: Harvard University Press.

———. 1983. "English Population History from Family Reconstitution: Summary Results 1600–1799." *Population Studies* 37(2):157–84.

Wrong, Dennis H. 1980. *Class Fertility Trends in Western Nations*. New York: Arno Press.

Wylie, Laurence, ed. 1966. *Chanzeaux: A Village in Anjou*. Cambridge: Harvard University Press.

Young, Arthur. [1792] 1929. *Travels in France during the Years 1787, 1788 and 1789*. Cambridge: Cambridge University Press.

Zeldin, Theodore. 1982. *The French*. New York: Pantheon and Sons.

Zolberg, Aristide R. 1974. "The Making of Flemings and Walloons: Belgium 1830–1914." *Journal of Interdisciplinary History* (Fall): 179–235.

———. 1977. "Splitting the Difference: Federalization without Federalism in Belgium." In Milton J. Esman, ed., *Ethnic Conflict in the Western World*, pp. 103–42. Ithaca, N.Y.: Cornell University Press.

Index